# THE
# METRIC
# TIDE

**SAGE** was founded in 1965 by Sara Miller McCune to support the dissemination of usable knowledge by publishing innovative and high-quality research and teaching content. Today, we publish over 900 journals, including those of more than 400 learned societies, more than 800 new books per year, and a growing range of library products including archives, data, case studies, reports, and video. SAGE remains majority-owned by our founder, and after Sara's lifetime will become owned by a charitable trust that secures our continued independence.

Los Angeles | London | New Delhi | Singapore | Washington DC

# THE METRIC TIDE

## THE INDEPENDENT REVIEW OF THE ROLE OF METRICS IN RESEARCH ASSESSMENT & MANAGEMENT

INTRODUCTION BY
## JAMES WILSDON

REPORT AUTHORS
JAMES WILSDON, LIZ ALLEN, ELEONORA BELFIORE,
PHILIP CAMPBELL, STEPHEN CURRY, STEVEN HILL,
RICHARD JONES, ROGER KAIN, SIMON KERRIDGE,
MIKE THELWALL, JANE TINKLER, IAN VINEY,
PAUL WOUTERS, JUDE HILL AND BEN JOHNSON

Los Angeles | London | New Delhi
Singapore | Washington DC

Los Angeles | London | New Delhi
Singapore | Washington DC

SAGE Publications Ltd
1 Oliver's Yard
55 City Road
London EC1Y 1SP

SAGE Publications Inc.
2455 Teller Road
Thousand Oaks, California 91320

SAGE Publications India Pvt Ltd
B 1/I 1 Mohan Cooperative Industrial Area
Mathura Road
New Delhi 110 044

SAGE Publications Asia-Pacific Pte Ltd
3 Church Street
#10-04 Samsung Hub
Singapore 049483

Typeset by: C&M Digitals (P) Ltd, Chennai, India
Printed and bound by Ashford Colour Press Ltd.

**Library of Congress Control Number: 2015960254**

**British Library Cataloguing in Publication data**

A catalogue record for this book is available from
the British Library

ISBN 978-1-47397-306-0 (pbk)

# CONTENTS

**Published separately**

*The Metric Tide: Literature Review* (Supplementary Report I to the Independent Review of the Role of Metrics in Research Assessment and Management)

*The Metric Tide: Correlation Analysis of REF2014 Scores and Metrics* (Supplementary Report II to the Independent Review of the Role of Metrics in Research Assessment and Management)

# FOREWORD[1]

Metrics evoke a mixed reaction from the research community. A commitment to using data and evidence to inform decisions makes many of us sympathetic, even enthusiastic, about the prospect of granular, real-time analysis of our own activities. If we as a sector can't take full advantage of the possibilities of big data, then who can?

Yet we only have to look around us, at the blunt use of metrics such as journal impact factors, h-indices and grant income targets to be reminded of the pitfalls. Some of the most precious qualities of academic culture resist simple quantification, and individual indicators can struggle to do justice to the richness and plurality of our research.

Too often, poorly designed evaluation criteria are "dominating minds, distorting behaviour and determining careers."[2] At their worst, metrics can contribute to what Rowan Williams, the former Archbishop of Canterbury, calls a "new barbarity" in our universities.[3] The tragic case of Stefan Grimm, whose suicide in September 2014 led Imperial College to launch a review of its use of performance metrics, is a jolting reminder that what's at stake in these debates is more than just the design of effective management systems.[4] Metrics hold real power: they are constitutive of values, identities and livelihoods.

How to exercise that power to positive ends is the focus of *The Metric Tide*. Based on fifteen months of evidence gathering, analysis and consultation, we propose here a framework for responsible metrics, and make a series of targeted recommendations.

Together these are designed to ensure that indicators and underlying data infrastructure develop in ways that support the diverse qualities and impacts of research. Looking

---

[1]This foreword was updated and expanded in December 2015 for the book edition of *The Metric Tide*.

[2]Lawrence, P.A. (2007). The mismeasurement of science. *Current Biology,* 17 (15): R583–R585.

[3]Annual Lecture to the Council for the Defence of British Universities, January 2015.

[4]https://www.timeshighereducation.co.uk/news/stefan-grimms-death-leads-imperial-to-review-performance- metrics/2019381.article. (Retrieved 22 June 2015.)

to the future, we show how responsible metrics can be applied in research management, by funders, and in the next cycle of the UK's Research Excellence Framework (REF).

## FROM REF TO TEF

When *The Metric Tide* was first published in July 2015, it sparked an energetic debate between researchers, managers, funders and metrics providers.[5] But despite the spread of opinion and evidence that we encountered over the course of the review, we were also encouraged by the degree of consensus in support of our main recommendations. From editorials in *Nature*, *Times Higher Education* and *Research Fortnight*, to formal reactions by Elsevier, PLOS, Jisc, Wellcome Trust and many universities, the idea of 'responsible metrics' has been widely endorsed. Internationally too, there has been interest in the review's findings from policymakers and funders who are grappling with similar dilemmas in their own research systems.

In the UK, recent months have seen a raft of proposed reforms to the higher education and research system. A November 2015 Green Paper outlines a new regulatory architecture, including the replacement of HEFCE with a new Office for Students, and (most controversially) the introduction of a Teaching Excellence Framework (TEF) to "identify and incentivise the highest quality teaching." [6] Metrics are portrayed as crucial to the TEF, albeit with some scope for expert judgement alongside, and there are now fierce arguments raging across the sector about whether we need a TEF at all, and if so, how it should be designed, and what mix of quantitative indicators it should employ.

On the research side of the system, the green paper revisits the question of whether metrics should be used in future cycles of the Research Excellence Framework (REF) – an issue we explore in some depth in *The Metric Tide*. And a further, more comprehensive review of the REF, led by Lord Stern, President of the British Academy, is now underway, and expected to report its findings in July 2016.[7]

So whether for research or for teaching, the metric tide continues to rise. But unlike King Canute, we have the agency and opportunity – and in this report, a serious body of evidence – to influence how that tide washes through higher education and research.

Efforts over the next decade should focus on improving the robustness, coverage and interoperability of the indicators that we have, and applying them responsibly. We should make sure that lessons learned on the research side are used to properly inform any uses of metrics for teaching. And we should build stronger connections between

---

[5]A good range of responses were published by the LSE Impact Blog at http://blogs.lse.ac.uk/impactofsocialsciences/hefcemetrics-review/

[6]Department for Business, Innovation and Skills (2015) *Fulfilling our Potential: Teaching Excellence, Social Mobility and Student Choice*. November 2015.

[7]https://www.gov.uk/government/news/government-launches-review-to-improve-university-research-funding

recent initiatives in this area – of which the San Francisco Declaration on Research Assessment, the Leiden Manifesto, and *The Metric Tide* are just three examples. Plans by the European Commission to examine metrics in 2016 as part of its Open Science Policy Platform provide a further opportunity to build responsible metrics into whatever framework for European research funding follows Horizon 2020.

Let me end on a note of personal thanks to my steering group colleagues, to the team at HEFCE, and to all those across the community who have contributed to our deliberations.

James Wilsdon, Chair
December 2015

# ACKNOWLEDGMENTS

The steering group would like to extend its sincere thanks to the numerous organisations and individuals who have informed the work of the review. Metrics can be a contentious topic, but the expertise, insight, challenge and open engagement that so many across the higher education and research community have brought to this process has made it both enjoyable and instructive.

Space unfortunately limits us from mentioning everyone by name. But particular thanks to David Willetts for commissioning the review and provoking us at the outset to frame it more expansively, and to his ministerial successors Greg Clark and Jo Johnson for the interest they have shown in its progress and findings. Thanks also to Dr Carolyn Reeve at BIS for ensuring close government engagement with the project.

The review would not have been possible without the outstanding support that we have received from the research policy team at HEFCE at every stage of research, evidence-gathering and report drafting; notably Jude Hill, Ben Johnson, Alex Herbert, Kate Turton, Tamsin Rott and Sophie Melton-Bradley. Thanks also to David Sweeney at HEFCE for his advice and insights.

We are indebted to all those who responded to our call for evidence; attended, participated in and spoke at our workshops and focus groups; and contributed to online discussions. Thanks also to those organisations who hosted events linked to the review, including the Universities of Oxford, Sheffield, Sussex, UCL and Warwick, the Higher Education Policy Institute and the Scottish Funding Council.

The review has hugely benefited from the quality and breadth of these contributions. Any errors or omissions are entirely our own.

# STEERING GROUP AND SECRETARIAT

The review was chaired by James Wilsdon FAcSS, Professor of Research Policy at the University of Sheffield (orcid.org/0000-0002-5395-5949; @jameswilsdon).

Professor Wilsdon was supported by an independent steering group with the following members:

Dr Liz Allen, Head of Evaluation, Wellcome Trust (orcid.org/0000-0002-9298-3168; @allen_liz);

Dr Eleonora Belfiore, Associate Professor in Cultural Policy, Centre for Cultural Policy Studies, University of Warwick (orcid.org/0000-0001-7825-4615; @elebelfiore);

Sir Philip Campbell, Editor-in-Chief, Nature (orcid.org/0000-0002-8917-1740; @NatureNews);

Professor Stephen Curry, Department of Life Sciences, Imperial College London (orcid.org/0000-0002-0552-8870; @Stephen_Curry);

Dr Steven Hill, Head of Research Policy, HEFCE (orcid.org/0000-0003-1799-1915; @stevenhill);

Professor Richard Jones FRS, Pro-Vice-Chancellor for Research and Innovation, University of Sheffield (orcid.org/0000-0001-5400-6369; @RichardALJones) (representing the Royal Society);

Professor Roger Kain FBA, Dean and Chief Executive, School of Advanced Study, University of London (orcid.org/0000-0003-1971-7338; @kain_SAS) (representing the British Academy);

Dr Simon Kerridge, Director of Research Services, University of Kent, and Chair of the Board of the Association of Research Managers and Administrators (orcid.org/0000-0003-4094-3719; @SimonRKerridge);

Professor Mike Thelwall, Statistical Cybermetrics Research Group, University of Wolverhampton (orcid.org/0000-0001-6065-205X; @mikethelwall);

Jane Tinkler, Social Science Adviser, Parliamentary Office of Science and Technology (orcid.org/0000-0002-5306-3940; @janetinkler);

Dr Ian Viney, MRC Director of Strategic Evaluation and Impact, Medical Research Council head office, London (orcid.org/0000-0002-9943-4989, @MRCEval);

Paul Wouters, Professor of Scientometrics & Director, Centre for Science and Technology Studies (CWTS), Leiden University (orcid.org/0000-0002-4324-5732, @paulwouters).

The following members of HEFCE's research policy team provided the secretariat for the steering group and supported the review process throughout: Jude Hill, Ben Johnson, Alex Herbert, Kate Turton, Tamsin Rott and Sophie Melton-Bradley. Hannah White and Mark Gittoes from HEFCE's Analytical Services Directorate also contributed, particularly to the REF2014 correlation exercise (see Supplementary Report II). Vicky Jones from the REF team also provided advice.

# EXECUTIVE SUMMARY

This report presents the findings and recommendations of the Independent Review of the Role of Metrics in Research Assessment and Management. The review was chaired by Professor James Wilsdon, supported by an independent and multidisciplinary group of experts in scientometrics, research funding, research policy, publishing, university management and administration.

## SCOPE OF THE REVIEW

This review has gone beyond earlier studies to take a deeper look at potential uses and limitations of research metrics and indicators. It has explored the use of metrics across different disciplines, and assessed their potential contribution to the development of research excellence and impact. It has analysed their role in processes of research assessment, including the next cycle of the Research Excellence Framework (REF). It has considered the changing ways in which universities are using quantitative indicators in their management systems, and the growing power of league tables and rankings. And it has considered the negative or unintended effects of metrics on various aspects of research culture.

Our report starts by tracing the history of metrics in research management and assessment, in the UK and internationally. It looks at the applicability of metrics within different research cultures, compares the peer review system with metric-based alternatives, and considers what balance might be struck between the two. It charts the development of research management systems within institutions, and examines the effects of the growing use of quantitative indicators on different aspects of research culture, including performance management, equality, diversity, interdisciplinarity, and the 'gaming' of assessment systems. The review looks at how different funders are using quantitative indicators, and considers their potential role in research and innovation policy. Finally, it examines the role that metrics played in REF2014, and outlines scenarios for their contribution to future exercises.

The review has drawn on a diverse evidence base to develop its findings and conclusions. These include: a formal call for evidence; a comprehensive review of the literature (Supplementary Report I); and extensive consultation with stakeholders at focus groups, workshops, and via traditional and new media.

The review has also drawn on HEFCE's recent evaluations of REF2014, and commissioned its own detailed analysis of the correlation between REF2014 scores and a basket of metrics (Supplementary Report II).

## Headline findings[8]

**There are powerful currents whipping up the metric tide.** These include growing pressures for audit and evaluation of public spending on higher education and research; demands by policymakers for more strategic intelligence on research quality and impact; the need for institutions to manage and develop their strategies for research; competition within and between institutions for prestige, students, staff and resources; and increases in the availability of real-time 'big data' on research uptake, and the capacity of tools for analysing them.

**Across the research community, the description, production and consumption of 'metrics' remains contested and open to misunderstandings.** In a positive sense, wider use of quantitative indicators, and the emergence of alternative metrics for societal impact, could support the transition to a more open, accountable and outward-facing research system. But placing too much emphasis on narrow, poorly-designed indicators – such as journal impact factors (JIFs) – can have negative consequences, as reflected by the 2013 San Francisco Declaration on Research Assessment (DORA), which now has over 570 organisational and 12,300 individual signatories.[9] Responses to this review reflect these possibilities and pitfalls. The majority of those who submitted evidence, or engaged in other ways, are sceptical about moves to increase the role of metrics in research management. However, a significant minority are more supportive of the use of metrics, particularly if appropriate care is exercised in their design and application, and the data infrastructure can be improved.

**Peer review, despite its flaws and limitations, continues to command widespread support across disciplines.** Metrics should support, not supplant, expert judgement. Peer review is not perfect, but it is the least worst form of academic governance we have, and should remain the primary basis for assessing research papers, proposals and individuals, and for national assessment exercises like the REF. However, carefully selected and applied quantitative indicators can be a useful complement to other forms of evaluation and decision-making. One size is unlikely to fit all: a mature research system needs a variable geometry of expert judgement, quantitative and qualitative indicators.

---

[8]These are presented in greater detail in Section 10.1 of the main report.

[9]www.ascb.org/dora. As of July 2015, only three UK universities are DORA signatories: Manchester, Sussex and UCL.

Research assessment needs to be undertaken with due regard for context and disciplinary diversity. Academic quality is highly context-specific, and it is sensible to think in terms of research *qualities,* rather than striving for a single definition or measure of quality.

**Inappropriate indicators create perverse incentives.** There is legitimate concern that some quantitative indicators can be gamed, or can lead to unintended consequences; journal impact factors and citation counts are two prominent examples. These consequences need to be identified, acknowledged and addressed. Linked to this, there is a need for greater transparency in the construction and use of indicators, particularly for university rankings and league tables. Those involved in research assessment and management should behave responsibly, considering and pre-empting negative consequences wherever possible, particularly in terms of equality and diversity.

**Indicators can only meet their potential if they are underpinned by an open and interoperable data infrastructure.** How underlying data are collected and processed – and the extent to which they remain open to interrogation – is crucial. Without the right identifiers, standards and semantics, we risk developing metrics that are not contextually robust or properly understood. The systems used by higher education institutions (HEIs), funders and publishers need to interoperate better, and definitions of research-related concepts need to be harmonised. Information about research – particularly about funding inputs – remains fragmented. Unique identifiers for individuals and research works will gradually improve the robustness of metrics and reduce administrative burden.

At present, further use of quantitative indicators in research assessment and management cannot be relied on to reduce costs or administrative burden. Unless existing processes, such as peer review, are reduced as additional metrics are added, there will be an overall increase in burden. However, as the underlying data infrastructure is improved and metrics become more robust and trusted by the community, it is likely that the additional burden of collecting and assessing metrics could be outweighed by the reduction of peer review effort in some areas – and indeed by other uses for the data. Evidence of a robust relationship between newer metrics and research quality remains very limited, and more experimentation is needed. Indicators such as patent citations and clinical guideline citations may have potential in some fields for quantifying impact and progression.

**Our correlation analysis of the REF2014 results at output-by-author level (Supplementary Report II) has shown that individual metrics give significantly different outcomes from the REF peer review process, and therefore cannot provide a like-for-like replacement for REF peer review.** Publication year was a significant factor in the calculation of correlation with REF scores, with all but two metrics showing significant decreases in correlation for more recent outputs. There is large variation in the coverage of metrics across the REF submission, with particular issues with coverage in units of assessment (UOAs) in REF Main Panel D (mainly arts & humanities). There is also evidence to suggest statistically significant differences in the correlation with REF scores for early-career researchers and women in a small number of UOAs.

**Within the REF, it is not currently feasible to assess the quality of UOAs using quantitative indicators alone.** In REF2014, while some indicators (citation counts, and supporting text to highlight significance or quality in other ways) were supplied to some panels to help inform their judgements, caution needs to be exercised when considering all disciplines with existing bibliographic databases. Even if technical problems of coverage and bias can be overcome, no set of numbers, however broad, is likely to be able to capture the multifaceted and nuanced judgements on the quality of research outputs that the REF process currently provides.

**Similarly, for the impact component of the REF, it is not currently feasible to use quantitative indicators in place of narrative impact case studies, or the impact template.** There is a danger that the concept of impact might narrow and become too specifically defined by the ready availability of indicators for some types of impact and not for others. For an exercise like the REF, where HEIs are competing for funds, defining impact through quantitative indicators is likely to constrain thinking around which impact stories have greatest currency and should be submitted, potentially constraining the diversity of the UK's research base. **For the environment component of the REF, there is scope to enhance the use of quantitative data in the next assessment cycle,** provided they are used with sufficient context to enable their interpretation.

**There is a need for more research on research. The study of research systems – sometimes called the 'science of science policy' – is poorly funded in the UK.** The evidence to address the questions that we have been exploring throughout this review remains too limited; but the questions being asked by funders and HEIs – *'What should we fund?' 'How best should we fund?' 'Who should we hire/promote/invest in?'* – are far from new and can only become more pressing. More investment is needed as part of a coordinated UK effort to improve the evidence base in this area. Linked to this, there is potential for the scientometrics community to play a more strategic role in informing how quantitative indicators are used across the research system, and by policymakers.

## Responsible metrics

In recent years, the concept of 'responsible research and innovation' (RRI) has gained currency as a framework for research governance. Building on this, we propose the notion of **responsible metrics** as a way of framing appropriate uses of quantitative indicators in the governance, management and assessment of research. Responsible metrics can be understood in terms of the following dimensions:

- **Robustness**: basing metrics on the best possible data in terms of accuracy and scope;
- **Humility**: recognising that quantitative evaluation should support – but not supplant – qualitative, expert assessment;
- **Transparency**: keeping data collection and analytical processes open and transparent, so that those being evaluated can test and verify the results;
- **Diversity**: accounting for variation by field, and using a range of indicators to reflect and support a plurality of research and researcher career paths across the system;
- **Reflexivity**: recognising and anticipating the systemic and potential effects of indicators, and updating them in response.

# RECOMMENDATIONS

This review has identified 20 specific recommendations for further work and action by stakeholders across the UK research system. These draw on the evidence we have gathered, and should be seen as part of broader attempts to strengthen research governance, management and assessment which have been gathering momentum, and where the UK is well positioned to play a leading role internationally. The recommendations are listed below, with targeted recipients in brackets:

## Supporting the effective leadership, governance and management of research cultures

1  **The research community should develop a more sophisticated and nuanced approach to the contribution and limitations of quantitative indicators.** Greater care with language and terminology is needed. The term 'metrics' is often unhelpful; the preferred term 'indicators' reflects a recognition that data may lack specific relevance, even if they are useful overall. *(HEIs, funders, managers, researchers)*

2  **At an institutional level, HEI leaders should develop a clear statement of principles on their approach to research management and assessment, including the role of quantitative indicators.** On the basis of these principles, they should carefully select quantitative indicators that are appropriate to their institutional aims and context. Where institutions are making use of league tables and ranking measures, they should explain why they are using these as a means to achieve particular ends. Where possible, alternative indicators that support equality and diversity should be identified and included. Clear communication of the rationale for selecting particular indicators, and how they will be used as a management tool, is paramount. As part of this process, HEIs should consider signing up to DORA, or drawing on its principles and tailoring them to their institutional contexts. *(Heads of institutions, heads of research, HEI governors)*

3  **Research managers and administrators should champion these principles and the use of responsible metrics within their institutions.** They should pay due attention to the equality and diversity implications of research assessment choices; engage with external experts such as those at the Equality Challenge Unit; help to facilitate a more open and transparent data infrastructure; advocate the use of unique identifiers such as ORCID iDs; work with funders and publishers on data interoperability; explore indicators for aspects of research that they wish to assess rather than using existing indicators because they are readily available; advise senior leaders on metrics that are meaningful for their institutional or departmental context; and exchange best practice through sector bodies such as ARMA. *(Managers, research administrators, ARMA)*

4  **HR managers and recruitment or promotion panels in HEIs should be explicit about the criteria used for academic appointment and promotion decisions.** These criteria should be founded in expert judgement and may reflect both the

academic quality of outputs and wider contributions to policy, industry or society. Judgements may sometimes usefully be guided by metrics, if they are relevant to the criteria in question and used responsibly; article-level citation metrics, for instance, might be useful indicators of academic impact, as long as they are interpreted in the light of disciplinary norms and with due regard to their limitations. Journal-level metrics, such as the JIF, should not be used. *(HR managers, recruitment and promotion panels, UUK)*

5   **Individual researchers should be mindful of the limitations of particular indicators** in the way they present their own CVs and evaluate the work of colleagues. When standard indicators are inadequate, individual researchers should look for a range of data sources to document and support claims about the impact of their work. *(All researchers)*

6   **Like HEIs, research funders should develop their own context-specific principles for the use of quantitative indicators in research assessment and management** and ensure that these are well communicated, easy to locate and understand. They should pursue approaches to data collection that are transparent, accessible, and allow for greater interoperability across a diversity of platforms. *(UK HE Funding Bodies, Research Councils, other research funders)*

7   **Data providers, analysts and producers of university rankings and league tables should strive for greater transparency and interoperability between different measurement systems.** Some, such as the Times Higher Education (THE) university rankings, have taken commendable steps to be more open about their choice of indicators and the weightings given to these, but other rankings remain 'black-boxed'. *(Data providers, analysts and producers of university rankings and league tables)*

8   **Publishers should reduce emphasis on journal impact factors as a promotional tool, and only use them in the context of a variety of journal-based metrics that provide a richer view of performance.** As suggested by DORA, this broader indicator set could include 5-year impact factor, EigenFactor, SCImago, editorial and publication times. Publishers, with the aid of Committee on Publication Ethics (COPE), should encourage responsible authorship practices and the provision of more detailed information about the specific contributions of each author. Publishers should also make available a range of article-level metrics to encourage a shift toward assessment based on the academic quality of an article rather than JIFs. *(Publishers)*

## Improving the data infrastructure that supports research information management

9   **There is a need for greater transparency and openness in research data infrastructure. A set of principles should be developed for technologies, practices and cultures that can support open, trustworthy research information management.** These principles should be adopted by funders, data providers, administrators and researchers as a foundation for further work. *(UK HE Funding Bodies, RCUK, Jisc, data providers, managers, administrators)*

10  **The UK research system should take full advantage of ORCID as its preferred system of unique identifiers. ORCID iDs should be mandatory for all researchers in the next REF.** Funders and HEIs should utilise ORCID for grant applications, management and reporting platforms, and the benefits of ORCID need to be better communicated to researchers. *(HEIs, UK HE Funding Bodies, funders, managers, UUK, HESA)*

11  **Identifiers are also needed for institutions, and the most likely candidate for a global solution is the ISNI, which already has good coverage of publishers, funders and research organisations.** The use of ISNIs should therefore be extended to cover all institutions referenced in future REF submissions, and used more widely in internal HEI and funder management processes. One component of the solution will be to map the various organisational identifier systems against ISNI to allow the various existing systems to interoperate. *(UK HE Funding Bodies, HEIs, funders, publishers, UUK, HESA)*

12  **Publishers should mandate ORCID iDs and ISNIs and funder grant references for article submission, and retain this metadata throughout the publication lifecycle.** This will facilitate exchange of information on research activity, and help deliver data and metrics at minimal burden to researchers and administrators. *(Publishers and data providers)*

13  **The use of digital object identifiers (DOIs) should be extended to cover all research outputs.** This should include all outputs submitted to a future REF for which DOIs are suitable, and DOIs should also be more widely adopted in internal HEI and research funder processes. DOIs already predominate in the journal publishing sphere – they should be extended to cover other outputs where no identifier system exists, such as book chapters and datasets. *(UK HE Funding Bodies, HEIs, funders, UUK)*

14  **Further investment in research information infrastructure is required.** Funders and Jisc should explore opportunities for additional strategic investments, particularly to improve the interoperability of research management systems. *(HM Treasury, BIS, RCUK, UK HE Funding Bodies, Jisc, ARMA)*

## Increasing the usefulness of existing data and information sources

15  **HEFCE, funders, HEIs and Jisc should explore how to leverage data held in existing platforms to support the REF process, and vice versa.** Further debate is also required about the merits of local collection within HEIs and data collection at the national level. *(HEFCE, RCUK, HEIs, Jisc, HESA, ARMA)*

16  **BIS should identify ways of linking data gathered from research-related platforms (including Gateway to Research, Researchfish and the REF) more directly to policy processes in BIS and other departments,** especially around foresight, horizon scanning and research prioritisation. *(BIS, other government departments, UK HE Funding Bodies, RCUK)*

## Using metrics in the next REF

17   For the next REF cycle, we make some specific recommendations to HEFCE and the other HE Funding Bodies, as follows. *(UK HE Funding Bodies)*

    a  **In assessing outputs, we recommend that quantitative data – particularly around published outputs – continue to have a place in informing peer review judgements of research quality.** This approach has been used successfully in REF2014, and we recommend that it be continued and enhanced in future exercises.

    b  **In assessing impact, we recommend that HEFCE and the UK HE Funding Bodies build on the analysis of the impact case studies from REF2014 to develop clear guidelines for the use of quantitative indicators in future impact case studies.** While not being prescriptive, these guidelines should provide suggested data to evidence specific types of impact. They should include standards for the collection of metadata to ensure the characteristics of the research being described are captured systematically; for example, by using consistent monetary units.

    c  **In assessing the research environment, we recommend that there is scope for enhancing the use of quantitative data, but that these data need to be provided with sufficient context to enable their interpretation.** At a minimum this needs to include information on the total size of the UOA to which the data refer. In some cases, the collection of data specifically relating to staff submitted to the exercise may be preferable, albeit more costly. In addition, data on the structure and use of digital information systems to support research (or research and teaching) may be crucial to further develop excellent research environments.

## Coordinating activity and building evidence

18   **The UK research community needs a mechanism to carry forward the agenda set out in this report. We propose the establishment of a Forum for Responsible Metrics, which would bring together research funders, HEIs and their representative bodies, publishers, data providers and others to work on issues of data standards, interoperability, openness and transparency.** UK HE Funding Bodies, UUK and Jisc should coordinate this forum, drawing in support and expertise from other funders and sector bodies as appropriate. The forum should have preparations for the future REF within its remit, but should also look more broadly at the use of metrics in HEI management and by other funders. This forum might also seek to coordinate UK responses to the many initiatives in this area across Europe and internationally – and those that may yet emerge – around research metrics, standards and data infrastructure. It can ensure that the UK system stays ahead of the curve and continues to make real progress on this issue, supporting research in the most intelligent and coordinated way, influencing debates

in Europe and the standards that other countries will eventually follow. *(UK HE Funding Bodies, UUK, Jisc, ARMA)*

19   **Research funders need to increase investment in the science of science policy.** There is a need for greater research and innovation in this area, to develop and apply insights from computing, statistics, social science and economics to better understand the relationship between research, its qualities and wider impacts. *(Research funders)*

20   **One positive aspect of this review has been the debate it has generated. As a legacy initiative, the steering group is setting up a blog (www.ResponsibleMetrics.org) as a forum for ongoing discussion of the issues raised by this report.** The site will celebrate responsible practices, but also name and shame bad practices when they occur. Researchers will be encouraged to send in examples of good or bad design and application of metrics across the research system. Adapting the approach taken by the Literary Review's "Bad Sex in Fiction" award, every year we will award a "Bad Metric" prize to the most egregious example of an inappropriate use of quantitative indicators in research management. *(Review steering group)*

# ONE

## MEASURING UP

### CHAPTER CONTENTS

"The standing of British science, and the individuals and institutions that comprise it, is rooted firmly in excellence... Much of the confidence in standards of excellence promoted comes from decisions being informed by peer-review: leading experts assessing the quality of proposals and work."

Our Plan for Growth: science and innovation,
HM Treasury/BIS, December 2014[1]

"We have more top ranking universities in London than in any other city in the world. With 4 universities in the global top 10, we rank second only to the US."

Jo Johnson MP, Minister for
Universities and Science, 1 June 2015[2]

---

[1]https://www.gov.uk/government/publications/our-plan-for-growth-science-and-innovation

[2]Speech to 'Going Global' 2015 conference https://www.gov.uk/government/speeches/international-higher-education

Citations, journal impact factors, h-indices, even tweets and Facebook likes – there are no end of quantitative measures that can now be used to try to assess the quality and wider impacts of research. But how robust and reliable are such metrics, and what weight – if any – should we give them in the future management of research systems at the national or institutional level?

These are questions that have been explored over the past year by the Independent Review of the Role of Metrics in Research Assessment. The review was announced by David Willetts, then Minister for Universities and Science, in April 2014, and has been supported by the Higher Education Funding Council for England (HEFCE).

As the 2014 BIS/HM Treasury science and innovation strategy reminds us, the UK has a remarkable breadth of excellent research across the sciences, engineering, social sciences, arts and humanities. These strengths are often expressed in metric shorthand: "with just 3% of global research spending, 0.9% of global population and 4.1% of the world's researchers, the UK produces 9.5% of article downloads, 11.6% of citations and 15.9% of the world's most highly-cited articles".[3]

The quality and productivity of our research base is, at least in part, the result of smart management of the dual-support system of research funding. Since the introduction of the Research Assessment Exercise (RAE) in 1986, the UK has been through six cycles of evaluation and assessment, the latest of which was the 2014 Research Excellence Framework (REF2014). Processes to ensure and improve research quality, and more recently its wider impacts, are also used by the UK Research Councils, by other funders such as the Wellcome Trust, and by universities themselves.

The quality and diverse impacts of research have traditionally been assessed using a combination of peer review and a variety of quantitative indicators. Peer review has long been the most widely used method, and underpins the academic system in the UK and around the world. The use of metrics is a newer approach, but has developed rapidly over the past 20 years as a potential method of measuring research quality and impact in some fields. How best to do this remains the subject of considerable debate.

There are powerful currents whipping up the metric tide. These include growing pressures for audit and evaluation of public spending on higher education and research; demands by policymakers for more strategic intelligence on research quality and impact; the need for institutions to manage and develop their strategies for research; competition within and between institutions for prestige, students, staff and resources; and increases in the availability of real-time 'big data' on research uptake, and the capacity of tools for analysing them.

In a positive sense, wider use of quantitative indicators, and the emergence of alternative metrics for societal impact, can be seen as part of the transition to a more open, accountable

---

[3]Elsevier. (2013). *International Comparative Performance of the UK Research Base – 2013; A report prepared by Elsevier for the UK's Department of Business, Innovation and Skills (BIS)*, p2. https://www.gov.uk/government/uploads/system/uploads/attachment_data/file/263729/ bis-13-1297-international-comparative-performance-of-the-UK-research-base-2013.pdf. Retrieved 1 May 2015.

and outward-facing research system.[4] But this has been accompanied by a backlash against the inappropriate weight being placed on particular indicators – such as journal impact factors (JIFs) – within the research system, as reflected by the 2013 San Francisco Declaration on Research Assessment (DORA), which now has over 570 organisational and 12,300 individual signatories.[5] As DORA argues, "The outputs from scientific research are many and varied… Funding agencies, institutions that employ scientists, and scientists themselves, all have a desire, and need, to assess the quality and impact of scientific outputs. It is thus imperative that scientific output is measured accurately and evaluated wisely."[6]

## 1.1 OUR TERMS OF REFERENCE

Our work builds on an earlier pilot exercise in 2008 and 2009, which tested the potential for using bibliometric indicators of research quality in REF2014. At that time, it was concluded that citation information was insufficiently robust to be used formulaically or as a primary indicator of quality, but that there might be scope for it to enhance processes of expert review.

This review has gone beyond the earlier pilot study to take a deeper and broader look at the potential uses and limitations of research metrics and indicators. It has explored the use of metrics across different disciplines, and assessed their potential contribution to the development of research excellence and impact within higher education. It has also analysed their role in processes of research assessment, including the next cycle of the REF. And it has considered the changing ways in which universities are using metrics, particularly the growing power of league tables and rankings. Finally, it has considered the relationship between the use of indicators and issues of equality and diversity, and the potential for 'gaming' that can arise from the use of particular indicators in systems of funding and evaluation.

To give structure and focus to our efforts, clear terms of reference were established at the outset. The review was asked to examine:

- The relative merits of different metrics in assessing the academic qualities and diverse impacts of research;
- The advantages and disadvantages of using metrics, compared with peer review, in creating an environment that enables and encourages excellent research and diverse impact, including fostering inter- and multidisciplinary research;

---

[4]Royal Society. (2012). *Science as an Open Enterprise*. The Royal Society Science Policy Centre report 02/12 https://royalsociety.org/~/media/policy/projects/sape/2012-06-20-saoe.pdf. Retrieved 1 June 2015.

[5]www.ascb.org/dora. As of June 2015, only three UK universities are DORA signatories: Manchester, Sussex and UCL.

[6]Ibid.

- How metrics-based research assessment fits within the missions of universities and research institutes, and the value that they place on published research outputs in relation to the portfolio of other activities undertaken by their staff, including training and education;
- The appropriate balance between peer review and metrics in research assessment, and the consequences of shifting that balance for administrative burden and research cultures across different disciplines;
- What is not, or cannot, be measured by quantitative metrics;
- The differential impacts of metrics-based assessment on individual researchers, including the implications for early-career researchers, equality and diversity;
- Ethical considerations, and guidance on how to reduce the unintended effects and inappropriate use of metrics and university league-tables, including the impact of metrics-based assessment on research culture;
- The extent to which metrics could be used in novel ways by higher education institutions (HEIs) and research funders to support the assessment and management of research;
- The potential contribution of metrics to other aspects of research assessment, such as the matching of reviewers to proposals, or research portfolio analysis;
- The use of metrics in broader aspects of government science, innovation and industrial policy.

Reflecting the evidence we received, this report focuses in greater depth on some aspects of these terms of reference than others (notably, the use of metrics in the REF, by other funders and in HEI management). However, we hope that the report provides a clear framework for thinking about the broader role of metrics, data and indicators within research management, and lays helpful foundations for further work to be carried out by HEFCE, the Research Councils and others.

The review has been conducted in an open and consultative manner, with the aim of drawing in evidence, views and perspectives from across the higher education and research system. There has been a strong emphasis on transparency and plurality throughout the project, and the make-up of the review's steering group itself reflects a diversity of disciplines and perspectives. In addition, the group has engaged actively with stakeholders from across the research community through numerous workshops, meetings, talks and other channels, including the review's website and social media. Papers from steering group meetings have been made publicly available at every stage, as have other resources, including evidence received and slides presented at workshops.[7]

## 1.2 DEFINITIONS AND TERMINOLOGY

The research assessment landscape is contested, contentious and complex. Researchers, funders and managers face an ever-expanding menu of indicators, metrics and assessment methods in operation, many of which are explored in this review. Some are founded on

---

[7]All of this material is available at the review's website: https://www.hefce.ac.uk/rsrch/metrics/

peer review, others on quantitative indicators such as citation counts, or measures of input, such as research funding or student numbers.

The term 'metric' is itself open to misunderstanding, because something can be a metric in one context but not in another. For example, the number of citations received by a researcher's publications is a citation metric but not an impact metric because it does not directly measure the impact of that researcher's work. In other words, it can imply 'measurement' of a quantity or quality which has not in fact been measured. The term *indicator* is preferable in contexts in which there is the potential for confusion. To reduce the scope of possible misunderstanding, this report will adopt the following definitions and terminology throughout.

| | |
|---|---|
| **Indicators** | A measurable quantity that 'stands in' or substitutes for something less readily measurable and is presumed to associate with it without directly measuring it. For example, citation counts could be used as indicators for the scientific impact of journal articles even though scientific impacts can occur in ways that do not generate citations. Similarly, counts of online syllabi mentioning a particular book might be used as an indicator of its educational impact. |
| **Bibliometrics** | Bibliometrics focuses on the quantitative analysis of scientific and scholarly publications, including patents. Bibliometrics is part of the field of scientometrics: the measurement of all aspects of science and technology, which may encompass information about any kind of research output (data, reagents, software, researcher interactions, funding, research commercialisation, and other outputs).[8] |
| **Citation impact** | The most widely exploited bibliometric relies on counts of citations. Citation counts are sometimes used as an indicator of academic impact in the sense that citations from other documents suggest that the cited work has influenced the citing work in some way. Bibliometric indicators might normalise these citation counts by research field and by year, to take into account the very different citation behaviours between disciplines and the increase in citations over time. It has to be emphasised that as bibliometrics often do not distinguish between negative or positive citation, highly cited literature might attract attention due to controversy or even error. High numbers of citations might also result from a range of different contributions to a field e.g. including papers that establish new methodologies or systematically review the field, as well as primary research articles. |
| **Alternative or altmetrics** | Altmetrics are non-traditional metrics that cover not just citation counts but also downloads, social media shares and other measures of impact of research outputs. The term is variously used to mean 'alternative metrics' or 'article level metrics', and it encompasses webometrics, or cybermetrics, which measure the features and relationships of online items, such as websites and log files. The rise of new social media has created an additional stream of work under the label altmetrics. These are indicators derived from social websites, such as Twitter, Academia.edu, Mendeley, and ResearchGate with data that can be gathered automatically by computer programs. |

*(Continued)*

---

[8]Definitions adapted from *Encyclopedia of Science Technology and Ethics,* 2nd Edition (2014). Macmillan.

*(Continued)*

| | |
|---|---|
| **Peer review** | A process of research assessment based on the use of expert deliberation and judgement.[9] |
| **Academic or scholarly impact** | Academic or scholarly impact is a recorded or otherwise auditable occasion of influence from academic research on another researcher, university organisation or academic author. Academic impacts are most objectively demonstrated by citation indicators in those fields that publish in international journals.[10] |
| **Societal impact** | As for academic or scholarly impact, though where the effect or influence reaches beyond scholarly research, e.g. on education, society, culture or the economy. Research has a societal impact when auditable or recorded influence is achieved upon non-academic organisation(s) or actor(s) in a sector outside the university sector itself – for instance, by being used by one or more business corporations, government bodies, civil society organisations, media or specialist/professional media organisations or in public debate. As is the case with academic impacts, societal impacts need to be demonstrated rather than assumed. Evidence of external impacts can take the form of references to, citations of or discussion of a person, their work or research results.[11] |
| **REF impact** | For the purposes of the REF2014,[12] impact was defined as an effect on, change or benefit to the economy, society, culture, public policy or services, health, the environment or quality of life, beyond academia. REF2014 impact includes, but was not limited to, an effect on, change or benefit to:<br><br>• the activity, attitude, awareness, behaviour, capacity, opportunity, performance, policy, practice, process or understanding<br>• of an audience, beneficiary, community, constituency, organisation or individuals<br><br>in any geographic location whether locally, regionally, nationally or internationally. |
| **REF environment** | Within REF2014, the research environment was assessed in terms of its 'vitality and sustainability', including its contribution to the vitality and sustainability of the wider discipline or research base. |
| **REF outputs** | Within REF2014, panels assessed the quality of submitted research outputs in terms of their 'originality, significance and rigour', with reference to international research quality standards.[13] |

[9]Adapted from: Council of Canadian Academies. (2012). *Informing Research Choices: Indicators and Judgment*, p11. www.scienceadvice.ca/uploads/eng/assessments%20and%20publications%20and%20news%20releases/science%20performance/science performance_fullreport_en_web.pdf. Retrieved 6 December 2014.

[10]Taken from LSE Public Policy Group (2011) *Maximising the Impacts of Your Research: A Handbook for Social Scientists*. London: PPG. http://blogs.lse.ac.uk/impactofsocialsciences/the-handbook/.

[11]Ibid.

[12]REF 02. 2011. *Assessment framework and guidance on submissions*, p26, para 141. www.ref.ac.uk/media/ref/content/pub/assessmentframeworkandguidanceonsubmissions/GOS%20including%20addendum.pdf. Retrieved 2 April 2015.

[13]Ibid, p23, para 118, notes that permitted 'types' of outputs included: Books (or parts of books); Journal articles and conference contributions; Physical artefacts; Exhibitions and performances; Other documents; Digital artefacts (including web content); Other.

## 1.3 DATA COLLECTION AND ANALYSIS

The review drew on an extensive range of evidence sources, including:

### 1.3.1 A formal call for evidence

A call for evidence was launched on 1 May 2014, with a response deadline of 30 June 2014.[14] The steering group appealed for evidence from a wide range of sources, including written summaries or published research. Respondents were asked to focus on four key themes and associated questions, as follows:

A   Identifying useful metrics for research assessment.
B   How metrics should be used in research assessment.
C   'Gaming' and strategic use of metrics.
D   International perspective.

In total, 153 responses were received to the call for evidence: 67 from HEIs, 42 from individuals, 27 from learned societies, 11 from publishers and data providers, three from HE mission groups, and three from other respondents. An analysis of the evidence received can be found at www.hefce.ac.uk/rsrch/metrics/call/.

### 1.3.2 A literature review

Two members of the Steering Group, Paul Wouters and Michael Thelwall, researched and wrote a comprehensive literature review to inform the review's work. The findings of the literature review have been incorporated into this report at appropriate points, and the full review is available as Supplementary Report I.[15]

### 1.3.3 Community and stakeholder engagement

The review team engaged actively with stakeholders across the higher education and research community. These activities included a series of six workshops, organised by the steering group, on specific aspects of the review, such as the role of metrics within the arts and humanities, and links to equality and diversity. Members of the steering group also gave talks and presentations about the work of the review at around 30 conferences, roundtables and workshops. Findings and insights from these events have

---

[14]The call for evidence letter is available at: www.hefce.ac.uk/media/hefce/content/What,we,do/Research/How,we,fund,research/Metrics/Letter-call-for-evidence-metrics-review.pdf

[15]Wouters, P., et al. (2015). *Literature Review: Supplementary Report to the Independent Review of the Role of Metrics in Research Assessment and Management.* HEFCE. DOI: 10.13140/RG.2.1.5066.3520.

been incorporated into the report wherever appropriate. A full itinerary of events linked to the review can be found in the 'Annex of tables' at the end of this report (Table 2).

### 1.3.4 Media and social media

Over the course of the review, the steering group sought to encourage wider discussion of these issues in the sector press (particularly Times Higher Education and Research Fortnight) and through social media. There was extensive use of the #HEFCEmetrics hashtag on Twitter. Members of the steering group, including Stephen Curry,[16] also wrote blog posts on issues relating to the review, and a number of other blog posts and articles were written in response to the review.[17]

### 1.3.5 Focus groups with REF2014 panel members

The steering group participated in a series of focus group sessions for REF2014 panel members, organised by HEFCE, to allow panellists to reflect on their experience, and wider strengths and weaknesses of the exercise. Specific sessions explored the pros and cons of any uses of metrics within REF2014, and their potential role in future assessment exercises.

### 1.3.6 REF2014 evaluations

Where relevant, the steering group also engaged with and analysed findings from HEFCE's portfolio of REF2014 evaluation projects, including:

- The nature, scale and beneficiaries of research impact: an initial analysis of REF2014 case studies;[18]

---

[16]Curry, S. (2014). Debating the role of metrics in research assessment. Blog posted at http://occamstypewriter.org/scurry/2014/10/07/debating-the-role-of-metrics-in-research-assessment/. Retrieved 1 June 2015.

[17]Numerous blog posts, including contributions from steering group members, have been featured at http://blogs.lse.ac.uk/impactofsocialsciences/2014/04/03/reading-list-for-hef cemetrics/. Retrieved 1 June 2015. We have referred to some of these posts within this report. Others discussing the review through blog posts include: David Colquhoun, www.dcscience.net/2014/06/18/should-metrics-be-used-to-assess-research-performance-a-submission-to-hefce/. Retrieved 1 June 2015. Also see contributors to: http://thedisorderofthings.com/tag/metrics/. Retrieved 1 June 2015.

[18]King's College London and Digital Science. (2015). *The Nature, Scale and Beneficiaries of Research Impact: An Initial Analysis of Research Excellence Framework (REF ) 2014 impact case studies*. www.hefce.ac.uk/pubs/rereports/Year/2015/analysisREFimpact/. Retrieved 1 June 2015.

- Preparing impact submissions for REF2014;[19]
- Assessing impact submissions for REF2014;[20]
- Evaluating the 2014 REF: Feedback from participating institutions;[21]
- REF Manager's report;[22]
- REF panel overview reports;[23]
- REF Accountability Review: costs, benefits and burden project report.[24]

### 1.3.7  Relating REF2014 outcomes to indicators

A final element of our evidence gathering was designed to assess the extent to which the outcome of the REF2014 assessment correlated with 15 metrics-based indicators of research performance. For the first time, we were able to associate anonymised REF authors by paper outputs to a selection of metric indicators, including ten bibliometric indicators and five alternative metric indicators. Previous research in this area has been restricted to specific subject areas and departmental level metrics, as the detailed level of data required for this analysis was destroyed before publication of the REF2014 results. This work is summarised in Chapter 9, and presented in detail in Supplementary Report II.[25]

[19]Manville, C., Morgan Jones, M, Frearson, M., Castle-Clarke, S., Henham, M., Gunashekar, S. and Grant, J. (2015). *Preparing Impact Submissions for REF2014: Findings and Observations*. Santa Monica, CA: RAND Corporation. RR-727-HEFCE. www.hefce.ac.uk/media/HEFCE,2014/Content/Pubs/Independentresearch/2015/REF,impact,submissions/REF_impact_prep_process-findings.pdf

[20]Manville, C., Guthrie, S., Henham, M., Garrod, B., Sousa, S., Kirtley, A., Castle-Clark, S. and Ling, T. (2015). *Assessing Impact Submissions for REF2014: An Evaluation*. Santa Monica, CA: RAND Corp. www.hefce.ac.uk/media/HEFCE,2014/Content/Pubs/Independentresearch/2015/REF,impact,submissions/REF_assessing_impact_submissions.pdf

[21]HEFCE. (2015). *Evaluating the 2014 REF: Feedback from Participating Institutions*. www.hefce.ac.uk/media/HEFCE,2014/Content/Research/Review,of,REF/2014_REF_sector_feedback.pdf

[22]HEFCE. (2015). *Research Excellence Framework 2014: Manager's Report*. www.ref.ac.uk/media/ref/content/pub/REF_managers_report.pdf. Retrieved 25 May 2015

[23]HEFCE's Panel overview reports can be downloaded from www.ref.ac.uk/panels/paneloverviewreports/

[24]Technopolis, 2015.

[25]HEFCE (2015). Correlation analysis of REF2014 scores and metrics: *Supplementary Report II to the Independent Review of the Role of Metrics in Research Assessment and Management*. HEFCE. DOI: 10.13140/RG.2.1.3362.4162.

## 1.4 THE STRUCTURE OF THIS REPORT

This opening chapter has provided a summary of the aims and working methods of the review, and the range of evidence sources on which this final report draws.

**Chapter 2** (*The rising tide*) gives a brief history of the role of metrics in research management, and the evolution of data infrastructure and standards to underpin more complex and varied uses of quantitative indicators. It also surveys the main features of research assessment systems in a handful of countries: Australia, Denmark, Italy, the Netherlands, New Zealand and the United States.

**Chapter 3** (*Rough indications*) looks in greater detail at the development, uses and occasional abuses of four categories of quantitative indicators: bibliometric indicators of research quality; alternative indicators of quality; input indicators; and indicators of impact.

**Chapter 4** (*Disciplinary dilemmas*) maps the diversity in types of research output, publication practices and citation cultures across different disciplines, and the implications these have for any attempts to develop standardised indicators across the entire research base. It also considers the extent to which quantitative indicators can be used to support or suppress multi- or interdisciplinary research.

**Chapter 5** (*Judgement and peer review*) compares the strengths and weaknesses of the peer review system with metric-based alternatives, and asks how we strike an appropriate balance between quantitative indicators and expert judgement.

**Chapter 6** (*Management by metrics*) charts the rise of more formal systems of research management within HEIs, and the growing significance that is being placed on quantitative indicators, both within institutions and as a way of benchmarking performance against others. It looks specifically at university rankings and league tables as a visible manifestation of these trends, and considers how these might be applied in more responsible ways across the sector.

**Chapter 7** (*Cultures of counting*) assesses the wider effects a heightened emphasis on quantitative indicators may have on cultures and practices of research, including concerns over systems for performance management, and negative effects on interdisciplinarity, equality and diversity. It also considers the extent to which metrics exacerbate problems of gaming and strategic approaches to research assessment.

**Chapter 8** (*Sciences in transition*) looks beyond HEIs to examine changes in the way key institutions in the wider research funding system are using quantitative indicators, including the Research Councils, research charities such as the Wellcome Trust, and the national academies. It also looks to developments at the European level, within Horizon2020. Finally, it considers how government could make greater use of available quantitative data sources to inform horizon scanning and policies for research and innovation.

**Chapter 9** (*Reflections on REF*) provides a detailed analysis of the modest role that quantitative indicators played in REF2014, and considers a range of scenarios for their use in future assessment exercises. It also outlines the results of our own quantitative analysis, which correlated the actual outcomes of REF2014 against 15 metrics-based indicators of research performance.

Finally, **Chapter 10** (*Responsible metrics*) summarises our headline findings, and makes a set of targeted recommendations to HEIs, research funders (including HEFCE), publishers and data providers, government and the wider research community. Within a framework of *responsible metrics*, the report concludes with clear guidance on how quantitative indicators can be used intelligently and appropriately to further strengthen the quality and impacts of UK research.

# TWO

## THE RISING TIDE

## CHAPTER CONTENTS

"The institutionalization of the citation is the culmination of a decades-long process start-ing with the creation of the Science Citation Index. The impact of this emergence of a new social institution in science and scholarship is often underestimated..."

Paul Wouters[1]

"A timid, bureaucratic spirit has come to suffuse every aspect of intellectual life. More often than not, it comes cloaked in the language of creativity, initiative and entrepreneurialism."

David Graeber[2]

---

[1]Wouters, P. (2014). The Citation: From Culture to Infrastructure. In Cronin, B. and Sugimoto, C. R. (eds.) *Beyond Bibliometrics: Harnessing Multidimensional Indicators of Scholarly Impact*. MIT Press.

[2]Graeber, D. (2015). *The Utopia of Rules: On Technology, Stupidity, and the Secret Joys of Bureaucracy*. London: Melville House.

The quantitative analysis of scientific papers and scholarly articles has been evolving since the early 20th century. Lotka's Law, dating back to 1926, first highlighted that within a defined area over a specific period, a low number of authors accounted for a large percentage of publications.[3] From this point, the field of scientometrics[4] developed rapidly, especially after the creation of the Science Citation Index (SCI), and over time we have seen a proliferation of quantitative indicators for research. This chapter provides a brief history of the use of metrics in research management and assessment, focusing on bibliometrics, alternative metrics and the role of data providers and data infrastructure. We then offer a brief outline of research assessment approaches from six countries.

## 2.1 BIBLIOMETRICS

The SCI was created in 1961, by Eugene Garfield.[5] Initially, it was mainly used by scientometric experts, rather than by the wider research community. In this early stage of scientometrics, data were generally used to describe the development and direction of scientific research, rather than to evaluate its quality.

In the 1980s, new approaches to public management, particularly in the UK and US, led to a growing emphasis on measurable indicators of the value of research. The 1990s gave rise to increasingly strategic forms of research policy and management, accompanied by greater use of bibliometric indicators, including JIF scores. These were developed in 1955 by Eugene Garfield, and became available through Journal Citation Reports from 1975,[6] but were used quite infrequently initially, and have only seen a real explosion in usage since the 1990s.

Citation analysis has been much more readily available since 2001, when the Web of Science (WoS) became easily accessible to all, followed by Scopus in 2003 and Google Scholar (GS) in 2004. J.E. Hirsch invented the Hirsch or h-index in 2005, and this led to a surge of interest in individual level metrics.

---

[3] Elsevier (2007). Scientometrics from Past to Present. *Research Trends*, 1. September 2007. www.researchtrends.com/issue1-september-2007/sciomentrics-from-past-to-present/. Retrieved 1 March 2015.

[4] "Scientometric research [is] the quantitative mathematical study of science and technology, encompassing both bibliometric and economic analysis." Ibid.

[5] Garfield founded the Institute for Scientific Information (ISI), which is now part of Thomson Reuters.

[6] Garfield, E. (2006). The history and meaning of the journal impact factor. *Journal of the American Medical Association*, 295(1): 90–93.

## 2.2 ALTERNATIVE METRICS

From the mid-1990s, as advances in information technology created new ways for researchers to network, write and publish, interest grew in novel indicators better suited to electronic communication and to capturing impacts of different kinds.[7]

These *alternative metrics* include *web citations* in digitised scholarly documents (e.g. eprints, books, science blogs or clinical guidelines) and, more recently, *altmetrics* derived from social media (e.g. social bookmarks, comments, ratings and tweets). Scholars may also produce and use non-refereed academic outputs, such as blog posts, datasets and software, where usage-based indicators are still in the early stages of development. Significant developments in this area include the establishment of F1000Prime in 2002, Mendeley in 2008 and Altmetric.com in 2011.

## 2.3 APPROACHES TO EVALUATION

Research assessment has traditionally focused on input and output indicators, evaluating academic impact through bibliometric measures such as citation counts. However, there is now far greater focus on the wider impacts, outcomes and benefits of research, as reflected in exercises such as REF2014. The measurement of societal impact, with robust indicators and accurate, comparable data, is still in its relative infancy.

Neither research quality nor its impacts are straightforward concepts to pin down or assess. Differing views on what they are, and how they can be measured, lie at the heart of debates over research assessment. In this report, we take research quality to include all scholarly impacts. But what constitutes quality remains contested.[8] As PLOS noted in its submission to this review, "it is unclear whether any unique quality of research influence or impact is sufficiently general to be measured".

In the context of research evaluation, quality typically denotes the overall calibre of research based on the values, criteria or standards inherent in an academic community.[9] However, those values and standards are highly dependent on context: for instance, views

---

[7]Ingwersen, P. (1998). The calculation of Web impact factors. *Journal of Documentation*, 54 (2): 236–243; Borgman, C., and Furner, J. (2002). Scholarly communication and bibliometrics. *Annual Review of Information Science and Technology*, 36. Medford, NJ: Information Today Inc., pp3–72; Priem, J., Taraborelli,, D., Groth, P. and Neylon, C. (2010). *Altmetrics: A Manifesto*, 26 October 2010. http://altmetrics.org/manifesto. Retrieved 1 June 2015.

[8]Halevi, G. and Colledge, L. (2014). Standardizing research metrics and indicators – perspectives and approaches. *Research Trends*, 39. December 2014. www.researchtrends.com/issue-39-december-2014/standardizing-research-metrics-and-indicators/. Retrieved 4 January 2015.

[9]Council of Canadian Academies (2012) *Informing Research Choices: Indicators and Judgment. Report of the Expert Panel on Science Performance and Research Funding*. Ottawa: CCA, p43.

vary enormously across and indeed within certain disciplines, as a result of different research cultures, practices and philosophical approaches. It is more productive to think in terms of research *qualities*, rather than striving for a singular definition.

## 2.4 DATA PROVIDERS

As scientometrics has developed, and evaluation systems have become more sophisticated, so the range of data providers and analysts has grown.[10] Those now engaged with the production of quantitative data and indicators include government agencies at the international, national and local level, HEIs, research groups, and a wide range of commercial data providers, publishers and consultants.

Funding agencies in the US, France, UK and the Netherlands were pioneers in using bibliometrics for research evaluation and monitoring, and the Organisation for Economic Co-operation and Development (OECD) set global standards for national science and technology indicators in its *Frascati Manual*.[11]

Today, leading universities around the world have adopted, or are in the process of developing, comprehensive research information systems in which statistical and qualitative evidence of performance in research, teaching, impact and other services can be recorded.[12] These include benchmarking tools such as SciVal and InCites, management systems such as PURE and Converis, and data consultancy from companies such as Academic Analytics, iFQ, Sciencemetrix and CWTS. Assisted by reference linking services like CrossRef, these enable users to link sophisticated bibliometric and other indicator-based analyses with their information infrastructure at all levels, to monitor institutional, departmental and individual performance. Research funders, such as RCUK, are also adopting new systems like Researchfish, which gather new information about research progress, while other funders are using systems such as UberResearch which aggregate existing information and add value to it.

## 2.5 DATA INFRASTRUCTURE

Systems for data collection and analysis have developed organically and proliferated over the past decade. In response to this review, many HEIs noted the burden associated with

---

[10]Whitley, R. (2010). Reconfiguring the public sciences: the impact of governance changes on authority and innovation in public science systems, in *Reconfiguring Knowledge Production: Changing Authority Relationships in the Sciences and their Consequences for Intellectual Innovation*, edited by R. Whitley et al. Oxford: Oxford University Press.

[11]www.oecd.org/innovation/inno/frascatimanualproposedstandardpracticeforsurveyson-researchandexperimentaldevelopment6thedition.htm

[12]DINI AG Research Information Systems (2015). Research information systems at universities and research institutions – Position Paper of DINI AG FIS. https://zenodo.org/record/17491/files/DINI_AG-FIS_Position_Paper_english.pdf. Retrieved 1 July 2015.

populating and updating multiple systems, and the need for more uniform standards and identifiers that could work across all of them. Others raised concerns that under-pinning systems may become overly controlled by private providers, whose long-term interests may not align with those of the wider research community.

Underpinning infrastructure has to be fit for the purpose of producing robust and trustworthy indicators.[13] Wherever possible, data systems also need to be open and transparent[14] and provide principles for 'open' scholarly infrastructures.[15] To produce indicators that can be shared across platforms, there are a number of prerequisites: *unique identifiers; defined data standards; agreed data semantics;* and *open data processing methods.* These are discussed in turn below. In addition, the infrastructure must be able to present the relevant suites of indicators to optimise forms of assessment that are sensitive to specific research missions and context. They should not 'black-box' particular indicators or present them as relevant for all fields and purposes.

## SOME KEY PLAYERS IN RESEARCH INFORMATION

**Converis** (owned by Thomson Reuters) is an integrated research information system. It provides support for universities, other research institutions and funding offices in collecting and managing data through the research lifecycle. http://converis.thomsonreuters.com/

**CrossRef** is a collaborative reference linking service that functions as a sort of digital switchboard. Its specific mandate is to be the citation linking backbone for all scholarly information in electronic form. It holds no full text content, but effects linkages through CrossRef Digital Object Identifiers (CrossRef DOI), which are tagged to article metadata supplied by the participating publishers. www.crossref.org/

**Elements** (owned by Symplectic) is designed to gather research information to reduce the administrative burden placed on researchers, and to support research organisation librarians and administrators. http://symplectic.co.uk/

**InCites** (owned by Thomson Reuters) is a customised, web-based research evaluation tool that allows users to analyse institutional productivity and benchmark output against peers

*(Continued)*

---

[13]Jacso, P. (2006). Deflated, inflated and phantom citation counts. *Online Information Review*, 30(3): 297–309; Abramo, G. and D'Angelo, C. A. (2011). Evaluating research: from informed peer review to bibliometrics. *Scientometrics*, 87: 499–514. DOI:10.1007/s11192-011-0352-7.

[14]Bilder, G., Lin, J. and Neylon, C. (2015). *Principles for Open Scholarly Infrastructure-v1.* http://cameronneylon.net/blog/principles-for-open-scholarly-infrastructures/. Retrieved 1 June 2015. http://dx.doi.org/10.6084/m9.figshare.1314859

[15]Royal Society. (2012). *Science as an Open Enterprise.* The Royal Society Science Policy Centre report 02/12. https://royalsociety.org/~/media/policy/projects/sape/2012-06-20-saoe.pdf. Retrieved 1 June 2015.

18 | the metric tide

*(Continued)*

worldwide, through access to customised citation data, global metrics, and profiles on leading research institutions. http://researchanalytics.thomsonreuters.com/incites/

**PURE** (owned by Elsevier) is a research information system. It accesses and aggregates internal and external sources, and offers analysis, reporting and benchmarking functions. www.elsevier.com/solutions/pure

**Researchfish** is an online database of outputs reported by researchers linked to awards, now widely used by UK funding agencies and being taken up by funders in Denmark and Canada. It aims to provide a structured approach to prospectively capturing outputs and outcomes from as soon as funding starts, potentially to long after awards have finished. The information is used by funders to track the progress, productivity and quality of funded research, and as a way of finding examples of impact. https://www.researchfish.com/

**SciVal** (owned by Elsevier) provides information on the research performance of research institutions across the globe. This can be used for analysis and benchmarking of performance. www.elsevier.com/solutions/scival

**UberResearch** provides services aimed at science funders including information tools based on natural language processing. www.uberresearch.com/

---

## 2.5.1 Unique identifiers

In order for an indicator to be reliable, it is important to be able to collect as much as possible of the underlying data that the indicator purports to represent. For example, if we consider citations to academic outputs, it is clear that the main databases do not include all possible citations, and that numbers of citations within them can vary. As PLOS noted in its response to our call for evidence, "there are no adequate sources of bibliometric data that are publicly accessible, useable, auditable and transparent."

In order to correctly count the number of citations that an article has, all other articles must be checked to see if they cite the article in question. This can be achieved through manual processes, but is subject to error. With unique identifiers for articles, the process can be automated (reducing sources of error to original mis-citation by the author).

The most commonly used identifier is the Digital Object Identifier (DOI).[16] While still not universal, DOIs have gained considerable traction across the sector. For instance, looking at the 191,080 outputs submitted to REF2014, 149,670 of these were submitted with DOIs (see Supplementary Report II, Table 1). Use of DOIs varies by discipline, and is still less common in the arts and humanities than in other areas.

DOIs in themselves are not sufficient for robust metrics. As well as article identifiers, a robust management and evaluation system needs unique identifiers for journals, publishers, authors and institutions. This would enable answers to more sophisticated

---

[16]www.doi.org/

questions, such as: How many articles has a particular author produced with citations above the average for the journal in question?

*Journals* have, in general, adopted the International Standard Serial Number (ISSN[17]) system. However, there is still a small proportion that have not. Journals which appear in more than one format (e.g. print and online) will have an ISSN for each media type, but one is the master (ISSN-L), to which the other ISSNs link.

*Publisher and institutional identifiers* are more problematic. There are various options for uniquely identifying organisations. One 2013 study found 22 organisational identifiers currently in use in the higher education sector in the UK.[18] But while none of these is wholly authoritative, both the International Standard Name Identifier (ISNI[19]) and UK Provider Reference Number (UKPRN[20]) have traction. The former is international, and the latter is more UK-centric and does not include funders; so it would seem that ISNI is the preferred route for developing an authoritative list of publishers.

## ORCID (OPEN RESEARCHER AND CONTRIBUTOR ID)

ORCID is a non-proprietary alphanumeric code to uniquely identify academic authors. Its stated aim is to aid "the transition from science to e-Science, wherein scholarly publications can be mined to spot links and ideas hidden in the ever-growing volume of scholarly literature". ORCID provides a persistent identity for humans, similar to that created for content-related entities on digital networks by DOIs.

ORCID launched its registry services and started issuing user identifiers on 16 October 2012. It is now an independent non-profit organisation, and is freely usable and fully interoperable with other ID systems. ORCID is also a subset of the International Standard Name Identifier (ISNI). The two organisations are cooperating: ISNI has reserved a block of identifiers for use by ORCID, so it is now possible for an individual to have both an ISNI and an ORCID.

By the end of 2013 ORCID had 111 member organisations and over 460,000 registrants. As of 1 June 2015, the number of registered accounts reported by ORCID was 1,370,195. Its organisational members include publishers, such as Elsevier, Springer, Wiley and Nature Publishing Group, funders, learned societies and universities.

*Author identifiers* are particularly important, as a particular scholar's contributions to the scientific literature can be hard to recognise, as personal names are rarely unique,

---

[17]www.issn.org/understanding-the-issn/the-issn-international-register/

[18]Hammond, M. and Curtis, G. (2013). Landscape study for CASRAI-UK Organisational ID. http://casrai.org/423

[19]www.isni.org/

[20]https://www.ukrlp.co.uk/

can change (e.g. through marriage), and may have cultural differences in name order or abbreviations. Several types of author identifiers exist, and a detailed analysis of the pros and cons of these was undertaken in 2012 by Jisc.[21] The ORCID system is widely regarded as the best, and uptake of ORCID is now growing rapidly in the UK and internationally. The same analysis recommended that the UK adopted ORCID, and many of the key players in the UK research system endorsed this proposal in a joint statement in January 2013.[22] A similar initiative in the US funded by the Alfred P. Sloan Foundation highlighted the importance of advocacy and improved data quality.[23] A recent Jisc-ARMA initiative has successfully piloted the adoption of ORCID in a number of UK HEIs[24], and an agreement negotiated by Jisc Collections will enable UK HEIs to benefit from reduced ORCID membership costs and enhanced technical support.[25] UK uptake will also be driven by the Wellcome Trust's decision to make ORCID iDs a mandatory requirement for funding applications from August 2015,[26] and by the strong support shown by Research Councils UK. ORCID also recently announced an agreement with ANVUR (National Agency for the Evaluation of University and Research Institutes) and CRUI (Conference of Italian University Rectors) to implement ORCID on a national scale in Italy.[27]

For outputs other than journal articles, ISBNs (International Standard Book Numbers)[28] for books are analogous to ISSNs for journals. A longstanding issue here is that different editions (e.g. hardback and paperback) have different ISBNs, but retailers such as Amazon have made progress in disambiguating this information.

---

[21] JISC Researcher Identifier Task and Finish Group. (2012). *Researcher Identifier Recommendations – Sector Validation.* www.serohe.co.uk/wp-content/uploads/2013/10/Clax-for-JISC-rID-validation-report-final.pdf. Retrieved 1 June 2015.

[22] Signatories to this joint statement include ARMA, HEFCE, HESA, RCUK, UCISA, Wellcome Trust and Jisc.

[23] Brown, J., Oyler, C. and Haak, L. (2015). *Final Report: Sloan ORCID Adoption and Integration Program 2013–2014.* http://figshare.com/articles/Final_Report_Sloan_ORCID_Adoption_and_Integration_Program_2013_2014/1290632.http://dx.doi.org/10.6084/m9.figshare.1290632. Retrieved 25 May 2015.

[24] http://orcidpilot.jiscinvolve.org/wp/. ORCID is also discussed in Anstey, A. (2014). How can we be certain who authors really are? Why ORCID is important to the British Journal of Dermatology. *British Journal of Dermatology*, 171(4): 679–680. DOI 10.1111/bjd.13381. Also Butler, D. (2012) Scientists: your number is up. *Nature*, 485, 564. DOI: 10.1038/485564a.

[25] http://jisc.ac.uk/news/national-consortium-for-orcid-set-to-improve-uk-research-visibility-and-collaboration-23-jun. Retrieved 28 June 2015.

[26] http://blog.wellcome.ac.uk/2015/06/30/who-are-you-recognising-researchers-with-orcid-identifiers/

[27] https://orcid.org/blog/2015/06/19/italy-launches-national-orcid-implementation. Retrieved 28 June 2015.

[28] www.isbn.nielsenbook.co.uk/controller.php?page=158#What_is_an_ISBN_

Funder references are important unique identifiers for contracts between research-performing and research-funding organisations. This information is required by most funders to be included in acknowledgement sections within manuscripts submitted for publication. However despite efforts to encourage standard forms for this acknowledgement,[29] there is a need for authoritative sources for funder names (as with institutional names above), and for authenticating the funding references (although Europe PubMed Central provides a post-publication grant lookup tool populated by those agencies that fund it).[30]

Increasingly, other forms of output, such as datasets and conference proceedings, are issued with DOIs, or DOIs can be obtained retrospectively, for example through platforms such as ResearchGate. Similarly DOIs can also resolve to ISBNs.

Other systems of unique identifiers have been proposed to support the sharing of research equipment[31] and to improve the citation of research resources.[32]

## 2.5.2 Defined data standards

Once unique and disambiguated identifiers for objects in the research information arena have been agreed, the next issue is how to represent them and their associated metadata. Various standards for data structure and metadata have been proposed over time. Across Europe, one standard for research information management, the Common European Research Information Format (CERIF),[33] has been adopted. In 1991 the European Commission recommended CERIF to the member states, and in 2002 handed stewardship of the standard to euroCRIS.[34] There have been a number of iterations since then.[35]

In 2009, Jisc commissioned a report, *Exchanging Research Information in the UK*,[36] which proposed the use of CERIF as the UK standard for research information exchange. This was

---

[29]www.rin.ac.uk/our-work/research-funding-policy-and-guidance/acknowledgement-funders-journal-articles Retrieved 1 June 2015.

[30]http://europepmc.org/GrantLookup/. Retrieved 1 June 2015.

[31]For example, see the N8 Shared Equipment Inventory System www.n8equipment.org.uk/. Retrieved 1 June 2015.

[32]Bandrowski, A., Brush, M., Grethe, J.S. et al. The Resource Identification Initiative: A cultural shift in publishing [v1; ref status: awaiting peer review, http://f1000r.es/5fj] *F1000Research 2015*, 4: 134. DOI:10.12688/f1000research.6555.1. Retrieved 1 June 2015.

[33]http://eurocris.org/cerif/main-features-cerif

[34]EuroCRIS is a not-for-profit association with offices in The Hague, The Netherlands, that brings together experts on research information in general and research information systems (CRIS) in particular. The organisation has 200+ members, mainly coming from Europe, but also from some countries outside of Europe. www.eurocris.org/

[35]http://eurocris.org/cerif/feature-tour/cerif-16

[36]Rogers, N., Huxley, L. and Ferguson, N. (2009). *Exchanging Research Information in the UK*. http://repository.jisc.ac.uk/448/1/exri_final_v2.pdf. Retrieved 1 June 2015.

followed by several Jisc-funded initiatives[37] and a further report: *Adoption of CERIF in Higher Education Institutions in the UK*[38] which noted progress but a lack of UK expertise. The majority of off-the-shelf research information management systems used in UK HEIs today are CERIF-compliant and able to exchange data in the agreed format. To date the CERIF standard covers around 300 entities and 2000 attributes, including: people, organisations (and sub units), projects, publications, products, equipment, funders, programmes, locations, events and prizes, although fully describing research qualities in this way is an ongoing task.

### 2.5.3 Agreed data semantics

An agreed approach to the semantics of data elements is required to ensure that everyone interprets data in the same way. One example is the titles used for academic staff. In the UK, it might be possible to agree on a standard scale of lecturer, senior lecturer, reader and professor, but this does not translate to other countries where other titles like 'associate professor' are commonly used and 'readers' are unknown. Clearly the context is important to the semantics. In order to compare research items from different databases, we need to have a standard vocabulary that we can match to, ideally at the international level, or else on a country basis. The Consortia Advancing Standards in Research Administration Information (CASRAI) is an international non-profit organisation that constructs such dictionaries, working closely with other standards organisations.

---

### CASRAI

The Consortia Advancing Standards in Research Administration Information (CASRAI) is an international non-profit organisation dedicated to reducing the administrative burden on researchers and improving business intelligence capacity of research institutions and funders. CASRAI works by partnering with funders, universities, suppliers and sector bodies to define a dictionary and catalogue of exchangeable business 'data profiles'. These create an interoperable 'drawbridge' between collaborating organisations and individuals. http://casrai.org/

---

### 2.5.4 More than pure semantics

Once all these elements are in place, it is possible to build robust indicators and metrics. But here again, agreed definitions are key. Take the example of proposal success rates.

---

[37]Russell, R. (2011). *Research Information Management in the UK: Current Initiatives Using* CERIF. www.ukoln.ac.uk/rim/dissemination/2011/rim-cerif-uk.pdf. Retrieved 1 June 2015.

[38]Russell, R. (2012). *Adoption of CERIF in Higher Education Institutions in the UK: A Landscape Study.* www.ukoln.ac.uk/isc/reports/cerif-landscape-study-2012/CERIF-UK-landscape-report-v1.0.pdf. Retrieved 1 June 2015.

If an institution has submitted ten proposals for funding and three have been funded, it may claim to have a 30% success rate. This indicator could be benchmarked against other institutions. However, if two of those proposals were yet to be reviewed, a three in eight or 37.5% success rate could also be claimed. Alternatively, the success rate might be calculated based on the financial value of applications and awards rather than the number submitted, each definition producing potentially different 'success rates' from the same data.[39]

The semantics of any metrics must also be clear and transparent. Progress in this area has been made by the UK-led Snowball Metrics consortium, which has specified 24 metrics 'recipes' to date, in areas such as publications and citations, research grants, collaboration, and societal impact. Snowball is also gaining some traction in the USA and Australia.[40]

---

## SNOWBALL METRICS

Snowball Metrics is a bottom-up academia-industry initiative. The universities involved aim to agree on methodologies that are robustly and clearly defined, so that the metrics they describe enable the confident comparison of apples with apples. These metrics (described by recipes) are data source- and system-agnostic, meaning that they are not tied to any particular provider of data or tools. The resulting benchmarks between research-intensive universities provide reliable information to help understand research strengths, and thus to establish and monitor institutional strategies. www.snowballmetrics.com/

---

## 2.6 INTERNATIONAL PERSPECTIVES

Although this review has focused on the UK, we have taken a keen interest in how other countries approach these issues. At several of our workshops and steering group meetings, we heard presentations and considered questions from international perspectives.[41]

---

[39]Kerridge, S. (2015). Questions of identity. *Research Fortnight*. 27 May 2015. https://www.researchprofessional.com/0/rr/news/uk/views-of-the-uk/2015/5/Questions-of-identity.html. Retrieved 1 June 2015.

[40]For relevant discussion, see US Research Universities Futures Consortium (2013). *The Current State and Recommendations for Meaningful Academic Research Metrics among American Research Universities*. www.researchuniversitiesfutures.org/us-research-metrics-working-group-current-state-and-recommendations-oct2013.pdf. Retrieved 1 March 2015.

[41]For example, Clare Donovan presented insights from her research in Australia and elsewhere at our Arts and Humanities workshop hosted by Warwick University; www.hefce.ac.uk/media/hefce/content/news/Events/2015/HEFCE,metrics,workshop,Warwick/Donovan.pdf. Donovan also contributed to one of the Review group's early steering group meetings. Academic Analytics, who presented at our workshops in Sheffield and Sussex, discussed their approach and use of data in US and UK contexts. www.hefce.ac.uk/media/hefce/content/

A handful of the responses to our call for evidence came from overseas, and our schedule of stakeholder events included meetings or presentations in Paris, Melbourne, Barcelona and Doha (see Table 2 in the 'Annex of tables').

Dialogue, learning and exchange across different systems are important, and any moves that the UK makes in respect of greater use of metrics are likely to be watched closely. The UK system continues to attract the attention of research leaders, managers and policymakers worldwide – particularly since the introduction of the impact element for REF2014.[42] Here we offer a brief outline of some of the striking features of research assessment in a handful of other countries – Australia, Denmark, Italy, the Netherlands, New Zealand and the United States – chosen to reflect the diversity of systems in operation worldwide.

### 2.6.1 Australia

The Australian Research Council administers *Excellence in Research for Australia* (ERA), which aims to identify and promote excellence in research across Australian HEIs. There is no funding attached to its outcomes. The first full round of ERA (in 2010–11) was the first time a nationwide stocktake of disciplinary strengths had been conducted in Australia. Data submitted by 41 HEIs covered all eligible researchers and their research outputs.

ERA is based upon the principle of expert review informed by citation-based analysis, with the precise mix depending on discipline; citations are used for most science, engineering and medical disciplines, and peer review for others. It aims to be "a dynamic and flexible research assessment system that combines the objectivity of multiple quantitative indicators with the holistic assessment provided by expert review...."[43]

ERA 2012[44] evaluations were informed by four broad categories of indicators:

- **Of research quality**: publishing profile, citation analysis, ERA peer review and peer reviewed research income;
- **Of research volume and activity**: total research outputs, research income and other items within the profile of eligible researchers;
- **Of research application**: commercialisation income and other applied measures;
- **Of recognition**: based on a range of esteem measures.

---

news/Events/2014/Metrics,we,trust/HEFCEMetrics_Olejniczak.pdf. The suppliers invited to our Sussex workshop operate at the global level, these being Academic Analytics, Altmetric, PLOS, Snowball Metrics, Elsevier and The Conversation, Plum Analytics and Thomson Reuters.

[42]See relevant discussion on internationalising the REF: www.researchresearch.com/index.php?option=com_news&template=rr_2col&view=article&articleId=1342955. Retrieved 1 June 2015.

[43]www.arc.gov.au/era/faq.htm#Q6. Retrieved 1 June 2015.

[44]www.arc.gov.au/pdf/era12/report_2012/ARC_ERA12_Introduction.pdf

Evaluation of the data submitted was undertaken by eight evaluation committees, representing different disciplinary clusters. The next ERA round will take place in 2015.[45]

## 2.6.2 Denmark

Danish public university funding is allocated according to four parameters: education based on study credits earned by the institution (45%); research activities measured by external funding (20%); research activities measured by the 'BFI', a metrics-based evaluation system (25%)[46]; and number of PhD graduates (10%). The current system was gradually implemented from 2010 to 2012 following agreement in 2009 to follow a new model. It is primarily a distribution model, based on the Danish Agency for Science, Technology and Innovation's count of peer reviewed research publications. The goal was to allocate an increasing proportion of the available research funding according to the outcomes of the national research assessment exercise. Given the methodology employed, the BFI has been described as a primarily quantitative distribution system, as opposed to a quality measurement system.[47]

Due to the limitations of existing publications databases (see Chapter 3), the Danish government decided to create its own. This enables the BFI to be defined by Danish researchers, with 67 expert groups of academics involved in selecting items for inclusion in two authority lists, one of series (journals, book series or conference series) and one of publishers. These are then ranked each year by the panels, and this is then used as the basis of a points system for researchers.

The scoring system includes monographs, articles in series and anthologies, doctoral theses and patents. Peer review is a prerequisite for inclusion on an authoritative list. These lists decide what publishers and what journals are recognised as being worth to publish in, and what level this recognition has – Level 1 or Level 2. Level 2 channels generate more points. These lists effectively decide which publication channels contain serious research. All eligible research outputs can be attributed BFI-points as they are entered into the system. Different weights are applied for different sorts of output and publication channel, so the system aims to assess performance and not just volume of production.

## 2.6.3 Italy

In 2013, Italy's National Agency for the Evaluation of the University and Research Systems (ANVUR) completed its largest ever evaluation initiative, known as the 'eValuation of

---

[45]Submission guidelines are provided at the following. Australian Research Council (2014) ERA 2015 Submission Guidelines. www.arc.gov.au/pdf/ERA15/ERA%202015%20Submission%20Guidelines.pdf. These include changes to the process since 2012, outlined on pp7–9.

[46]Veterager Pedersen, C. (2010). The Danish bibliometric research indicator – BFI: Research publications, research assessment, university funding. *ScieCom Info*, 4: 1–4.

[47]Ibid.

the Quality of Research' (VQR), across 95 universities, 12 public research bodies and 16 voluntary organisations.[48] The aim was to construct a national ranking of universities and institutes, based on key indicators, including: research outcomes obtained from 2004 to 2010; ability to attract funding; number of international collaborations; patents registered; spin-offs; and other third-party activities.

The results of the VQR are being used by the education and research ministry to award €540 million in 'prize funds' from the government's university budget. The process included the evaluation of approximately 195,000 publications, using a hybrid approach of two methodologies:

- Bibliometric analysis: based on the impact factor (IF) of the journal[49] and the number of citations received in a year, divided by articles published;
- Peer review: assigned to around 14,000 external reviewers, more than 4,000 of whom were from outside Italy.

Bibliometric analysis was used in the natural sciences and engineering; whereas for social sciences and humanities (Panels 10–14), only peer review was used. The overall evaluation of institutions was based on a weighted sum of various indicators: 50% for the quality of the research products submitted (for faculty members, the maximum number of products was three); and the remaining 50% based on a composite score from six indicators. These are: capacity to attract resources (10%); mobility of research staff (10%); internationalisation (10%); PhD programmes (10%); ability to attract research funds (5%); and overall improvement from the last VQR (5%). ANVUR used 14 panels to undertake evaluations, divided by disciplinary area.

### 2.6.4 Netherlands

Since 2003, it has been the responsibility of individual Dutch university boards and faculties to organise research assessment on a six-yearly cycle, in line with a 'Standard Evaluation Protocol' (SEP).[50] Assessments are made by expert committees, which may

---

[48]A useful analysis of the VQR is provided by Abramo, G. and D'Angelo, C.A. (2015). The VQR, Italy's Second National Research Assessment: Methodological Failures and Ranking Distortions. *Journal of the Association for Information, Science and Technology.*

[49]For those indexed in Web of Science, or the SCImago Journal Rank for those indexed in Scopus.

[50]The Standard Evaluation Protocol (SEP) was jointly developed by the Royal Netherlands Academy of Arts and Sciences (KNAW), The Association of Universities in the Netherlands (VSNU) and the Netherlands Organisation for Scientific Research (NWO). The goal of the SEP is to provide common guidelines for the evaluation and improvement of research and research policy to be used by university boards, institutes and the expert evaluation committees.

use qualitative and quantitative indicators to score research groups or programmes on a scale. The distribution of government research funds is not explicitly linked to this assessment process.[51]

From 2015 onwards, the assessment involves three criteria: quality, societal relevance, and viability.[52] Productivity was previously a criterion, but has now been removed as a goal in itself (and subsumed under the quality criterion) to put less emphasis on the number of publications and more on their quality. The review also looks at the quality of PhD training, and management of research integrity (including how an institution has dealt with any cases of research misconduct). The research unit's own strategy and targets are guiding principles for the evaluation. In addition, the evaluation should provide feedback to the evaluated research institutes and groups on their research agendas for the near future.

## 2.6.5 New Zealand

New Zealand's evaluation system is known as the 'Performance-Based Research Fund' (PBRF), and is used to assess the performance of all Tertiary Education Organisations (TEOs).[53] Its four objectives are: to increase the quality of basic and applied research at degree-granting TEOs; to support world-leading teaching and learning at degree and postgraduate levels; to assist TEOs to maintain and lift their competitive rankings relative to their international peers; and to provide robust public information to stakeholders about research performance within and across TEOs.

The PBRF is carried out every six years; most recently in 2012,[54] when 27 institutions participated (eight universities, ten institutes of technology and polytechnics, one wānanga,[55] and eight private training establishments.) The amount of funding that a participating institution receives is based on three elements: quality evaluation (55%); research degree completions (25%); and external research income (20%).

The quality element of the process rests on the submission and evaluation of evidence portfolios. Twelve specialist peer-review panels assess and evaluate these portfolios with

---

[51]Key Perspectives Ltd. (2009). *A Comparative Review of Research Assessment Regimes in Five Countries and the Role of Libraries in the Research Assessment Process*: Report Commissioned by OCLC Research. www.oclc.org/research/publications/library/2009/2009-09.pdf

[52]https://www.knaw.nl/nl/actueel/publicaties/standard-evaluation-protocol-2015-2021

[53]www.tec.govt.nz/Funding/Fund-finder/Performance-Based-Research-Fund-PBRF-/. Retrieved 30 March 2015.

[54]Details of the 2012 exercises can be downloaded from www.tec.govt.nz/Funding/Fund-finder/Performance-Based-Research-Fund-PBRF-/quality-evaluation/2012-Quality-Evaluation/

[55]In the New Zealand education system, a wānanga is a publicly-owned tertiary education organisation that provides education in a Māori cultural context.

additional advice from expert advisory groups and specialists as needed.[56] The PBRF is unusual in that it takes the individual (rather than the department or school) as the unit of assessment, so provides very detailed performance information that can inform strategic planning and resource allocation within institutions. It does not systematically measure research impacts outside academia.

## 2.6.6 United States

The US does not have a centralised national assessment system for its universities and research institutes; however, in recent years, it has actively supported projects including STAR METRICS (Science and Technology for America's Reinvestment: Measuring the Effects of Research, Innovation and Competitiveness and Science).[57] This was launched in 2010 and is led by the National Institute of Health (NIH), the National Science Foundation (NSF), and the Office of Science and Technology Policy (OSTP). It aims to create a repository of data and tools to help assess the impact of federal research investments.

STAR METRICS focus at two different levels:

- Level I: Developing uniform, auditable and standardised measures of the impact of science spending on job creation, using data from research institutions' existing database records; [58]
- Level II: Developing measures of the impact of federal science investment on scientific knowledge (using metrics such as publications and citations), social outcomes (e.g. health outcomes measures and environmental impact factors), workforce outcomes (e.g. student mobility and employment), and economic growth (e.g. tracing patents, new company start-ups and other measures). This is achieved through the Federal RePORTER[59] tool, thus developing an open and automated data infrastructure that will enable the documentation and analysis of a subset of the inputs, outputs, and outcomes resulting from federal investments in science.

The STAR METRICS project involves a broad consortium of federal R&D funding agencies with a shared vision of developing data infrastructures and products to support evidence-based analyses of the impact of research investment.[60] It aims to utilise existing administrative data from federal agencies and their grantees, and match them with existing research databases of economic, scientific and social outcomes. It has recently been announced that from 2016 onwards resources will be redirected away from STAR

---

[56]PBRF Quality evaluation guidance 2012 is provided at www.tec.govt.nz/Documents/Publications/PBRF-Quality-Evaluation-Guidelines-2012.pdf

[57]https://www.starmetrics.nih.gov/

[58]STAR METRICS will be discontinuing Level I activities as of 1 January 2016.

[59]http://federalreporter.nih.gov

[60]But not all funders are involved, e.g. the National Endowment for the Humanities.

METRICS data scraping to focus on the RePORTER tool, which has similarities to the UK Gateway to Research approach.[61]

## 2.7 ADDING IT UP

As these snapshots reveal, the ways that metrics and indicators are conceived and used varies by country, often significantly. The nature of the assessment approach, and the choice, use and relative importance of particular indicators, reflect particular policies, and usually involve compromises around fairness across disciplines, robustness, administrative and/or cost burdens and sector buy in.

Two recent studies provide further discussion of how national approaches differ:

- A 2012 report by the Council of Canadian Academies looks at the systems used in ten different countries.[62] It emphasises the importance of national research context in defining a given research assessment, underlining that no single set of indicators for assessment will be ideal in all circumstances. The report also highlights a global trend towards national research assessment models that incorporate both quantitative indicators and expert judgement.
- A 2014 study by Technopolis examined 12 EU member states and Norway.[63] This includes a comparative consideration of systems using performance-based research funding (PRF systems). The report shows that Czech Republic is the only country that limits the indicators used to the output of research, (even though it is the PRF system that covers research and innovation-related outputs in the most detailed and comprehensive manner). In a second group of countries – Denmark, Finland, Norway (PRI), Belgium/PL (BOF), Norway (HEI) and Sweden – the PRFs include both output and systemic indicators; (in Denmark, Finland and Norway this includes indicators related to innovation-oriented activities). Only a few countries also examine research impacts: Italy, UK (REF), France (AERES) and Belgium/FL (IOF). While the PRFs in France and Belgium focus on impacts in the spheres of research and innovation, Italy and the UK also consider societal impacts.

---

[61]http://gtr.rcuk.ac.uk/

[62]Council of Canadian Academies (2012) work included analysis of research assessment systems employed in ten countries including Australia, China, Finland, Germany, the Netherlands, Norway, Singapore, South Korea, USA and the UK.

[63]Technopolis. (2014). *Measuring Scientific Performance for Improved Policy Making*. www.europarl. europa.eu/RegData/etudes/etudes/join/2014/527383/IPOL-JOIN_ET(2014)527383(SUM01)_ EN.pdf Published for the European Parliamentary Research Service. This examined Norway, Sweden, the UK, Spain, France, Belgium/FL, Italy, Czech Republic, Denmark, the Netherlands, Slovakia, Austria and Finland. A third report published in 2010, by the expert group on assessment in university-based research (AUBR), provided case studies of 16 different countries, which again represent a breadth of approaches and objectives: http://ec.europa.eu/research/science-society/ document_library/pdf_06/assessing-europe-university-based-research_en.pdf.

It is valuable to learn from the approaches being used by different countries, particularly as research and data infrastructure are increasingly global. However, context is also crucial to good assessment, and there will be elements that are specific to the design, operation and objectives of the UK system. Overall though, we are likely to see greater harmonisation of approaches, certainly across EU member states. Recent initiatives, such as the 2014 'Science 2.0' White Paper from the European Commission point towards a more integrated architecture for research funding, communication, dissemination and impact. The UK has been at the forefront of these debates since the 1980s, and over that same period its research system, across many indicators, has grown significantly in strength. Ensuring that the UK is positioned well for the next wave of change in how the research system operates – in terms of data infrastructure, standards and systems of assessment – is a vital part of our overall leadership in research. Moves by HEFCE to explore the potentially increased internationalisation of research assessment are to be welcomed, although such steps are not without strategic and operational challenges. Proceeding cautiously, in an exploratory way, seems an appropriate approach.

# THREE

## ROUGH INDICATIONS

### CHAPTER CONTENTS

"The answer to the Great Question of Life, the Universe and Everything is... forty-two', said Deep Thought, with infinite majesty and calm."

Douglas Adams, *The Hitchhiker's*
*Guide to the Galaxy*

Having charted the development of research metrics and indicators and their usage internationally, this chapter turns the focus on their application. It looks in detail at the current development, uses and occasional abuses of four broad categories of indicator: bibliometric indicators of quality (3.1); alternative indicators (3.2); input indicators (3.3); and indicators of impact (3.4).

## 3.1 BIBLIOMETRIC INDICATORS OF QUALITY

The most common approaches to measuring research quality involve bibliometric methods, notably weighted publication counts; and citation-based indicators, such as the JIF or h-index. As the Canadian Council of Academies report states: "Bibliometric indicators are the paradigmatic quantitative indicators with respect to measurement of scientific research."[1]

This section gives a brief overview of the technical possibilities of bibliometric indicators. Many points raised here are addressed in greater detail in our literature review (Supplementary Report I), reflecting the breadth of existing literature on citation impact indicators, the use of scientometric indicators in research evaluation[2], and in measuring the performance of individual researchers[3].

Several considerations need to be borne in mind when working with bibliometric analyses, including: differences between academic subjects/disciplines; coverage of sources within databases; the selection of the appropriate unit of analysis for the indicator in question; the question of credit allocation where outputs may include multiple authors, and accounting for self-citations.

### 3.1.1 Bibliographic databases

The three most important multidisciplinary bibliographic databases are Web of Science, Scopus, and Google Scholar. Scopus has a broader coverage of the scholarly literature than Web of Science. Some studies report that journals covered by Scopus but not by Web of Science tend to have a low citation impact and tend to be more nationally oriented, suggesting that the most important international academic journals are usually covered by both databases. Certain disciplines, especially the Social Sciences and Humanities (SSH) create special challenges for bibliometric analyses.[4] Google Scholar is generally found to outperform both Web of Science and Scopus in terms of its coverage of the literature. However, there are a few fields, mainly in the natural sciences, in which some studies have reported the coverage of Google Scholar to be worse than the coverage of Web of Science and Scopus. On the other hand, the coverage of Google Scholar has been improving over time, so it is not clear the same still applies today.

### 3.1.2 Basic citation impact indicators

A large number of citation impact indicators have been proposed in the literature. Most of these indicators can be seen as variants or extensions of a limited set of basic indicators: the total and the average number of citations of the publications of a research unit

---

[1]Council of Canadian Academies (2012). pp53–54.

[2]Vinkler, P. (2010). *The Evaluation of Research by Scientometric Indicators*. Oxford: Chandos Publishing.

[3]Wildgaard, L., Schneider, J. W. and Larsen, B. (2014). A review of the characteristics of 108 author-level bibliometric indicators. *Scientometrics*, 101(1): 125–158.

[4]See Sections 1.1 and 1.4.1 of the literature review (Supplementary Report I).

(e.g. of an individual researcher, a research group, or a research institution); the number and the proportion of highly cited publications of a research unit; and a research unit's h-index. There is criticism in the literature of the use of indicators based on total or average citation counts. Citation distributions tend to be highly skewed, and therefore the total or the average number of citations of a set of publications may be strongly influenced by one or a few highly cited publications ('outliers'). This is often considered undesirable. Indicators based on the idea of counting highly cited publications are suggested as a more robust alternative to indicators based on total or average citation counts.

### 3.1.3 Exclusion of specific types of publications and citations

When undertaking bibliometric analyses, one needs to decide which types of publications and citations are included and which are not. In Web of Science and Scopus, each publication has a document type. It is clear that research articles, which simply have the document type 'article', should be included in bibliometric analyses. However, publications of other document types, such as 'editorial material', 'letter', and 'review' may be either included or excluded.

Most bibliometric researchers prefer to exclude author self-citations from bibliometric analyses. There is no full agreement in the literature on the importance of excluding these citations. In some bibliometric analyses, the effect of author self-citations is very small, suggesting that there is no need to exclude these citations. In general, however, it is suggested that author self-citations should preferably be excluded, at least in analyses at low aggregation levels, for instance at the level of individual researchers. However, as self-citation is a common and acceptable practice in some disciplines but frowned upon in others, choosing to exclude them will affect some subject areas more than others.

### 3.1.4 Normalisation of citation impact indicators

In research assessment contexts, there is often a requirement to make comparisons between publications from different fields. There is agreement in the literature that citation counts of publications from different fields should not be directly compared with each other, because there are large differences among fields in the average number of citations per publication. Researchers have proposed various approaches to normalise citation impact indicators for differences between field, between older and more recent publications, and between publications of different types.

Most attention in the literature has been paid to normalised indicators based on average citation counts. Recent discussions focus on various technical issues in the calculation of these indicators, for instance whether highly cited publication indicators count the proportion of the publications of a research unit that belong to the top 10% or the top 1% of their field, and more sophisticated variants thereof, including the position of publications within the citation distribution of their field.

A key issue in the calculation of normalised citation impact indicators is the way in which the concept of a research field is operationalised. The most common approach is to work with the predefined fields in a database such as Web of Science, but this approach is heavily criticised. Some researchers argue that fields may be defined at different levels of aggregation and that each aggregation level offers a legitimate but different viewpoint on the citation impact of publications. Other researchers suggest the use of disciplinary classification systems (e.g. Medical Subject Headings or Chemical Abstracts sections) or sophisticated computer algorithms to define fields, typically at a relatively low level of aggregation. Another approach is to calculate normalised citation impact indicators without defining fields in an explicit way. This idea is implemented in so-called 'citing-side normalisation' approaches, which represent a recent development in the literature.

### 3.1.5 Considerations of author position on scholarly published work

In the absence of other reliable indicators of research contribution or value, the contribution of a particular researcher to a piece of scholarly published work has been estimated by consideration of the inclusion of a researcher as a listed author on published work – and the relative position in the list. However, the average number of authors of publications in the scholarly literature continues to increase, partly due to the pressure to publish to indicate research progression and also due to a trend, in many disciplines, toward greater collaboration and 'team science'[5]. Research in many disciplines is increasingly collaborative, and original research papers with a single author are – particularly in the natural sciences – becoming rarer.

This trend makes it increasingly difficult to determine who did what, and who had a particularly pivotal role or contribution, to scholarly published work. It is currently difficult to decipher individual contributions by consulting the author lists, acknowledgements or contributions sections of most journals; and the unstructured information is difficult to text-mine.

There has been a mixture of approaches to identifying contributions of 'authors'. One example works on the assumption that any listing of an author is valuable, known as 'full counting'. The citations to a multi-author publication are counted multiple times, once for each of the authors, even for authors who have made only a small contribution. Because the same citations are counted more than once, the full counting approach has a certain inflationary effect, which is sometimes considered undesirable. A number of alternative credit allocation approaches have therefore been proposed, including the fractional counting approach, where the credit for a publication is divided equally among all authors.

Another approach frequently used as short-hand is to assume that the first and/or last authors in a list have played the most pivotal role in the production of the scholarly outputs. However this does not apply across disciplines (e.g. economics and high energy

---

[5]An extreme case is the recent physics paper with more than 5,000 authors, as discussed at: www.nature.com/news/physics-paper-sets-record-with-more-than-5-000-authors-1.17567. Retrieved 1 June 2015.

physics where author-listing protocols are frequently alphabetical). An alternative possibility is to fully allocate the credits of a publication to the corresponding author instead of the first author. A final approach discussed in the literature is to allocate the credits of a publication to the individual authors in a weighted manner, with the first author receiving the largest share of the credits, the second author receiving the second-largest share, and so on.

Developments in digital technology present opportunities to address the challenge of deriving contributions to published work. A collaboration between the Evaluation team at the Wellcome Trust, Harvard University and Digital Science has made steps to address this challenge by working across the research community to develop a simply structured taxonomy of contributions to scholarly published work which capture what has traditionally been masked as 'authorship'. The taxonomy is currently being trialled within publishing manuscript submissions systems and by several organisations interested to help research gain more visibility around the work that they do.[6] The UK's Academy of Medical Sciences is also exploring how enabling greater visibility and credit around contributions to research might help to incentivise, encourage and sustain 'team science' in disciplines where this is highly valuable.[7]

For researchers, the ability to better describe what they contributed would be a more useful currency than being listed as a specific 'author number'. Researchers could draw attention to their specific contributions to published work to distinguish their skills from those of collaborators or competitors, for example during a grant-application process or when seeking an academic appointment. This could benefit junior researchers in particular, for whom the opportunities to be a 'key' author on a paper can prove somewhat elusive. Methodological innovators would also stand to benefit from clarified roles – their contributions are not reliably apparent in a conventional author list. It could also facilitate collaboration and data sharing by allowing others to seek out the person who provided, for example, an important piece of data or statistical analysis.

Through the endorsement of individuals' contributions, researchers could move beyond 'authorship' as the dominant measure of esteem. For funding agencies, better information about the contributions of grant applicants would aid the decision-making process. Greater precision could also enable automated analysis of the role and potential outputs of those being funded, especially if those contributions were linked to an open and persistent researcher profile or identifier. It would also help those looking for the most apt peer reviewers. For institutions, understanding a researcher's contribution is fundamental to the academic appointment and promotion process.

### 3.1.6 Indicators of the citation impact of journals

The best-known indicator of the citation impact of journals is the JIF. This is an annual calculation of the mean number of citations to articles published in any given journal in

---

[6]See http://credit.casrai.org/

[7]www.acmedsci.ac.uk/policy/policy-projects/team-science/

the two preceding years.[8] There is a lot of debate about the JIF, both regarding the way in which it is calculated (which skews the JIF towards a minority of well-cited papers)[9] and the way in which it is used in research assessment contexts (as discussed more in Chapter 7).

Various improvements of and alternatives to the JIF have been proposed in the literature. It is for instance suggested to take into account citations during a longer time period, possibly adjusted to the specific citation characteristics of a journal, or it is proposed to consider the median instead of the average number of citations of the publications in a journal. Another suggestion is to calculate an h-index for journals as an alternative or complement to the JIF.

Researchers also argue that citation impact indicators for journals need to be normalised for differences in citation characteristics among fields. A number of normalisation approaches have been suggested, such as the SNIP indicator available in Scopus.[10]

Another idea proposed in the literature is that in the calculation of citation impact indicators for journals more weight should be given to citations from high-impact sources, such as citations from *Nature* and *Science*, than to citations from low-impact sources, for instance from a relatively unknown national journal that receives hardly any citations itself. This principle is implemented in the EigenFactor and article influence indicators reported, along with the JIF, in the Journal Citation Reports. The same idea is also used in the SJR indicator included in Scopus.[11]

The JIF and other citation impact indicators for journals are often used not only in the assessment of journals as a whole but also in the assessment of individual publications in a journal. Journal-level indicators then serve as a substitute for publication-level citation statistics. The use of journal-level indicators for assessing individual publications is rejected by many bibliometricians. It is argued that the distribution of citations over the publications in a journal is highly skewed, which means that the JIF and other journal-level indicators are not representative of the citation impact of a typical publication in a journal. However, some bibliometricians agree with the use of journal-level indicators in the assessment of very recent publications. In the case of these publications, citation statistics at the level of the publication itself provide hardly any information.

---

[8]Curry, S. (2012). Sick of impact factors. Post on Reciprocal Space blog. http://occamstype writer.org/scurry/2012/08/13/sick-of-impact-factors/. Retrieved 1 June 2015.

[9]Seglen, P. (1992). The skewness of science. *Journal of the Association for Information Science and Technology*, 43: 628–638. DOI: 10.1002/(SICI)1097-4571(199210)43:9<628::AID-ASI5>3.0.CO;2-0.

[10]According to its provider, "SNIP corrects for differences in citation practices between scientific fields, thereby allowing for more accurate between-field comparisons of citation impact." www.journalindicators.com/

[11]www.scimagojr.com/

### 3.1.7 Future developments

RCUK has extended its bibliometric analysis beyond an examination of citation counts, having an interest in the qualities of the literature that *cites* RCUK-funded research and the qualities of the literature *cited by* RCUK-funded research. RCUK has obtained this data from Thomson Reuters, drawn from Web of Science. Using this approach, it is possible to analyse the body of knowledge that authors draw upon, and also the diversity of research fields that subsequently draws on these results. This quantification of the 'diffusion of ideas' and mapping of the distance between research subject areas has been pioneered by Rafols *et al.* and has contributed to the discussion of how to measure interdisciplinary research.[12]

Another area that is developing fast is analysis of the influence of a given work within a particular network. In the area of citations this is exemplified by the EigenFactor.[13] In social media analyses the concept of reach or page impressions can be more informative than simple counts. Within this network conception of the spread of knowledge and ideas it is also possible to use knowledge of the types of connections. Once again this is illustrated by citations in analyses that categorise citations into types by both function (citing an idea, data) and sentiment (agree or disagree). These much richer indicators will make it possible to track and understand the way that research outputs spread and influence activities ranging from further research to public discussion of policy.[14]

## 3.2 ALTERNATIVE INDICATORS

Here we consider the more influential of the alternative indicators now in circulation, many of which are discussed in more detail in Section 3 of our literature review (Supplementary Report I). Throughout this section, we generally treat alternative indicators in relation to their potential to indicate scholarly impacts, but in some cases, we also cover wider impacts as well. Table 3 in the 'Annex of tables' provides a summary of key alternative indicators.

---

[12]Rafols, I., Porter, A.L. and Leydesdorff, L. (2010). Science overlay maps: A new tool for research policy and library management. *Journal of the American Society for Information Science and Technology*, 61(9): 871–887.

[13]See www.eigenfactor.com

[14]Shotton, D., Portwin, K., Klyne, G. and Miles, A. (2009). Adventures in Semantic Publishing: Exemplar Semantic Enhancements of a Research Article. *PLOS Comput Biol*, 5(4). e1000361. DOI:10.1371/journal.pcbi.1000361; Shotton, D. (2010). Introducing the Semantic Publishing and Referencing (SPAR) Ontologies. Post on Open Citations and Related Work blog. https://open citations.wordpress.com/2010/10/14/introducing-the-semantic-publishing-and-referencing-spar-ontologies/. Retrieved 1 June 2015; Moed, H. and Halevi, G. (2014). Research assessment: Review of methodologies and approaches. *Research Trends*, 36. March 2014. www.researchtrends.com/issue-36-march-2014/research-assessment/. Retrieved 1 June 2015.

The most common method to help assess the value of altmetrics is to investigate their correlation with citations, despite the hope that they may indicate different aspects of scholarly impact. This is because it would be strange for two valid impact indicators, no matter how different, to be completely uncorrelated.

### 3.2.1 Open access scholarly databases

The internet now contains a range of websites hosting free general scholarly databases, such as Google Scholar (discussed above in 3.1.1) and Google Books, as well as institutional and subject repositories, some of which form new sources of citation or usage data. These inherit many of the strengths and limitations of traditional bibliometric databases, but with some important differences. Although Google Scholar was not primarily developed to rival conventional citation indexes, many studies have now compared it with them for research assessment, as covered by Appendix A of the literature review (Supplementary Report I).

### 3.2.2 Usage indicators from scholarly databases

Usage data is a logical choice to supplement citation counts and digital readership information can be easily and routinely collected, except for paper copies of articles. Bibliometric indicators do not show the usage of a published work by non-authors, such as students, some academics, and non-academic users who do not usually publish but may read scholarly publications. Usage-based statistics for academic publications may therefore help to give a better understating of the usage patterns of documents and can be more recent than bibliometric indicators.

Many studies have found that correlations between usage and bibliometric indicators for articles and usage data could be extracted from different sources such as publishers, aggregator services, digital libraries and academic social websites. Nonetheless, the usage statistics could be inflated or manipulated and some articles may be downloaded or printed but not read or may be read offline or via different websites such as authors' CVs and digital repositories.[15] Integrated usage statistics from different sources such as publishers' websites, repositories and academic social websites would be optimal for global usage data if they are not manipulated in advance. However, this does not seem to be practical at present because of differences in how they are collected and categorised.

### 3.2.3 Citations and links from the general web

It is possible to extract information from the web in order to identify citations to publications, hence using the web as a huge and uncontrolled de-facto citation database.

---

[15]Thelwall, M. (2012). Journal impact evaluation: A webometric perspective. *Scientometrics*, 92(2): 429–441.

This data collection can be automated, such as through the Bing API, making the web a practical source of this type of citation data. Web and URL citations to publications can be located by commercial search engines (Google manually and Bing automatically) from almost any type of online document, including blog posts, presentations, clinical guidelines, technical reports or document files (e.g. PDF files) and there is evidence (although not recent) that they can be indicators of research impact. In theory, then, web and URL citations could be used to gather evidence about the scholarly impact of research if they were filtered to remove non-scholarly sources. In contrast, unfiltered web or URL citation counts are easy to manipulate and many citations are created for navigation, self-publicity or current awareness and so it does not seem likely that they would genuinely reflect the wider impacts of research, without time-consuming manual filtering out of irrelevant sources.

In addition to searching for citations from the general web, citations can be counted from specific parts of the web, including types of website and types of document. This information can be extracted from appropriate searches in commercial search engines and automated, for example via the Bing API. The discussions below cover online presentations, syllabi and science blogs, although there is also some evidence that mentions in news websites and discussion forums may also be useful.[16] Citations from online 'grey' literature seem to be an additional useful source of evidence of the wider impact of research,[17] but there do not seem to be any systematic studies of these.

Statistics about the uptake of academic publications in academic syllabi may be useful in teaching-oriented and book-based fields, where the main scholarly outputs of teaching staff are articles or monographs for which students are an important part of the audience, or textbooks. It is practical to harvest such data from the minority of syllabi that have been published online in the open web and indexed by search engines, but it seems that such syllabus mentions may be useful primarily to identify publications with a particularly high educational impact rather than for the systematic assessment of the educational impact of research. Syllabus mentions have most potential for the humanities and social sciences, where they are most common and where educational impact may be most important.

Research may be cited and discussed in blogs by academics or non-academics in order to debate with or inform other academics or a wider audience. Blog citations can perhaps be considered as evidence of a combination of academic interest and a potential wider social interest, even if the bloggers themselves tend to be academics. In addition, the evidence that more blogged articles are likely to receive more formal citations shows that

[16]Costas, R., Zahedi, Z. and Wouters, P. (2014). Do altmetrics correlate with citations? Extensive comparison of altmetric indicators with citations from a multidisciplinary perspective. arXiv preprint arXiv:1401.4321; Thelwall, M., Haustein, S., Larivière, V. and Sugimoto, C. (2013). Do altmetrics work? Twitter and ten other candidates. *PLOS ONE*, 8(5), e64841. DOI:10.1371/journal.pone.0064841.

[17]Wilkinson, D., Sud, P. and Thelwall, M. (2014). Substance without citation: Evaluating the online impact of grey literature. *Scientometrics*, 98(2): 797–806.

blog citations could be used for early impact evidence. Nevertheless, blog citations can be easy to manipulate, and are not straightforward to collect, so may need to be provided by specialist altmetric software or organisations.

In addition to the types of web citations discussed above, preliminary research is evaluating online clinical guidelines, government documents and encyclopaedias. Online clinical guidelines could be useful for medical research funders to help them to assess the societal impact of individual studies.[18] In support of this, one study extracted 6,128 cited references from 327 documents produced by the National Institute of Health and Clinical Excellence (NICE) in the UK, finding articles cited in guidelines tend to be more highly cited than comparable articles.[19]

### 3.2.4 Altmetrics: citations, links, downloads and likes from social websites

The advent of the social web has seen an explosion in both the range of indicators that could be calculated as well as the ease with which relevant data can be collected (even in comparison to web impact metrics). Of particular interest are comments, ratings, social bookmarks, and microblogging,[20] although there have been many concerns about validity and the quality of altmetric indicators due to the ease with which they can be manipulated.[21] Elsevier (via Scopus), Springer, Wiley, BioMed Central, PLOS and Nature

---

[18]For a discussion of issues see Manchikanti, L., Benyamin, R., Falco, F., Caraway, D., Datta, S. and Hirsch, J. (2012). Guidelines warfare over interventional techniques: is there a lack of discourse or straw man? *Pain Physician*, 15: E1–E26; also Kryl, D., Allen, L., Dolby, K., Sherbon, B., and Viney, I. (2012). Tracking the impact of research on policy and practice: investigating the feasibility of using citations in clinical guidelines for research evaluation. *BMJ Open*, 2(2), e000897. DOI:10.1136/bmjopen-2012-000897.

[19]Thelwall, M., and Maflahi, N. (in press). Guideline references and academic citations as evidence of the clinical value of health research. *Journal of the Association for Information Science and Technology*. www.scit.wlv.ac.uk/~cm1993/papers/GuidelineMetricsPreprint.pdf

[20]For instance: Taraborelli, D. (2008). Soft peer review: Social software and distributed scientific evaluation. *Proceedings of the Eighth International Conference on the Design of Cooperative Systems*. Carry–Le–Rouet, 20–23 May. http://nitens.org/docs/spr_coop08.pdf; Neylon, C. and Wu. S. (2009). Article-level metrics and the evolution of scientific impact. *PLOS Biol*, 7(11). DOI: 10.1371/journal.pbio.1000242; Priem, J., and Hemminger, B. M. (2010). Scientometrics 2.0: Toward new metrics of scholarly impact on the social web. *First Monday*, 15(7). http://firstmonday.org/ojs/index.php/fm/article/view/2874/2570

[21]Birkholz, J., and Wang, S. (2011). Who are we talking about?: the validity of online metrics for commenting on science. Paper presented in: altmetrics11: Tracking scholarly impact on the social Web. An ACM Web Science Conference 2011 Workshop, Koblenz (Germany), 14–15. http://altmetrics.org/workshop2011/birkholz-v0; Rasmussen, P. G., and Andersen, J.P. (2013). Altmetrics: An alternate perspective on research evaluation. *Sciecom Info*, 9(2). http://journals.lub.lu.se/index.php/sciecominfo/article/view/7292/6102

Publishing Group have all added article-level altmetrics to their journals, and uptake is rising among other publishers.

Although the term 'altmetrics' refers to indicators for research assessment derived from the social web,[22] the term *alternative metrics* seems to be gaining currency as a catch-all for web-based metrics.

A range of altmetrics have been shown to correlate significantly and positively with bibliometric indicators for individual articles,[23] giving evidence that, despite the uncontrolled nature of the social web, altmetrics may be related to scholarly activities in some way.[24] This is perhaps most evident when the altmetrics are aggregated to entire journals[25] rather than to individual articles. Social usage impact can be extracted from a range of social websites that allow users to upload, or register information about, academic publications, such as Mendeley, Twitter, Academia and ResearchGate. These sites can be used for assessing an aspect of the usage of publications based on numbers of downloads, views or registered readers. Fuller information on the following are included within the literature review (Supplementary Report I): Faculty of 1000 Web Recommendations; Mendeley and other Online Reference Managers; Twitter and microblog citations.

### 3.2.5 Book-based indicators

Research evaluation in book-oriented fields is more challenging than for article-based subject areas because counts of citations *from* articles, which dominate traditional citation indexes, seem insufficient to assess the impact of books. The Book Citation Index

---

[22]Priem, J., Taraborelli, D., Groth, P., and Neylon, C. (2010). *Altmetrics: A Manifesto*. Retrieved from http://altmetrics.org/manifesto/

[23]Priem, J., Piwowar, H., and Hemminger, B. (2012). *Altmetrics in the Wild: Using Social Media to Explore Scholarly Impact*. Retrieved from http://arXiv.org/html/1203.4745v1; Thelwall, M., Haustein, S., Larivière, V., and Sugimoto, C. (2013). Do altmetrics work? Twitter and ten other candidates. *PLOS ONE*, 8(5), e64841. DOI:10.1371/journal.pone.0064841; Costas, R., Zahedi, Z., and Wouters, P. (2014). How well developed are altmetrics? A cross-disciplinary analysis of the presence of 'alternative metrics' in scientific publications. *Scientometrics*, 101(2): 1491–1513.

[24]However, recent research suggests that some factors driving social media and citations are quite different: (1) while editorials and news items are seldom cited, these types of document are most popular on Twitter; (2) longer papers typically attract more citations, but the converse is true of social media platforms; (3) SSH papers are most common on social media platforms, the opposite to citations. Haustein, S., Costas, R., and Larivière, V. (2015). Characterizing Social Media Metrics of Scholarly Papers: The Effect of Document Properties and Collaboration Patterns. *PLOS ONE*, 10(3), e0120495. DOI:10.1371/journal.pone.0120495.

[25]Alhoori, H. and Furuta, R. (2014). Do altmetrics follow the crowd or does the crowd follow altmetrics? in *Proceedings of the IEEE/ACM Joint Conference on Digital Libraries* (JCDL) (2014). Los Alamitos: IEEE Press. http://people.tamu.edu/~alhoori/publications/alhoori2014jcdl.pdf; Haustein, S. and Siebenlist, T. (2011). Applying social bookmarking data to evaluate journal usage. *Journal of Informetrics*, 5(3): 446–457.

within Web of Science is a recent response to this issue[26] since journal citations on their own might miss about half of the citations to books.[27] However, some academic books are primarily written for teaching (e.g. textbooks) or cultural purposes (e.g. novels and poetry) and citation counts of any kind may be wholly inappropriate for these.

In REF2014, books (authored books, edited books, scholarly editions and book chapters) were more frequently submitted to Main Panels C and D (29.4%) than to Main Panels A and B (0.4%), and many of these books (art, music and literary works) may have merits that are not reflected by conventional bibliometric methods (see Table 3 in the 'Annex of tables' for the full distribution of results in REF2014). Moreover, the main sources of citations to humanities books are other books.[28] Even today, the Thomson Reuters Book Citation Index and Scopus index a relatively small number of books (50,000[29] and 40,000[30] as of September 2014, respectively) and this may cause problems for bibliometric analyses of books.[31] Expert peer judgement of books seems to be by far the best method but it is even more time-consuming and expensive than article peer assessment because books are generally much longer.[32] In response, alternative sources have been investigated for book impact assessment, including syllabus mentions, library holding counts, book reviews and publisher prestige.

Many of the indicators discussed elsewhere in the full literature review (Supplementary Report I) can also be used for books but have not yet been evaluated for this purpose. However, since academic books are still mainly read in print form, download indicators are not yet so relevant.

---

[26]Previously noted in Garfield, E. (1996). *Citation Indexes for Retrieval and Research Evaluation.* Consensus Conference on the Theory and Practice of Research Assessment, Capri.

[27]Hicks, D. (1999). The difficulty of achieving full coverage of international social science literature and the bibliometric consequences. *Scientometrics*, 44(2): 193–215.

[28]Thompson, J. W. (2002). The death of the scholarly monograph in the humanities? Citation patterns in literary scholarship. *Libri*, 52(3): 121–136; Kousha, K., and Thelwall, M. (2014). An automatic method for extracting citations from Google Books. *Journal of the Association for Information Science and Technology.* DOI: 10.1002/asi.23170.

[29]http://wokinfo.com/products_tools/multidisciplinary/webofscience

[30]http://blog.scopus.com/posts/scopus-content-book-expansion-project-update

[31]For example: Gorraiz, J., Purnell, P. J., and Glänzel, W. (2013). Opportunities for and limitations of the book citation index. *Journal of the American Society for Information Science and Technology*, 64(7): 1388–1398; Torres-Salinas, D., Robinson-García, N., Jiménez-Contreras, E., and Delgado López-Cózar, E. (2012). Towards a 'Book Publishers Citation Report'. First approach using the 'Book Citation Index'. *Revista Española de Documentación Científica*, 35(4): 615–620; Torres-Salinas, D., Rodríguez-Sánchez, R., Robinson-García, N., Fdez-Valdivia, J., and García, J. A. (2013). Mapping citation patterns of book chapters in the Book Citation Index. *Journal of Informetrics*, 7(2): 412–424.

[32]See Weller, A. C. (2001). *Editorial peer review: Its strengths and weaknesses.* Medford, NJ: Information Today.

Google Books[33] contains a large number of academic and non-academic books based upon digitising the collections of over 40 libraries around the world as well as partnerships with publishers.[34] Several studies have shown that the coverage of Google Books is quite comprehensive, but, due to copyright considerations, Google Books does not always reveal the full text of the books that it has indexed.[35]

Although Google Books is not a citation index and provides no citation statistics of any kind, it is possible to manually search it for academic publications and hence identify citations to these publications from digitised books.[36] Google Books could be useful because citations from books have been largely invisible in traditional citation indexes and the current book citation search facilities in Scopus and Web of Science cover relatively few books that are predominantly in English and from a small number of publishers, which is problematic for citation impact assessment in book-based disciplines.[37]

National or international library holdings statistics can indicate library interest in books and seem to reflect a different type of impact to that of citations, perhaps including educational and cultural impacts. These statistics are relatively simple to collect automatically from the OCLC WorldCat library holding catalogue,[38] with more than 2.2 billion items from over 72,000 libraries in 170 countries. These data, which are based upon book holdings and hence would be costly to manipulate, seem promising for assessing the wider influence of books in SSH based on the information needs of users, teaching staff and researchers. While more detailed borrowing statistics might be even more useful, these data do not seem to be currently available.

---

[33]http://books.google.com

[34]http://books.google.com/intl/en/googlebooks/about/

[35]Chen, X. (2012). Google Books and WorldCat: A comparison of their content. *Online Information Review*, 36(4): 507–516. Weiss, A., and James, R. (2013). Assessing the coverage of Hawaiian and pacific books in the Google Books digitization project. *OCLC Systems and Services*, 29(1): 13–21.; Weiss, A., and James, R. (2013a). 'An examination of massive digital libraries' coverage of Spanish language materials: Issues of multilingual accessibility in a decentralized, mass-digitized world'. Paper presented at the Proceedings – 2013 International Conference on Culture and Computing. pp10–14.

[36]Kousha, K., and Thelwall, M. (2009). Google Book Search: Citation analysis for social science and the humanities. *Journal of the American Society for Information Science and Technology*, 60(8): 1537–1549; Kousha, K., Thelwall, M., and Rezaie, S. (2011). Assessing the citation impact of books: The role of Google Books, Google Scholar, and Scopus. *Journal of the American Society for Information Science and Technology*, 62(11): 2147–2164.

[37]Gorraiz, J., Purnell, P., and Glänzel, W. (2013). Opportunities and limitations of the book citation index. *Journal of the American Society for Information Science and Technology*, 64(7): 1388–1398; Torres-Salinas, D., Rodriguez-Sánchez, R., Robinson-Garcia, N., Fdez-Valdivia, J. and Garcia, J. A. (2013). Mapping citation patterns of book chapters in the book citation index. *Journal of Informetrics*, 7(2): 412–424.

[38]www.worldcat.org; http://oclc.org/worldcat/catalog.en.html

Publisher prestige, reputational surveys, libcitation and citation indicators can also help to identify prestigious scholarly publishers. A combination of all of the above may be more useful for rating (rather than ranking) academic publishers of books or monographs as long as other factors, such as geographical, language and disciplinary differences, are taken into consideration when they are used.

### 3.2.6 Varieties of outputs

While much of this discussion tends to focus on text-based outputs in peer-reviewed publications, it is common for scholars across all disciplines to produce a wider variety of outputs from their research processes. These range from research datasets, software, images, videos and patents, through to exhibitions, compositions, performances, presentations and non-refereed publications (such as policy documents or 'grey' literature). For some of these there may be plausible indicators of impact, such as audience size, art gallery prestige, composition commissioner prestige, art sales or sales prices. In most cases, however, it is likely that the contributions of individual works are so varied that any data presented to support an impact case would not be directly comparable with other available data, although they could be presented as evidence to support a specific argument about the contribution of a work.

### 3.2.7 How robust are alternative quality metrics?

There is empirical evidence that a wide range of indicators derived from the web for scholars or their outputs are related to scholarly activities in some way because they correlate positively and significantly with citation counts. In many cases these metrics can also be harvested on a large scale in an automated way with a high degree of accuracy (see Appendix B of the literature review, Supplementary Report I, for methods to obtain alternative metric data). Nevertheless, most are easy to manipulate[39] and nearly all are susceptible to spam to some extent. Thus, alternative metrics do not seem to be suitable as a management tool with any kind of objective to measure, evaluate or manage research.[40] Even if no manipulation took place, which seems unlikely, the results would be suspected of being affected by manipulation and in the worst case scenario the results would be extensively manipulated and researchers would waste their time and money on this manipulation.

In our call for evidence, 19 respondents (of which 15 were HEIs) proposed that altmetrics could be used as a research assessment tool; while 12 responses (of which eight were HEIs), argued that altmetrics are not reliable enough to be used as a measure of research

---

[39] For example: Dullaart, C. (2014). High Retention, Slow Delivery. (Art piece: 2.5 million Instagram followers bought and distributed to artists. See e.g. http://jeudepaume.espacevirtuel.org/, http://dismagazine.com/dystopia/67039/constant-dullaart-100000-followers-for-everyone/).

[40] Wouters, P., and Costas, R. (2012). Users, narcissism and control: Tracking the impact of scholarly publications in the 21st century. SURFfoundation. Retrieved 29 November 2014, from https://www.surf.nl/kennis-en-innovatie/kennisbank/2012/rapport-users-narcissism-and-control.html [in Dutch].

quality. This reflects the uncertainties often associated with these indicators which are at an early stage of development. For an altmetric to be taken seriously, empirical evidence of its value is needed in addition to evidence of a reasonable degree of robustness against accidental or malicious spam.

## 3.3 INPUT INDICATORS

In some contexts, there is support for the measurement of research quality through the use of proxy indicators including: external research income (recognising that organisations are in competition for these funds, so success is a marker of quality); research student enrolments; and research student completion data. These were all mentioned by a number of respondents to our call for evidence as potential measures of quality, but more often as a useful means to measure 'environment' or 'vitality' or the research base, along the lines of the REF's environment component.[41]

In UK HEIs, the maturity of current research information systems (CRISs) varies markedly between institutions. Some HEIs have fully fledged systems that are completely integrated with other core systems, others have stand-alone systems, and some rely on non-specific systems such as generic databases and spreadsheets. Some UK HEIs capture or wish to capture data associated with all of the above items (and more) for internal or external purposes. Publication information is most commonly collected in central systems. Grant information, commercialisation, and PhD numbers and completions tend to be collected centrally and most can produce information by staff member/FTE. On the other hand, prizes, editorships, other esteem indicators and international visitors might more commonly only be collected locally within departments. Information on research infrastructure is perhaps the most variable and, anecdotally at least, least likely to be comprehensive (though initiatives like equipment.data.ac.uk and the work of sharing consortiums like N8 show that infrastructure can be established and well-utilised).

## 3.4 INDICATORS OF IMPACT

Attempting to measure and capture broader societal or external impacts of academic work is a relatively new concern in the UK system. Originally emphasised by the UK Research Councils as a means of enhancing the external reach of their grant awards, impact became an established part of the UK's research assessment culture when it was introduced into the REF in 2011.[42] Impact is still a contested term, with a variety of definitions and understandings of its implications. The ways in which it can be assessed and measured are equally

---

[41]For instance, see the University of Durham's response to our call for evidence, available at www.hefce.ac.uk/media/hefce,2014/content/research/research,metrics/responses_to_metrics_review_call_for_evidence.pdf

[42]See www.ref.ac.uk/pubs/2011-01/. Arguably, the REF impact pilots (concluded 2010) marked the formal introduction of the impact element.

varied. Some definitions of impact highlight the importance of being able to evidence its reach and significance: "Research has an external impact when an auditable or recorded influence is achieved upon a non-academic organization or actor in a sector outside the university sector itself ... external impacts need to be demonstrated rather than assumed."[43]

One problem associated with the creation of impact indicators is that the model of impact seemingly supported by some definitions can be rather linear, when dissemination is in fact more broadly interspersed through the research cycle.[44] For example findings from the recent HEFCE review of monographs and open access show that arts and humanities scholars don't first research and then disseminate in a neat two-stage process.[45] This means that developing metrics for the ways in which impact is created in these disciplines is harder and the use of ad-hoc data that are contextualised by interpretation of their meaning may be more suitable.[46] Others also argue that academics who create impact by building long-lasting partnerships with groups and organisations will not be able to demonstrate the depth and detail of impacts through metrics or data alone. A key concern from some critics is that impact metrics focus on what is measurable at the expense of what is important.

Evidence of external impacts can take a number of forms – references to, citations of or discussion of an academic or their work; in a practitioner or commercial document; in media or specialist media outlets; in the records of meetings, conferences, seminars, working groups and other interchanges; in the speeches or statements of authoritative actors; or via inclusions or referencing or weblinks to research documents in an external organisation's websites or intranets; in the funding, commissioning or contracting of research or research-based consultancy from university teams or academics; and in the direct involvement of academics in decision-making in government agencies, government or professional advisory committees, business corporations or interest groups, and trade unions, charities or other civil society organisations.[47]

Journal articles and books are seen to be less impact relevant than other forms of publications such as research reports, briefing notes and conference papers. However research from

[43]LSE Public Policy Group (2011). Maximising the Impacts of Your Research. A Handbook for Social Scientists. London, LSE, p10. Available at: http://www.lse.ac.uk/government/research/resgroups/LSEPublicPolicy/Docs/LSE_Impact_Handbook_April_2011.pdf

[44]A recent report on whether altmetrics are useful measures of broader impact is: Adams, J. and Loach, T. (2015). Altmetric mentions and the communication of medical science: Disseminating research outcomes outside academia. Digital Science. www.digital-science.com/blog/news/digital-research-report-altmetric-mentions-and-the-identification-of-research-impact. Retrieved 1 June 2015.

[45]Crossick, G. (2015). Monographs and Open Access: A report to HEFCE. www.hefce.ac.uk/pubs/rereports/Year/2015/monographs/

[46]Thelwall, M. and Delgado, M. (2015). Arts and humanities research evaluation: No metrics please, just data. Journal of Documentation, 71(4).

[47]LSE Public Policy Group (2011). Maximising the Impacts of Your Research. A Handbook for Social Scientists. London, LSE, P. 10. Available at: http://www.lse.ac.uk/government/research/resgroups/LSEPublicPolicy/Docs/LSE_Impact_Handbook_April_2011.pdf

Talbot and Talbot found that journal articles were identified as the third most used route to find academic work by policymakers.[48] However, even where government documents, for example, quote academic work these references are not citations in the traditional sense and are therefore not picked up by bibliometric analysis. Grey literature produced by academics tends to be more used by policymakers but its impact is difficult to capture. Firstly citations are not made in the usual way and secondly academics have been slow to realise the importance of using tagging information such as DOIs in order to allow these references to be tracked.[49]

The development of a range of alternative indicators has created the potential to diversify away from a reliance upon counting citations to journal articles. Nevertheless, although a few alternative indicators are promising and do have the potential to enable a new view of the impact and reach of research, the 'science' is in its infancy and most of the alternative metrics can be easily gamed. Some of the most promising indicators are relevant to a much narrower range of research than are citations to journal articles (F1000 ratings, patent citations, syllabus mentions, citations from Google Books). Hence, the systematic use of alternative indicators as pure indicators of academic quality seems unlikely at the current time, though they have the potential to provide an alternative perspective on research dissemination, reach and 'impact' in its broadest sense.

The variety of evidence needed to build case studies of impact is such that, unlike scholarly impact, it is difficult to reach a consensus about which indicators to use to highlight particular kinds of impact. From the almost 7,000 impact case studies submitted to REF2014, there is little consistency in the indicators that case study authors used to evidence the impact of their research. An analysis of the impact case studies commissioned by HEFCE from Digital Science and King's College London concluded as follows:

"The quantitative evidence supporting claims for impact was diverse and inconsistent, suggesting that the development of robust impact metrics is unlikely. There was a large amount of numerical data (ie, c.170,000 items, or c.70,000 with dates removed) that was inconsistent in its use and expression and could not be synthesized. In order for impact metrics to be developed, such information would need to be expressed in a consistent way, using standard units. However, as noted above, the strength of the impact case studies is that they allow authors to select the appropriate data to evidence their impact. Given this, and based on our analysis of the impact case studies, we would reiterate...impact indicators are not sufficiently developed and tested to be used to make funding decisions." [50]

---

[48]Talbot, C. and Talbot, C. (2014). *Sir Humphrey and the Professors: What does Whitehall Want from Academics?* Policy@Manchester. www.policy.manchester.ac.uk/media/projects/policy manchester/1008_Policy@Manchester_Senior_Civil_Servants_Survey_v4%281%29.pdf. Retrieved 1 June 2015.

[49]See Ernesto Priego's contribution to our Warwick workshop on this point: https://epriego. wordpress.com/2015/01/16/hefcemetrics-more-on-metrics-for-the-arts-and-humanities/

[50]King's College London and Digital Science (2015). The nature, scale and beneficiaries of research impact. An initial analysis of Research Excellence Framework (REF) 2014 impact case studies. Available at: http://www.kcl.ac.uk/sspp/policy-institute/publications/Analysis-of-REF-impact.pdf p72.

Although the potential for a small subset of quantitative data to represent a diverse array of impacts is limited, we did receive a wealth of views on how the narrative elements of impact case studies could be enhanced. For example, the work carried out by King's College London examined the use of Quality Adjusted Life Years (QALYs) as a measure of health impact in the case studies, and concluded that in the future where this data was available it could allow better comparability between impact cases.

There are likely to be numerous additional examples of indicators that could be used in this way, but they are usually specific to certain types of impact and need to be interpreted in context. Sometimes these indicators may be measures of dissemination (e.g. webpage visits or YouTube views) that need to be considered alongside other evidence of impact. The reports from RAND Europe which analysed impact in the REF, also provide useful evidence, noting that HEIs could develop their own impact metrics and should be encouraged to do so in future, but any effort to define impact indicators up front risks unnecessary limitations on the exercise, as has been found to be the case in other pilot impact exercises.[51] Furthermore, the same metrics may not be applicable across main panels and might not work for all disciplines. For example, a subset of research users were concerned about measures when claiming an impact involving interaction with the public. As one panellist asked: "What is the right number of website hits to become 4-star?"[52]

## 3.5 INDICATING WAYS AHEAD

There are widespread concerns that quantitative indicators, such as citation-based data, cannot provide sufficiently nuanced or robust measures of quality when used in isolation. Bibliometricians generally see citation rates as a proxy measure of academic impact or of impact on the relevant academic communities. But this is only one of the dimensions of academic quality. Quality needs to be seen as a multidimensional concept that cannot be captured by any one indicator, and which dimension of quality should be prioritised may vary by field and mission.

During the process of our own review, we have found greater support for the use of (carefully chosen) indicators as a **complement** to other forms of assessment (in particular peer review), than as a means to assess research quality by themselves (this is discussed further in Chapter 5). Many recent studies also recommend opting for a combination of strategies, and it is crucial that these are tailored to the specific context in question.

---

[51]See for example Ovseiko, P., Oancea, A. and Buchan, A. (2012). Assessing research impact in academic clinical medicine: a study using Research Excellence Framework pilot impact indicators, *BMC Health Services Research* 2012, 12: 478. www.biomedcentral.com/1472-6963/12/478. Retrieved 1 June 2015.

[52]Manville, C., Guthrie, S., Henham, M., Garrod, B., Sousa, S., Kirtley, A., Castle-Clark, S. and Ling, T. (2015). Assessing impact submissions for REF 2014. An evaluation. Cambridge: RAND Europe, p34.

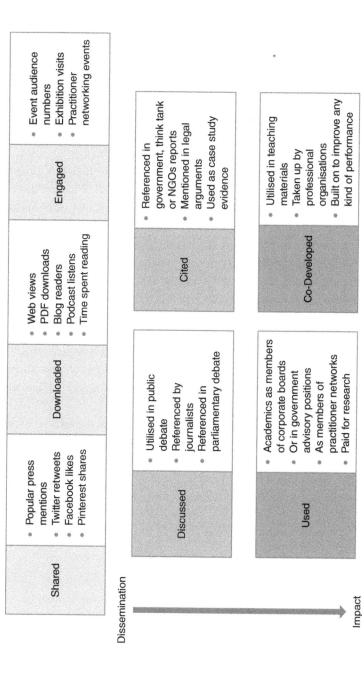

**Figure 1** Examples of types of impact metrics tracking how research has been used[53]

---

[53]This figure was designed by Jane Tinkler for the review.

It is crucial to consider what is best suited to the scale and focus of assessment. Concern over the application of indicators at inappropriate scales features prominently in recent statements, such as DORA and the Leiden Manifesto. Too often, managers and evaluators continue to rely on metrics that are recognised as unsuitable as measures of individual performance, such as journal-level indicators.

Using carefully chosen 'baskets' of (qualitative and quantitative) indicators is often deemed to provide the best way forward. "A single indicator cannot fully capture and represent the diversity and complexity of the relationships within a research funding ecosystem. Quantitative measures are a conduit of information that represents only very specific aspects of that ecosystem."[54]It is also important to emphasise that high quality bibliometric data are expensive. But we want high quality data, otherwise our analysis is not worth the effort.

Turning to indicators for impact, there is an increasing body of literature on how scholarly impact relates to broader external impact. Some examples of impact metrics are shown in Figure 1. Work by Altmetrics for example has shown that citations and altmetric indicators seem to be measuring different but possibly related aspects.[55]And early analysis from REF2014 highlights that the same units score well on outputs and impact, showing that these aspects may be constituent of each other.

Views that the impact agenda is problematic are found across all disciplines but are perhaps strongest in the arts and humanities where it is felt that it is impossible to be able to show the variety and depth of impact of the work in those fields. However, these disciplines have experience in developing possible indicators for, or data about, the impacts of arts and humanities research, particularly in REF impact terms.[56] It could be that experience from cultural organisations could be used in order to further develop impact metrics that are relevant for the outputs produced by arts and humanities researchers.

As noted elsewhere, the way that impact is assessed in the REF is through case studies alongside a broader narrative (see Section 9.3.2). These narrative-based outputs allow academics to outline in detail how their work has created impact and therefore can be crafted to take appropriate account of the context. As with peer review, case studies allow expert judgement to be used in determining successful research impact.

---

[54]Council of Canadian Academies (2012). 'Informing research choices: Indicators and judgment.' Report of the Expert Panel on Science Performance and Research Funding. Ottawa: CCA, p42.

[55]Also see Adams, J. and Loach, T. (2015). 'Altmetric 'mentions' and the identification of research impact.' Nesta Working Paper No. 15/03. Available at: https://www.nesta.org.uk/sites/default/files/nesta_altmetrics_working_paper.pdf. This compares altmetrics mentions and the communication of medical research. The authors call for more work to be done to better understand definitive outcomes in terms of the relationship between the content of biomedical research papers and the frequency with which they are mentioned in social media contexts.

[56]Thelwall, M. and Delgado, M. (2015). Arts and humanities research evaluation: No metrics please, just data. Journal of Documentation, 71(4).

The REF made use of external research users as part of assessing impact; they were actively involved in providing context to impact claims made by academics. For some, case studies are the only viable route to assessing impact; they offer the potential to present complex information and warn against more focus on quantitative metrics for impact case studies. Others however see case studies as "fairy tales of influence"[57] and argue for a more consistent toolkit of impact metrics that can be more easily compared across and between cases.

In sum, while some alternative metrics seem to reflect types of impact that are different from that of traditional citations, only Google patent citations and clinical guideline citations can yet be shown to reflect wider societal impact. In addition, as the range of impact metrics is so wide – rightly so to be able to show the range of impacts taking place – many of them would be too rare to help distinguish between the impacts of typical publications. But they could be useful to give evidence of the impact of the small minority of high impact articles. Overall, then, despite the considerable body of mostly positive empirical evidence reviewed above, although alternative metrics do seem to give indications of where research is having wider social impact they do not yet seem to be robust enough to be routinely used for evaluations in which it is in the interest of stakeholders to manipulate the results.

Recent work on the REF impact case studies indicates that interdisciplinary research is more likely to achieve greater impact, and it is to (inter)disciplinary differences and dilemmas that we now turn.[58]

---

[57]Dunleavy, P. (2012). REF Advice Note 1: Understanding HEFCE's definition of Impact, LSE Impact, 22 October. http://blogs.lse.ac.uk/impactofsocialsciences/2012/10/22/dunleavy-ref-advice-1/

[58]King's College London and Digital Science (2015). The nature, scale and beneficiaries of research impact. An initial analysis of Research Excellence Framework (REF) 2014 impact case studies. Available at: http://www.kcl.ac.uk/sspp/policy-institute/publications/Analysis-of-REF-impact.pdf, p24.

# FOUR

## DISCIPLINARY DILEMMAS

## CHAPTER CONTENTS

"Metrics have to be intertwined with the context of the discipline in question."

Martin Eve, University of Warwick Arts
and Humanities workshop

It is well known that practices of output production and research outlet selection vary significantly across disciplinary and subdisciplinary fields. These diverse practices are bound up with specific philosophical and methodological histories and practices, though the propensity to choose a particular type of output or outlet over others may also be influenced by other factors, such as a specific university or other policy environments.

This diversity has implications for how universally useful particular metrics are for some disciplines, not least because of their limited coverage, as already discussed, but also because differences in research practices across disciplines have deeper implications for the applicability of metrics.

The various emphases of existing metrics (at least as far as bibliometrics are concerned) has been on counting and analysing research outputs published predominately in journals, and for that reason the debate around metrics is often characterised by its identification of an 'arts and humanities problem', where practices differ considerably from this pattern. It is perhaps inevitable that the focus of this chapter is on how arts and humanities research might be distinctive, but we would sound a note of caution here. Research is diverse, right across the academy. Disciplinary differences are often broadly and unhelpfully characterised, but can in reality be quite subtle and entirely valid where they occur.

Metrics should not become the 'tail that wags the dog' of research practice in all disciplines. Rather, it is incumbent on those who design and use metrics to take a fuller account of the existing diversity of research, and design sensitive and meaningful metrics to reflect and support this.

## 4.1 VARIATIONS IN RESEARCH OUTPUTS

Researchers produce a variety of research outputs across the range of disciplines. Submissions to REF2014 revealed a wealth of types of output submitted across all units of assessment: journal articles, books, datasets, performances, compositions, artefacts, software, patents, exhibitions, installations, designs, digital media – the list goes on. RCUK's use of Researchfish has compiled a large structured dataset of outputs linked to research funded since 2006, and this demonstrates that a diverse range of outputs are produced across the breadth of research disciplines, and that certain outputs are not exclusive to particular disciplines.[1] For instance, although rare, it is not unheard of for life science researchers to write a play or devise a work inspired by their research, and interdisciplinary research often results in unusual or multimodal outputs. It is therefore important not to oversimplify. However, some general trends for output production, across broad disciplinary areas, can be noted as follows:[2]

- Journal articles are the primary output for many disciplines (on average half of all output reports captured in Researchfish[3]) but their importance varies, tending to play a less predominant role in the arts and humanities, and some areas of the social sciences;

---

[1]While the REF and RCUK have noted this diversity, this doesn't necessarily reflect what researchers actually do – instead it reflects what is considered important to submit to the various assessment or reporting systems.

[2]Other outputs might include audio-visual recordings, technical drawings, website content, software, designs or working models, exhibitions, patents, plant breeding rights, working papers, policy documents, research reports, legal cases, and translations, amongst others. Furthermore, the diversity of outputs being produced by academics is becoming increasingly broad due to digital and web-based technological developments.

[3]www.mrc.ac.uk/documents/pdf/Introduction/; also note the above point in Chapter 3's Footnote 51.

- Monographs and book chapters are particularly important for many disciplines within the humanities, and for some within the social sciences;[4]
- Conference contributions are particularly important for computer scientists and engineers;
- Products and prototypes are important outputs for some academics, particularly in the engineering sciences;
- Art works, artefacts and practice-based outputs are more likely to play an important role for arts-based disciplines.

While not entirely representative of output production across subject areas,[5] some idea of the trends in output production can be gained by looking at the spread of output types submitted to REF2014 across the 36 panels (see Table 3 in the 'Annex of tables').

As noted in Section 3.1 of the previous chapter, such trends are noteworthy as some outputs are less likely to be included within bibliographic databases, which are central to the formulation of many bibliometric indicators and analyses (see Section 3.1). In particular, book publications and publications in "niche"[6] or locally important journals play an important role in SSH but these publications are often not indexed in bibliographic databases. Bibliometric analyses in computer science and engineering involve similar difficulties, as many computer science and engineering publications appear in conference proceedings, but such literature is often less well covered by bibliographic databases, especially by Web of Science and Scopus, in comparison to journal articles, perhaps because of the costs and complexity of monitoring conference proceedings.

Publication patterns and practices also vary across discipline. For instance in some areas, academics might publish a number of articles per year, while in those disciplines where monographs are a favoured output, producing one book every few years might be seen as appropriate. The language in which outputs are likely to be produced can also vary; for some areas of SSH outputs are more likely to be produced in the relevant national language, which may not be English. Outputs that are not produced in English are less likely to be included in certain bibliographic databases, and may be less likely to be captured in bibliometric indicators.

The number of authors per publications also varies to some extent by subject area. For instance, outputs produced in the humanities are more likely to be single-authored,

---

[4]For a useful discussion of monographs, see Crossick, G. (2015). Monographs and open access. A report to HEFCE. January 2015. Available at: http://www.hefce.ac.uk/pubs/rereports/year/2015/monographs/. Retrieved 6 January 2016.

[5]Indeed see Adams, J. and Gurney, K. (2014). Evidence for excellence: Has the signal taken over the substance? An analysis of journal articles submitted to the RAE2008. *Digital Science*. www.digital-science.com/resources/digital-research-report-evidence-for-excellence-has-the-signal-overtaken-the-substance/. Retrieved 1 April 2015.

[6]Social sciences and humanities in particular have larger numbers of 'national' or 'niche' journals which are not indexed in bibliometric databases. Yet these may still have transnational contributions and readership, and despite a smaller audience may be highly significant for that specialist (sub)discipline.

whereas publications in some areas of science, such as medicine and biology, often have several. This will affect requirements for allocation of credit, which can be relevant to bibliometric and citation indicators.

## 4.2 VARIATIONS IN CITATION PRACTICES

There is significant disciplinary diversity in terms of citation practices, and linked to this, the use and acceptance of indicators for the assessment of research outputs. Such variations influence the interpretation of indicators such as the JIF. For instance, top ranked journals in mathematics have a JIF of three versus 30 for cell biology.

Some subject areas are more likely to rank their journals and publishers according to their JIFs, while in other areas, such as SSH, this practice is less common[7]. Thus, bibliometrics measures such as JIFs are more welcomed and embedded within certain disciplines than others.

Many humanities disciplines are characterised by internal debate, such that an output may be just as likely to be cited for its stance on a particular issue, or place in a broader debate, than for the quality of the thinking or research it describes. In STEM disciplines, methods papers may also attract large numbers of citations. Practices of citation are therefore more complex than is visible in the simplicity of citation numbers.

The time span over which a piece of research is deemed to be relevant can also vary by discipline, as some subject areas move faster than others. In general terms, research in SSH tends to remain relevant for longer periods than in the natural sciences, as noted by recent analysis of journal usage half-lives by the British Academy.[8] This will affect citation practices and therefore the relevance of certain indicators in particular contexts.

There are widespread concerns that indicators are less likely to capture the value of academic outputs from less popular or more obscure fields of work as these are cited less often, or works published in languages other than English and there are concerns that fields of enquiry, based on more theoretical and also applied outputs may fall foul of certain indicator-based assessment strategies (whatever the discipline).

## 4.3 DIFFERING DISCIPLINARY PERSPECTIVES

There is an extensive literature on these and related issues, and the review has captured detailed debate and commentary on these points, particularly in response to our call for

---

[7]With some exceptions, such as Business and Management, where the practice is more commonplace as per the ABS ranking.

[8]Darley, R, Reynolds, D. and Wickham, C. (2014). *Open access journals in Humanities and Social Science: A British Academy Research Project.* www.britac.ac.uk/templates/asset-relay. cfm?frmAssetFileID=13584. Retrieved 1 June 2015.

evidence. Thirty-five out of 153 respondents were concerned that indicators, in particular citation-based metrics, could unfairly disadvantage some disciplines, especially in the arts, humanities and social sciences. Some felt that in certain disciplines, including law, English literature, nursing and criminology, the use of such indicators would never be plausible. A number of respondents made the point that variations are often considerable within as well as between disciplines.

Throughout the course of the review, we have heard that assessment regimes must take different cultures of output and citation into account to ensure that diverse research practices and cultures are supported and captured appropriately.

This was certainly the case within discussions of the (potential) use of citation-based data within the REF during our focus groups with REF panellists (see Chapter 9). At our roundtable review workshop hosted by UCL in July 2014, a diversity of opinions on the potential use of (typically citation-based data) were aired, with considerable variation in views across disciplines, as summarised below:

- **Area studies**: Capturing metrics data for both outputs and impacts has proved very difficult in area studies;
- **Biological sciences**: Citation metrics can be helpful as a last resort to inform borderline decisions but are not currently seen as widely useful;
- **Built environment**: Some disciplines are more inclined to use quantitative data but they are in a minority. The use of metrics for assessment of architecture is flawed – most outputs are buildings, design projects, books, etc, which don't fit into metrics;
- **Computer science**: There are significant problems relating to coverage of citations by providers, for instance, indexing conference proceedings. Other computer science outputs include software, which are poorly captured. Downloads might be one option but it is unclear what these say about the excellence of research;
- **Education**: It was suggested that some quantitative measures in research assessment are appropriate, but there was a risk that reviewers might use metrics disproportionately within the peer review process;
- **Performing arts**: There is no formalised process of outputs, so a metrics-based approach based on this assumption would be unsuitable. More discursive elements of assessment would be welcome in these disciplines;
- **Physics** and **epidemiology**: Very large author groups can be an issue. Currently 'team science' and collaborative research is not well rewarded. It would be worth exploring whether metrics could address this. Current metrics and methods of assessment can create tensions in research practices for some disciplines;
- **Psychosocial studies**: There is an important question about why papers are cited and how to interpret the meaning of high citation counts – for example, something written provocatively can be cited many times despite being a paper well known to be poor. There are also issues about use of metrics in people's individual references, when these are not necessarily comparable and produce certain kinds of gaming and individualistic culture.

During the course of the review, we have found that the most serious concerns about certain bibliometric and citation-based indicators tended to be voiced by academics working in arts and humanities disciplines. Colleagues from the arts and humanities are not alone in their distrust of certain research assessment indicators, however the diversity of their research practice and their attendant methodologies and research cultures – which impact on views and attitudes surrounding what epitomises quality and thus how to best evaluate research – perhaps makes them well placed to articulate these concerns. Notwithstanding this, as pointed out in the literature review (Supplementary Report I), research conducted within the arts, humanities (and parts of the social sciences) often differs from much of the research conducted in the sciences in a number of fundamental ways, for instance:[9]

- It has a stronger national and regional orientation; for instance, more publications are likely to be written in languages other than English;
- It is often published in books and other outputs which are harder to measure quantitatively (e.g. objects, films and ephemeral works);
- It can have a different configuration of theoretical development that operates at a different pace; it is difficult to introduce quantitative metrics of incremental work that is undertaken over a long period of time and is slow to develop;
- It depends on the scholars working alone as well as in collaborative teams, so is sometimes less collaborative;
- It may be directed more at a non-scholarly public.

Therefore, we contend that the specificities of different disciplines and sub-disciplines including, but not limited to, the arts and humanities,[10] need to be accounted for within research assessment. We agree with the assertion by PLOS in their response to our call for evidence: "It is entirely appropriate that various research communities seek to articulate the value of their work in different ways."

## 4.4 TAILORED APPROACHES

As noted above, metrics or indicators are not discipline-specific, as such, but can be more or less relevant (or the data more complete) for particular forms of communication, interaction or re-use.

In research assessment contexts, comparison between publications from research fields is often a requirement, but this is a challenging task due to differing cultures of

---

[9]Concerns raised in the literature review (Supplementary Report I) echo several of the concerns and points raised by respondents to our call for evidence as well as contributors to our REF panel focus groups (from Main Panels C and D) who were largely sceptical about the use of citation indicators as a means to assess research quality.

[10]Also see the report produced by the BA and AHRC in (2006). *Use of research metrics in the arts and humanities: Report of the expert group set up jointly by the Arts and Humanities Research Council and HEFCE.*

output production and citation practice. For outputs, attempts to address these difficulties, through processes or normalisation, are often seen as crucial (see the literature review (Supplementary Report I) and Section 3.1.4 of this report). Indeed, the call to normalise indicators across fields is one of the ten guiding principles for research evaluation listed in the Leiden manifesto for research metrics.[11] However, processes of normalisation are not always straightforward and do not necessarily remove problems across all fields, including but not limited to those related to the coverage of metrics. Relatedly, many of the standard indicators currently on offer cannot adequately capture outputs from the arts, especially practice-based subjects, but also written products such as poetry and novels.

Attempts are being made to find alternative and altmetric solutions as a means to provide other routes forward, as discussed at our Sussex and Warwick workshops.[12] However, while increasingly sophisticated, these are not yet ready for widespread application in evaluations. Furthermore, difficulties in terms of their potential application across and between different disciplines would remain. For some disciplines, there is more (or less) of a culture of citing outputs online in ways that will be captured. For instance, at the arts and humanities workshop in Warwick, some concerns were raised that unless larger proportions of the arts and humanities community increase their use and understanding of social media, for instance to capture and circulate DOIs, then such altmetric projects are unlikely to succeed. As Ernesto Priego suggests, systems will not function unless communities buy into them and use associated platforms in effective ways.[13]

There are also residual concerns in relation to books, though improvements are being made (see Section 3.2.5). Perhaps further investment is required in these fields into the development of more suitable indicators. However, the challenge of making meaningful comparisons across subjects is likely to still remain and sufficient sensitivity to context would still be paramount.

One option would be to develop a 'basket' of appropriate metrics perhaps used alongside other forms of assessment such as peer review, and tailored to the community in question. For instance, at Warwick, we also heard that (perhaps) alternative measures/indicators need to be found given the different nature of research quality within the arts and humanities, in order to avoid the risk of using "inappropriate proxies, and bringing in unsuitable goals and objectives" (Jonathan Adams).

Most of the international case studies discussed in Section 2.6 tailor their approaches to research assessment to account for some disciplinary variations, as is also the case

[11]Hicks, D., Wouters, P., Waltman, L., de Rijcke, S., and Rafols, I. (2015). Bibliometrics: The Leiden Manifesto for research metrics. *Nature*, 520: 429–431. www.nature.com/news/bibliometrics-the-leiden-manifesto-for-research-metrics-1.17351. Retrieved 1 May 2015.

[12]Slides available at: www.hefce.ac.uk/media/hefce/content/news/Events/2014/Metrics,we,trust/Mike%20Thelwall%20Slides-%20In%20Metrics%20we%20Trust.pdf. Retrieved 1 February 2015; www.hefce.ac.uk/media/hefce/content/news/Events/2015/HEFCE,metrics,workshop,Warwick/Thelwall.pdf. Retrieved 1 May 2015.

[13]https://epriego.wordpress.com/2015/01/16/hefcemetrics-more-on-metrics-for-the-arts-and-humanities/. Retrieved 1 June 2015.

with the REF, in terms of citation data provision. However, the degree to which such systems have been adapted varies enormously, and primarily focuses on attempts to mitigate certain biases of bibliometric analyses. Snowball Metrics also attempts to provide clarity to the definition and use of metrics, such that disciplinary differences could be more readily accounted for.

However, use of tailored and varied approaches raises additional complexities in terms of cost and administration, has implications for interdisciplinary research (as discussed further in the next section), and could lead to potential disquiet between groups. Claire Donovan, who spoke at our Warwick arts and humanities workshop, discussed the use of different research assessment methods within the Australian system, where some subject areas just employed metrics and others used a mix; she warned that this was not without its attendant problems, and has the potential to lead to perceived hierarchies which may cause significant tension between disciplinary groups.[14]

## 4.5 INDICATORS OF INTERDISCIPLINARITY

In recent years, there has been an increasing emphasis on the importance of interdisciplinary research, but also a recognition that this isn't always easy to undertake effectively, or to support. Our literature review (Supplementary Report I, Section 1.3.2.2) highlights past attempts to establish whether certain modes of research assessment, including the 1996 RAE, have helped or hindered interdisciplinary working.

Throughout the review, a number of contributors have emphasised the need to pay due attention to supporting interdisciplinary working. For instance, a small number of responses to the call for evidence (eight in total) expressed concern that the use of discipline-led metrics could unfairly disadvantage interdisciplinary research. At the Sussex review workshop, several contributors suggested ways to encourage interdisciplinarity, including:

- Taking plurality seriously, calling for metrics to open up the debate rather than closing down the range of outputs within disciplines. It is argued that we need to resist strong demands to keep systems simple, given that the research system may be irreducibly complex. 'Baskets' of metrics that include qualitative and quantitative indicators are more likely to give a better picture of how systems work.
- Adopt new indicators that ask meaningful questions about the research enterprise that appreciate the multiplicity of qualities underpinning research. These would give due consideration to the type of research being carried out, who is using and doing the research and the networks involved.
- Evaluation processes could better be linked to the creative process. There is a need to create further novel research experiences, which could include work across and between disciplines.

---

[14]Slides available at www.hefce.ac.uk/media/hefce/content/news/Events/2015/HEFCE, metrics,workshop,Warwick/Donovan.pdf. Retrieved 1 June 2015.

- Some of the work that Academic Analytics have been undertaking to find indicators for discovery, for instance highlighting the interdisciplinary work of US academics through network analysis, may be useful in this context.

## 4.6 RESOLVING OUR DIFFERENCES

It is clear that research across disciplines, and within them, is diverse in practice and output. Variation in citation practices is the most obvious and striking example of this diversity, but the differences run deeper, drawing in questions of method, debate, epistemology, value, quality and documentation. The research system clearly displays a degree of complexity that is difficult to reduce to simple numbers, but approaches that take account of local practice within disciplines and sub-disciplines may prevent unhelpful or misleading comparisons being made between different types and modes of research and encourage – and perhaps even nurture – diversity. These approaches would carry significant costs, though, and may hamper interdisciplinary research and creative approaches more broadly. There are no quick fixes here, but the greatest potential for recognising differences may come in the form of 'baskets' of indicators – qualitative and quantitative – that can capture the valuable aspects of research practice, output and impact within all disciplines, however they are configured.

# FIVE

## JUDGEMENT AND PEER REVIEW

### CHAPTER CONTENTS

"Reputation is an idle and most false imposition, oft got without merit and lost without deserving."

William Shakespeare, Othello,

Act 2, Scene 3

There are three broad approaches to the assessment of research: a metrics-based model; peer review; and a mixed model, combining these two approaches. Choosing between these remains contentious.[1] In this chapter we explore the relationships, trade-offs and interdependencies between metrics, expert judgement and peer review. As Derek Sayer reminded us in his response to the review, it is important to avoid comparing "a crude caricature of metrics with an idealized chimera of peer review".[2]

---

[1]Technopolis. (2014). *Measuring scientific performance for improved policy making*, p8.

[2]Sayer, D. (2014). Time to abandon the gold standard?, LSE Impact. http://blogs.lse.ac.uk/ impactofsocialsciences/2014/11/19/peer-review-metrics-ref-rank-hypocrisies-sayer/. Retrieved 21 June 2015.

## 5.1 STRENGTHS AND WEAKNESSES OF PEER REVIEW

Peer review is a general umbrella term for a host of expert-based review practices including the review of journal manuscripts, peer review of applications for funding and career promotions, and national peer review-based research assessments such as the REF. It takes place at each stage of the research cycle: in the review of research proposals; the review of outputs (pre- and post-publication); and in broader retrospective assessments of outputs (such as the REF).

Peer review is arguably the most important method of quality control in all disciplines and can be characterised as a core family of mechanisms by which academic communities control themselves and maintain their social order, academic ethos and norms. As noted in a 2015 report commissioned by the Wellcome Trust, "peer review remains a bedrock of the scholarly communications system."[3]

The general respect for peer review was evident in the responses to our call for evidence. Although not explicitly sought in the call for evidence, a common theme that emerged was that peer review should be retained as the primary mechanism for evaluating research quality. Responses that were generally or supportive of the use of metrics both argued that metrics must not be seen as a substitute for peer review (26 responses, 13 of which were from learned societies), which should continue to be the 'gold standard' for research assessment. Sceptical responses generally argued that metrics could never become a realistic substitute for peer review, while many supportive responses stated that robust metrics could support peer reviewers in making nuanced judgements about research excellence. Many responses argued that changes should only be made to the established methods for research assessment where they could be demonstrated to provide improvement. However, it was recognised that peer review is not without its own flaws or disadvantages, and suggestions for its improvement included increasing the transparency and representativeness of the process.

Ethnographic studies of peer review processes have emerged only recently. They often focus on peer review in the context of funding decisions[4] and are often linked to policy-driven agendas and needs. There are often complaints about the lack of robust evidence to support the notion that peer review is the best method the research community has at its disposal.[5]

---

[3]Research Information Network. (2015). *Scholarly Communication and Peer Review: The Current Landscape and Future Trends*. A report commissioned by the Wellcome Trust. www.wellcome.ac.uk/stellent/groups/corporatesite/@policy_communications/documents/web_document/wtp059003.pdf, p27. Retrieved 1 May 2015.

[4]Lamont, M. (2009). *How Professors Think: Inside the Curious World of Academic Judgment*. Cambridge, MA: Harvard University Press.

[5]See Smith, R. (2015). The peer review drugs don't work. *Times Higher*, 28 May 2015. https://www.timeshighereducation.co.uk/content/the-peer-review-drugs-dont-work. Retrieved 1 June 2015.

In general, however, peer review is still considered the main quality control mechanism, arguably due to a lack of viable alternatives.[6]

The literature review (Supplementary Report I) discusses evaluations of peer review in much more detail, but the following summarises its key strengths and weaknesses as a mode of assessment.[7]

| Weaknesses of Peer Review | Strengths of Peer Review |
| --- | --- |
| • It is slow, inefficient and expensive, although most costs are hidden;<br>• Human judgement is subjective – which may however also be seen as a strength;[8]<br>• It is almost by definition not transparent;<br>• It is inconsistent, sometimes characterised as a lack of inter-rater reliability;<br>• It is a biased process (e.g. gender bias regarding career decisions, bias against negative studies in publication decisions, bias in favour of prestigious institutes, bias in favour of dominant paradigms);<br>• Its bias is strengthened by the Matthew effect;[9]<br>• The process can be abused (e.g. to block competitors, to plagiarise);<br>• It is not very good at identifying errors in data or even in detecting fraudulent research;[10] | • Its foundation in specialised knowledge of the subject, methodology and literature relevant for specific decisions;<br>• Its social nature;<br>• The subjectivity of this approach could be seen as a strength (as well as a weakness);<br>• It can help assess elements of research which are challenging to quantify e.g. novelty;<br>• It can deliver more nuanced and detailed understandings of research in the context of research production. |

*(Continued)*

[6]Kassirer, J. P. (1994). Peer Review. *JAMA*, 272(2): 96. DOI:10.1001/jama.1994.03520020022005; Smith, R. (2006). Peer review: a flawed process at the heart of science and journals. *Journal of the Royal Society of Medicine*, 99(4): 178–182. www.ncbi.nlm.nih.gov/pmc/articles/PMC1420798/. Retrieved 1 March 2015.

[7]The table also includes insights from: Council of Canadian Academies (2012). *Informing Research Choices: Indicators and Judgment. Report of the Expert Panel on Science Performance and Research Funding.* Ottawa: CCA.

[8]Lee, C. J., Sugimoto, C. R., Zhang, G., and Cronin, B. (2013). Bias in peer review. *Journal of the American Society for Information Science and Technology*, 64(1): 2–17. DOI:10.1002/asi.22784.

[9]Merton, R. K. (1968). The Matthew Effect in Science. *Science*, 159: 56–62; Merton, R. K. (1988). The Matthew Effect in Science, II: Cumulative Advantage and the Symbolism of Intellectual Property. *ISIS*, 79: 606–623.

[10]Martin, B. (1992). Scientific Fraud and the Power Structure of Science. *Prometheus*, 10(1): 83–98. DOI:10.1080/08109029208629515.

*(Continued)*

| Weaknesses of Peer Review | Strengths of Peer Review |
| --- | --- |
| <ul><li>It cannot process the complete research output of a nation and will therefore result in distorted rankings (since rankings are sensitive to the selection of submissions to the assessments);</li><li>It cannot provide information about the productivity and efficiency of the research system;</li><li>The selection of peer reviewers may create problems because of a variety of reasons (bias, lack of experts in emerging and interdisciplinary areas, lack of experts due to the speed of research areas, etc).</li></ul> | |

However, the identification of peer review's weaknesses has stimulated a series of experiments with different forms of peer review, especially in the area of journal publishing and grant reviews, and also, if less often, in the context of national research assessment exercises. Attempts to improve or enhance peer review include:[11]

- Single-blind or double-blind peer review to remedy the bias in favour of prestigious institutions;
- Post-publication review instead of pre-publication review;
- Open peer review to increase transparency and accountability and counter the risk of abuse;
- Training of reviewers to improve the quality of the reviews;
- Increasing interest in the provision of rewards in the form of scholarly credit and recognition for reviewers;
- Developing new standards of peer review (e.g. a focus on methodology rather than substantive quality criteria as developed by PLOS ONE in journals or other reader systems in grant review);
- Provision of article-level metrics, relating to comments and ratings, mentions in social media and bookmarking.

---

[11]Jayasinghe, U. W., Marsh, H. W., and Bond, N. (2006). A new reader trial approach to peer review in funding research grants: An Australian experiment. *Scientometrics*, 69(3): 591–606; Marsh, H. W., Jayasinghe, U. W., and Bond, N. W. (2008). Improving the peer-review process for grant applications: reliability, validity, bias, and generalizability. *The American Psychologist*, 63(3): 160–168. DOI:10.1037/0003-066X.63.3.160; Pontille, D., and Torny, D. (2014). The Blind Shall See! The Question of Anonymity in Journal Peer Review. *Ada: A Journal of Gender, New Media, and Technology*, ("4"): 1–15. DOI:10.7264/N3542KVW; Smith, R. (2006). Peer review: a flawed process at the heart of science and journals. *Journal of the Royal Society of Medicine*, 99(4): 178–182. Retrieved from www.ncbi.nlm.nih.gov/pmc/articles/PMC1420798/; Research Information Network. (2015).

## 5.2 CAN INDICATORS AND METRICS REPLACE PEER REVIEW?

A common refrain during the process of collecting evidence for this review has been the warning to avoid tensioning an idealised problem-free notion of peer review against an overly simplistic and negative construction of metrics. The picture is clearly far more complex than this, and once again it is crucial to emphasise the role that context must play when making decisions about research assessment processes and strategy.

However, the recognition that some aspects of peer review are problematic has led to calls to replace or supplement peer review with citation indicators and other metrics that may measure aspects of scholarly quality and impact. Similarly, there have been recent calls to rethink the REF in the light of concerns about the specific form of peer review as operated in this context.[12] Some critics have suggested the use of metrics as an alternative for peer review, e.g. a respondent to our call for evidence stated:

> "...greater use of quantitative evidence (metrics) could be seen as a fairer and more objective method of assessment [because] metrics are arguably more transparent than peer review as the basis for the score/grading can be verified independently."
>
> University of Southampton, HEI response

The literature review (Supplementary Report I) explores numerous attempts to undertake correlations between indicators (using various types and combinations of bibliometric measure) and outputs of peer review, and notes that the rise of national assessment exercises based on peer review in the UK, Italy, the Scandinavian countries, the Netherlands, Belgium and other countries, has created a novel opportunity to study the extent to which the outcome of peer review evaluations can be predicted by or correlated to assessments only based on bibliometric data.

A summary of recent studies focusing on the UK context can be found within the literature review (Supplementary Report I), but two HEFCE exercises are also relevant here as well. HEFCE's 2008 pilot project to explore the potential for bibliometrics[13] found they were insufficiently robust at that point in time to be used formulaically or to replace expert review in the REF. In areas where publication in journals was the main type of output being submitted to the exercise, bibliometrics were more representative of the research undertaken. Citation information could be used to inform expert review, but robustness varies across the fields of research covered by the pilot, with lower levels of coverage decreasing the representativeness of the citation information. Much more

---

[12]Sayer, D. (2014). Time to abandon the gold standard? Peer review for the REF falls far short of internationally accepted standards. http://blogs.lse.ac.uk/impactofsocialsciences/2014/11/19/peer-review-metrics-ref-rank-hypocrisies-sayer/. Retrieved 1 March 2015. Also see Section 9.1 of this report.

[13]Details of the pilot exercise are available at www.ref.ac.uk/about/background/bibliometrics/

recently, for this review, we have completed a detailed exercise correlating REF outputs with indicators (as detailed in Chapter 9, and Supplementary Report II).

## 5.3 A DELICATE BALANCE

In summary, the literature shows varying strengths of correlation between bibliometric indicators and peer review assessment. Correlation strengths vary between fields both within the natural sciences, the social sciences, and the humanities, and may even vary within fields. In some fields citation-based indicators are strong predictors of peer review outcomes, in other fields this may be research income, and in a number of fields there is no correlation. In general, the correlation between bibliometrics and peer review is weaker in most fields in the humanities, the applied fields, the technical sciences, and the social sciences. This is partly caused by lower coverage in the citation databases, but also by varying citation and publication cultures, as noted in Chapter 4.

Peer review and bibliometric data are not completely independent. Citation data are ultimately based on researchers who cite or do not cite particular publications. The same communities are the source of the peer review data. Although the meaning of the citation cannot be deduced from the role of the literature reference, it does explain any positive correlation there may be between peer review and bibliometrics. In addition, peer review decisions may have been influenced by prior knowledge of bibliometric data. This interaction may have increased due to the large-scale availability of bibliometric data and indicators.

## 5.4 INFORMED PEER REVIEW

Although no complete consensus exists in the bibliometric literature about what citation indicators and bibliometric measures exactly mean, the vast majority of bibliometric experts see citations as a proxy measure for the impact of the work on the relevant academic communities[14]. The act of counting citations abstracts from the substantive information in the scholarly literature based on the formal relationships among references and citations. By definition, many forms of peer review cannot be replaced by bibliometric indicators. This is clearly the case where the research has not yet been published, but in many other instances where substantive judgement is required.

This has given rise to the concept of informed peer review: the idea that the judicious application of specific bibliometric data and indicators may inform the process of peer

---

[14]Martin, B. R., and Irvine, J. (1983). Assessing basic research: Some partial indicators of scientific progress in radio astronomy. *Research Policy*, 12(2): 61–90; for an overview of citation theory see Nicolaisen, J. (2007). Citation Analysis, in *Annual Review of Information Science and Technology*, 41: 609–642. New York etc.: Interscience Publishers. Also see Chapter 3 of this report.

review, depending on the exact goal and context of the assessment. Informed peer review is in principle relevant for all types of peer review and at all levels of aggregation. Partly for this reason, the extent to which large-scale research assessment exercises should be based on peer review (whether informed by metrics or not), rather than metrics alone, remains a contested issue in the literature.

Some respondents to the call for evidence also suggested that the use of informed review within national assessments, such as the REF, was already or would be worth-while. As detailed in Chapter 9, a form of informed review was introduced within the process of REF2014 for 11 of the 36 sub-panels (see Table 6 in the 'Annex of tables'). This was generally seen as positive by those who used it, but viewed more critically by sub-panels who had not drawn in any way on citation data.

Within the literature on this topic, there are several studies exploring informed peer review. One analysis of the UK RAE[15] concluded that the future of research evaluation would need to be based on an intelligent combination of advanced metrics and informed peer review[16]. The paper argued that metrics, especially sophisticated forms of citation analysis, may provide tools to keep the peer review process more honest and transparent.

A further empirical argument in favour of informed peer review has been developed by Claire Donovan.[17] Her study argues that quantitative indicators are as infused with human values as qualitative approaches. Quality and impact metrics have followed a trajectory "away from the unreflexive use of standardised quantitative metrics divorced from expert peer interpretation, towards triangulation of quantitative data, contextual analysis and placing a renewed and greater value on peer judgement combined with stakeholder perspectives".

Another specific argument in favour of informed peer review is the limitation of citation analysis to predict future work. Mazloumian tested the assumption that cita-tion counts are reliable predictors of future success, analysing complete citation data on the careers of ~150,000 scientists.[18] The results show that among all citation indica-tors, annual citations at the time of prediction are the best predictor of future citations. However, future citations of *future* work are hardly predictable, and others argue that the impact of papers published in the past does not necessarily correlate with that of papers published in the future.[19]

---

[15]The UK Research Assessment Exercise was the predecessor to the REF.

[16]Moed, H. (2007). The future of research evaluation rests with an intelligent combination of advanced metrics and transparent peer review. *Science and Public Policy*, 34(8): 575–583. DOI:10.3152/030234207X255179.

[17]Donovan, C. (2007). The qualitative future of research evaluation. *Science and Public Policy*, 34(8): 585–597. DOI:10.3152/030234207X256538.

[18]Mazloumian, A. (2012). Predicting scholars' scientific impact. *PLOS One*, 7(11): e49246. DOI:10.1371/journal.pone.0049246.

[19]Penner, O., Petersen, A. M., Pan, R., and Fortunato, S. (2013). Commentary: The case for caution in predicting scientists' future impact. *Physics Today*, 66(4): 8. DOI:10.1063/PT.3.1928.

Informed peer review may also be used to provide feedback on the design of new performance indicators[20] and to develop improvements in systems of large-scale peer review. A recent study of ten different conferences in computer science (ca. 9,000 reviews on ca. 2,800 submitted contributions) explored possible improvements to conference peer review.[21]

Informed peer review can also be used to increase participation in review processes by non-academic stakeholders, particularly in policy or practice-oriented fields of research. One recent study across three countries (UK, Australia and Spain) argues that informed peer review can help us to move beyond a situation where evaluation is confined to a "hyper-specialised committee of 'experts', operating behind closed doors."[22]

## 5.5 COMPLEMENTS AND SUPPLEMENTS

Much of the literature appears to support the idea of supplementing peer review by bibliometrics (informed peer review), but this concept is yet to be fully operationalised. Bibliometric data may counter specific weaknesses of peer review (for instance, its selectivity, and certain forms of bias), but further work would need to be undertaken to decide on the best way forward in specific contexts.

This topic is part of an emerging literature in which the 'relevance gap'[23] or the 'evaluation gap'[24] is seen as a major shortcoming of the traditional disciplinary peer

---

[20]Hug, S. E., Ochsner, M., and Daniel, H.-D. (2013). Criteria for assessing research quality in the humanities: a Delphi study among scholars of English literature, German literature and art history. *Research Evaluation*, 22(5): 369–383. DOI:10.1093/reseval/rvt008; Ochsner, M., Hug, S. E., and Daniel, H. (2012). Indicators for Research Quality for Evaluation of Humanities Research: Opportunities and Limitations Quality criteria for research in the humanities. Collecting indicators for research in the humanities. The measurement of research quality in the humanities. *Bibliometrie – Praxis und Forschung*, 1(4): 1–17; Ochsner, M., Hug, S. E., and Daniel, H.-D. (2014). Setting the stage for the assessment of research quality in the humanities. Consolidating the results of four empirical studies. *Zeitschrift Für Erziehungswissenschaft*, 17(S6): 111–132. DOI:10.1007/s11618-014-0576-4.

[21]Ragone, A., Mirylenka, K., Casati, F., and Marchese, M. (2013). On peer review in computer science: analysis of its effectiveness and suggestions for improvement. *Scientometrics*, 97(2): 317–356. DOI:10.1007/s11192-013-1002-z.

[22]Derrick, G. E., and Pavone, V. (2013). Democratising research evaluation: Achieving greater public engagement with bibliometrics-informed peer review. *Science and Public Policy*, 40(5): 563–575. DOI:10.1093/scipol/sct007.

[23]Nightingale, P., and Scott, A. (2007). Peer review and the relevance gap: ten suggestions for policy-makers. *Science and Public Policy*, 34(8): 543–553. DOI:10.3152/030234207X254396.

[24]Wouters, P., Bar-Ilan, J., Thelwall, M., Aguillo, I. F., Must, Ü., Havemann, F. and Schneider, J. (2010). Academic Careers Understood through Measurement and Norms (ACUMEN). pp1–39.

review systems and practices. Although this literature is mainly in the area of science policy and higher education studies and not itself mainly concerned with bibliometrics, it may provide an important theoretical context for further developing concepts of informed peer review and informed expert review.[25] The decades of experience among bibliometricians with bibliometric databases, indicators, and deliberations with users of these data and indicators (sometimes under the flag of 'validation of bibliometrics') may prove to be useful in a wider sense than has previously been realised.

This development has recently become more pronounced by the increased need for guidance in the use of bibliometric and other performance indicators. A recent analysis of the bibliometric literature has shown an increased role of authors not affiliated within the bibliometric discipline.[26] In response to the growing availability of bibliometrics and to concerns about the potential for abuse and unintended effects, the bibliometric community started a number of initiatives to initiate principles of good evaluation practices, building on initiatives in the community that started decades ago.[27] Perhaps a new body of 'translational bibliometrics' literature to flesh out the concept of informed peer review will emerge from these initiatives.

As altmetrics are still emergent, understandings of their potential use (and abuse) remains nascent. Some suggestions to prevent gaming have been provided by Mike Thelwall[28] amongst others,[29] but more work needs to be done as this area develops.

---

[25]Etzkowitz, H., and Leydesdorff, L. (2000). The dynamics of innovation: from national systems and "Mode 2" to a triple helix of university-industry-government relations. *Research Policy*, 29: 109–123; Hemlin, S., and Rasmussen, S. B. (2006). The Shift in Academic Quality Control. *Science, Technology & Human Values*, 31(2): 173–198. DOI:10.1177/0162243905283639; Martin, B. R. (2011). What can bibliometrics tell us about changes in the mode of knowledge production? *Prometheus*, 29(4): 455–479; Nowotny, H., Scott, P., and Gibbons, M. (2001). *Re-thinking Science: Knowledge and the Public in an Age of Uncertainty*. Cambridge, UK: Polity Press.

[26]Jonkers, K., and Derrick, G. E. G. E. (2012). The bibliometric bandwagon: Characteristics of bibliometric articles outside the field literature. *Journal of the American Society for Information Science and Technology*, 63(4): 829–836. DOI:10.1002/asi.22620.

[27]Moed, H. F., and Glänzel, W. (2004). *Handbook of Quantitative Science and Technology Research: The Use of Publication and Patent Statistics in Studies of S&T Systems*. Dordrecht etc: Kluwer Academic Publishers; Noijons, E., and Wouters, P. (2014). Report on the 19th International Conference on Science and Technology Indicators. *ISSI Newsletter*, 10(4): 69–70; Wouters, P., Glänzel, W., Gläser, J., and Rafols, I. (2013). The dilemmas of performance indicators of individual researchers: an urgent debate in bibliometrics. *ISSI Newsletter*, 9(3): 48–53.

[28]Thelwall, M. (2014). Five recommendations for using alternative metrics in the future UK Research Excellence Framework. http://blogs.lse.ac.uk/impactofsocialsciences/2014/10/23/alternative-metrics-future-uk-research-excellence-framework-thelwall/. Retrieved 1 June 2015.

[29]NISO's initiative emphasises the importance of understanding factors that may lead to the greater likelihood of gaming and also the need for further research into improving data quality.

The emergence of DORA in 2013 is encouraging and demonstrates that more people are likely to be thinking about these issues.[30] Through its Alternative Assessment Metrics Initiative, NISO is also doing valuable work to identify and advance standards for altmetrics, and to develop assessment criteria for non-traditional research outputs, such as data sets, visualizations and software.[31]

---

[30]The San Francisco Declaration on Research Assessment can be found at: http://am.ascb.org/dora/

[31]www.niso.org/topics/tl/altmetrics_initiative/

# SIX

## MANAGEMENT BY METRICS

## CHAPTER CONTENTS

"Truly, evaluators can help do good things. They can increase the sensitivity of practition-
ers and decision makers to the effects and side effects in society of what they do... They
can connect what is otherwise disconnected in hypocritical organizations (such as goals
and activities, promises, and deeds)."

Peter Dahler-Larsen[1]

Over the past twenty years, pressures on universities to be more accountable to government
and public funders of research have intensified. Partly in reaction to this, universities (and
research institutes) have in turn developed more formal methods of research assessment at
the *institutional* level, characterised by a more formalised focus on outcomes at a strategic
level and the closer management of research at an operational level.

This greater focus on the management of outcomes has facilitated the import of more
corporate styles of management. Since 2000, university leadership, governance and management have become increasingly professionalised. In the UK, university finances and resources
are more strategically and professionally managed,[2] and vice-chancellors are increasingly

---

[1]Dahler-Larsen, P. (2012). *The Evaluation Society.* Stanford University Press.

[2]J M Consulting Ltd. (2006). Future needs for capital funding in higher education: A review of
the future of SRIF and learning and teaching capital. www.hefce.ac.uk/news/newsarchive/
2015/2006capitalreport/

seen as chief executive officers.[3] Within this cultural shift, metrics are often positioned as tools that can drive organisational financial performance as part of an institution's competitiveness. Coupled with greater competition for scarce resources more broadly, this is steering academic institutions and their researchers towards being more market-oriented.

These tendencies are strengthened by the fact that UK higher education is a significant export industry – whose strengths are neatly captured in impressive performance metrics that justify continued investment and stimulate student demand. All actors within the sector respond to this by gathering metrics and using them to inform decisions: vice-chancellors and research managers are analysing indicators to report to government and to inform institutional strategy; researchers contribute to an emergent performance culture that is dependent on JIFs and h-indices; students are turning more and more to information from public and private sources (league tables, the National Student Survey and the new Key Information Set being prominent examples) to guide their choices of degree programme.

The pressures to incorporate metrics into research assessment within universities may have originated in response to external forces – government policy, constrained funding and globalisation – but they have also assumed an internal life and dynamic within institutions. Some information-gathering exercises are voluntary, while others are the result of policy requirements or are motivated by the need to compete e.g. for students.

This chapter will focus on how the adoption of metric-based modes of assessment by universities has affected internal processes and research management practices within institutions. It will focus in particular on analysing the characteristics of university league tables and rankings, with a view to suggesting some ways forward in this area.

## 6.1 THE USE OF INDICATORS IN HEI MANAGEMENT

A recent European Commission report[4] provides a useful overview of the types of research assessment that are gathered, organised by the range of 'target' users of such information. These user groups include governments and government agencies, academic organisations, industrial partners, civic organisations, peer HEIs, benefactors and alumni, potential employees and students, and of course the originating HEI.

Within HEIs themselves (the focus of this chapter), the target users can be broken into three sub-sets, reflecting different tiers of management: (1) governing bodies or councils; (2) executives and university-level managers; (3) research groupings within universities (e.g. faculty and departmental heads). These sub-groups have extensive and overlapping needs for assessment information to underpin policy and planning, strategy-setting, investor confidence, quality assurance, publicity, student and academic recruitment, and benchmarking.

---

[3]McGettigan, A. (2013). *The Great University Gamble: Money, Markets and the Future of Higher Education*. Pluto Press.

[4]Expert group on assessment of University-based research (2010). Assessing Europe's University-Based Research. http://ec.europa.eu/research/science-society/document_library/pdf_06/assessing-europe-university-based-research_en.pdf

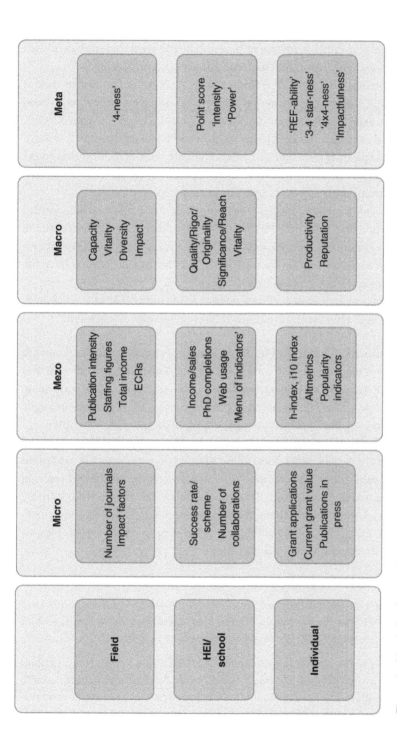

**Figure 2** Vocabulary for metrics at a range of levels and scales[5]

[5]Oancea, A. (2015). Universities and Society: Research Impacts and Ecologies of Value. Keynote address. European Foundation for Management Development, Higher Education Research Conference, 4 June 2015.

Alis Oancea (who spoke at our Warwick workshop) offers a helpful framework for thinking about research assessment strategies[6] at different levels and scales: see Figure 2.

To meet these information needs HEIs are turning to various forms of metrics to characterise institutional performance, including in research. The types and sources of such metrics are diverse[7] and practices at different institutions vary considerably.

These various datasets, or in most HEIs subsets thereof, are collected through various means, often including internal and external sources. For example citation counts tend to be collected from external databases such as Scopus, Web of Science or Google Scholar. However in external databases, the association of author with HEI tends not to be robust. HEIs normally combine their own staff lists with externally sourced citation data to get the most accurate picture of the institutional citation position (the problems associated with doing this author-matching are discussed in Section 2.5.1 of this report).

This however creates a problem for benchmarking: if an externally available institutional citation position does not match the one that the institution itself creates then the externally available benchmark data must also be called into question. To help address this situation there has been a recent increase in the number of CRISs which have the potential to produce and share benchmark data.

Looking at the three main HEI users of such metrics, while their needs vary, sometimes markedly, between and within institutions, the following overview is suggested:

1. **Governing bodies or councils** tend to be interested in institutional level compound metrics either over time or relative to comparator institutions, or both. For example they are more likely to be interested in the top-level view of an institution. Have we gone up in league table X since last year, or are we above our benchmark institutions in league table Y; and if not, why not? Perhaps leaving the detail to the university executive;

2. **Executives and university-level managers** are more likely to drill down into the components of the league tables, looking for areas of poor performance compared to benchmark institutions, for example weak citation counts, or external research income, or international faculty mix. This information is likely to feed into strategic investment decisions and institutional culture development, for example encouraging publication in higher profile outlets, or incentivising external research bids, or actively trying to recruit international faculty;

---

[6]The slides for this talk are available at: www.hefce.ac.uk/media/hefce/content/news/Events/2015/HEFCE,metrics,workshop,Warwick/16%20Jan%20A%20Oancea%20metrics%20rankings%20and%20governance.pdf. Retrieved 1 June 2015.

[7]Including: Counts of research publications/outputs; Research outputs per academic; Citation counts; Number of invited keynote addresses; Awards/prizes; International visiting research appointments; Editorships in 'prestigious' journals; External research income; Number and percentage of grants won; Research income per FTE; Total R&D investment; Employability of PhD graduates; Research students per research-active staff; PhD completions; Number/percentage of research-active staff; Commercialisation of IP; End user esteem; Number of collaborations/partnerships; Research infrastructure (number of labs, library and computing facilities).

3. **Research groupings within universities** may have targets set by the centre in terms of metrics and wish to be able to track (demonstrate) their progress towards them. In a more devolved scenario, a research group may develop their own research strategy and just having the metrics visible to colleagues can act as a reminder as to where efforts might be focused.

All of these needs are of course overlapping, and hopefully complimentary. Specifically in the UK there are pressures for research managers to provide additional information to help inform strategic decisions. There is no suggestion that metrics should be used in isolation but there is a growing trend to include them in order to make the decision-making process as evidence-based as possible. Having up to date and accurate research information also allows institutions to meet the various requirements of funders with regard to issues such as publication-funder acknowledgement and reporting, open access, and of course impact, academic and otherwise.

### 6.1.1 Commercial platforms

Within this context, a number of players have emerged to provide platforms, research information systems and data collection and analysis services to support institutional research management and metrics-driven decision making; some examples are provided in Section 2.4. These include CRISs provided by commercial providers, and analytical services from consultancies, academic bibliometric institutes and altmetrics providers. Commercial solutions such as these are complemented – and perhaps challenged – by the emergence of free services such as Google Scholar and Microsoft Academic Search, providing alternatives and competition within this growing marketplace.

Taken together, these services increasingly allow institutions to benchmark themselves against others in a number of performance dimensions. At the local level, approaches and methodologies appear to differ considerably, with no one tool or approach being universally adopted. There are therefore natural limits to the ability of institutions to assess relative performance against what are increasingly contested benchmarks. By way of illustration, the following was written in a US context, but is also relevant to the UK:

"Standardized processes are not available to connect, evaluate and share credible research performance data between universities. Standard definitions and information management systems are often available at the institutional level but tend to be unique to the individual university and of value only in evaluating changes in performance over time. When comparative benchmarking takes place it is often as a snapshot of a point in time and is not performed on an ongoing basis, so the university then returns to internal comparisons of progress on a yearly basis."[8]

---

[8]US Research Universities Futures Consortium (2013). The current state and recommendations for meaningful academic research metrics among American research universities. www.research universitiesfutures.org/us-research-metrics-working-group-current-state-and-recommenda tions-oct2013.pdf. Retrieved 1 March 2015.

Faced with a complex information collection regime (as described by the Higher Education Data & Information Improvement Programme, HEDIIP[9]), it is perhaps not surprising that institutions have increasingly come to rely on off-the-shelf commercial solutions, which has raised the question about whether there are risks to the information infrastructure within institutions becoming dominated by commercial providers. Partly driven by this, and partly by the need for greater consistency and transparency, the growing need for open technologies and standards has risen up the agendas of institutions, public research funders and information professionals. Cameron Neylon provides an outline discussion of this topic (and an ambitious suggestion that the research community gather together around some common principles) in a recent blog post, *Principles for Open Scholarly Infrastructures*.[10] This is not a new debate – moves towards open scholarly infrastructures and standards have been taking place for many years (the emergence of NISO standards being one of the more visible examples) – but the increasing adoption of metrics and the growing role of commercial or proprietary systems in this space has brought the issue to the fore.

## 6.2 UNIVERSITY RANKINGS AND LEAGUE TABLES

One of the most obvious outcomes of the greater interest in and drive towards data-driven decision-making is the burgeoning influence of league tables and rankings which compare universities on the basis of a variety of indicators, some of which are linked to research. The indicators used, and the weightings attributed to them vary between different rankings, and the methodologies underpinning many systems are often 'black-boxed' or not made public, although they are coming under increasing pressure to do so (either in response to broader endeavours from governments and others to increase transparency, or in response to specific initiatives such as U-Multirank[11]).

However, even when criteria are made public, they underline the problematic way in which these types of metric are being used (see below). Some HEIs effectively outsource crucial aspects of performance management to league table providers, by incorporating their rank position as a specific organisational target. For example, the first performance indicator in the University of Manchester's '2020 Vision' strategic plan is "To be in the top 25 of the Shanghai Jiao Tong Academic Ranking of World Universities by 2020."[12] Other institutions link VC and senior management remu-neration and bonuses to league table results. There are also examples of institutions (mostly outside the UK) incentivising behaviour to influence their position in specific league tables, for example by offering financial rewards to researchers for publication

---

[9]www.hediip.ac.uk/

[10]Bilder G., Lin J. and Neylon C. (2015). 'Principles for open scholarly infrastructure-v1. Available at: http://dx.doi.org/10.6084/m9.figshare.1314859.

[11]www.umultirank.org/. Retrieved 28 June 2015.

[12]www.manchester.ac.uk/discover/vision/

in *Nature* and *Science*, or awarding nominal 'visiting faculty' status to highly cited researchers from universities in other countries.[13]

Ellen Hazelkorn[14] has given a comprehensive description and analysis of university rankings, including describing their evolution in relation to four phases of development (since 1900), culminating in the emergence of supra-national rankings since 2008. We now have ten major global rankings and more than 150 national/specialist rankings. Two of these (Webometrics and U-Multirank) are government-sponsored:

- Academic Ranking of World Universities (*ARWU*) (Shanghai Jiao Tong University, China), 2003;
- Webometrics (Spanish National Research Council, Spain), 2004;
- National Taiwan University Rankings (formerly Performance Ranking of Scientific Papers for Research Universities, HEEACT), 2007;
- Leiden Ranking (Centre for Science and Technology Studies, University of Leiden), 2008;
- SCImago Journal and Country Rank (SJR) (Spain), 2009;
- University Ranking by Academic Performance (URAP) (Informatics Institute of Middle East Technical University, Turkey), 2009;
- QS World University Rankings (Quacquarelli Symonds, UK), 2010;
- THE World University Ranking (Times Higher Education, UK), 2010;
- U-Multirank (European Commission, Brussels), 2014;
- Best Global Universities rankings (USNWR, US), 2014.

A broad range of users takes notice of such league tables, including students, the public, government and institutions themselves. Within institutions, Hazelkorn reports that 84% of HEIs have a formal internal mechanism to review their institution's rank; in 40% of institutions this review is led by the vice-chancellor, president or rector.

Hazelkorn notes that there are some advantages associated with such rankings schemes, notably that: they provide a simple, quick and easy way to measure and compare higher education performance; they place higher education within a wider and global context and they may lead to improvement of performance. She also argues, however, that the biggest consumers are students, the public and government, all of whom are likely to be most negatively influenced by the results conveyed. The disadvantages of rankings are numerous; in particular, there are serious concerns around the methods and

---

[13]http://scholarlykitchen.sspnet.org/2011/04/07/paying-for-impact-does-the-chinese-model-make-sense/; https://www.timeshighereducation.co.uk/news/secondary-affiliations-lift-king-abdulaziz-university-in-rankings/2014546.article; www.dailycal.org/2014/12/05/citations-sale/. Retrieved 28 June 2015.

[14]As discussed by Hazelkorn in a presentation delivered to the World Bank 'The Obsession with Rankings in Tertiary Education: Implications for Public Policy', January 2015. Available at https://hepru.files.wordpress.com/2015/01/the-obsession-with-rankings-in-tertiary-education_wb_0115.pdf. Retrieved 1 June 2015.

often arbitrary weightings used to underpin global rankings, and there is also widespread scepticism about the tendency to compare whole universities (often in very different contexts), using single, aggregate, and often poorly explained scores.[15]

The rise of university league tables might be seen as the embodiment of international standards but each one is different so in reality a common standard of comparison has yet to emerge. Close inspection reveals varying degrees of arbitrariness in the weighting of different components in different league tables. The aggregate scores suffer from the same problems of all composite indicators in that their meaning or value is not clear.[16] Also, no effort is made to estimate errors and, with rare exceptions,[17] there is no clear acknowledgement that they might exist. Ranking in fact magnifies differences beyond statistical significance.[18] Rankings assume degrees of objectivity, authority and precision that are not yet possible to achieve in practice, and to date have not been properly justified by vendors.

Considering research more specifically, Hazelkorn notes a number of implications arising from the use of league tables, performance indicators and quantitative measures. The central problem identified here is that academic quality is a complex notion that cannot easily be reduced to quantification – the use of proxy variables runs the risk of misrepresenting the qualities of research contributions and may lead to unintended consequences. She contests that there is considerable difficulty obtaining meaningful indicators and comparative data (nationally and internationally), and that the adoption of rankings serves to embed a metrics culture and to down-weight features of research or teaching quality that cannot easily be captured with numbers. This is a perspective echoed by the European Commission's expert group on research assessment: "Unintended consequences can occur when indicators are taken in isolation and simple correlations are made. This may include over-concentrating on research, favouring particular disciplines of allocating resources and realigning priorities to match indicators."[19]

---

[15]In this context, the Times Higher Education should be commended for their current moves towards greater transparency and openness in terms of the indicators used to rank universities. However, it is not clear how familiar users within university management are with methodologies when they are made available. The methodological details are rarely mentioned in Times Higher Education news stories built on the league tables' transparency, for instance.

[16]Gingras. Y. (2014). Criteria for evaluating indicators. In Cronin, B. and Sugimoto, B. *Beyond Bibliometrics: Harnessing multidimensional indicators of scholarly impact*. Cambridge, MA: MIT.

[17]For example, as argued by Phil Baty, in Baty, P. (2014). The Times Higher Education World University Rankings, 2004–2012. *Ethics in Science and Environmental Politics*, 13(2): 125–130. http://doi.org/10.3354/esep00145

[18]Goldstein, H. and Spiegelhalter, D. (1996). League tables and their limitations: Statistical issues in comparisons of institutional performance. *Journal of the Royal Statistical Society. Series A (Statistics in Society)*, 159(3): 385–443. Available at www.bristol.ac.uk/media-library/sites/cmm/migrated/documents/statistical-issues-for-league-tables1.pdf. Retrieved 1 June 2015.

[19]European Commission (2010). Expert group on assessment of university-based research, assessing Europe's university-based research. European Commission Directorate General for Research, p21.

Further, the use of such indicators is felt by many to risk reinforcing a hierarchical system of institutions that may lead to simplistic comparisons. Such comparisons are hard to justify when aggregate scores show statistically insignificant differences – indeed, an over-emphasis on a small set of indicators risks encouraging perverse behaviour within and across institutions. Comparisons between institutions may lead to an unhelpful focus on the 'top' universities worldwide and foster a narrow definition of excellence; such a focus is not likely to be relevant to the institutional goals of universities, where the balance of research and teaching, the geographical focus and disciplinary distinctiveness may vary considerably. In fact, one of the specific concerns associated with rankings is their tendency to rely on certain bibliometric and citation databases, such as Scopus or WoS, which, as discussed in Chapter 3, benefit or disadvantage certain disciplines and types of research, ignoring the important role that distinctiveness can play in an institution's research and teaching missions. Thus, there is considerable concern that rankings "can misinform and mislead when used to influence decision-making by governments, universities and other stakeholders."[20]

All current rankings remain problematic to varying degrees, and further, only a very small percentage of the globe's universities and colleges feature within these listings.[21] We need to continue observing who undertakes rankings, how, and why, and to monitor the effects they may have. Furthermore, rankings should be fully transparent, and more closely aligned to the sort of information that is of real use to the higher education sector, with clear attempts made to avoid perverse effects.

## 6.2.1 Future uses of rankings and league tables

A key issue with university rankings is that they command a great deal of attention thanks to vigorous promotion. Furthermore, as many international students made choices on the basis of ranking positions, there are strong pressures for HEIs to focus on these metrics.

Although there is competition between vendors in this sector, the extant products are all vulnerable to Hazelkorn's critique and valid alternatives have yet to emerge: *their use takes place partly due to the absence of alternatives.* Faced with the challenge of objective and comparative performance assessment, rankings are easy measures to find and to use. As the US Research Universities Futures Consortium report notes:

"Universities have a difficult time objectively assessing their comparative research strengths and weaknesses in relation to their peers on both a program level as well as an institutional basis. This is not to say they do not collect data and construct positive narratives about how well they are doing, mostly as a means of self-promotion. The result is that

---

[20]Ibid. p20.

[21]US Research Universities Futures Consortium (2013). The current health and future wellbeing of the American Research University. Available at: https://www.elsevier.com/research-intelligence/research-initiatives/futures p7.

rather than having the ability to conduct objective analysis of their comparative productivity internally, institutions turn to external consultants to provide guidance on strategic planning decisions. Consultants often only have access to public information about other universities, as biased as that might be, but they have the time and experience in evaluating performance between universities."[22]

In response to this challenge, it is felt by many that universities and others should not delegate important judgements on quality to external ranking organisations, perhaps especially when these organisations have commercial interests to promote the validity of their products or where senior leaders from particular HEIs are influencing the design of such rankings. It is worth noting that the data assembled by the various rankers are often not subject to rigorous peer review or external input and critique, and the emphases of rankings on particular features (such as research) at the expense of others are not often drawn out in the broad analyses.

In this context, it may be sensible to suggest some measures to improve how rankings and league tables are to be used most effectively to support university leadership, governance and management. The most important and immediate suggestion here is that HEIs should make efforts to explain the reasons for using rankings – in particular whether they are using these as a means to achieve particular ends (and what these are), or whether the reverse is true. In particular they should explain to staff how rankings information is being used to inform the balance between academic activities, with an emphasis on explaining how the implications for those activities not captured in rankings are being managed. Transparency is vital.

In the medium term, initiatives such as Snowball and the work of the above US consortium may both offer possible ways forward for developing more locally sensitive performance indicators. As the US consortium notes, there is a growing need for "reliable and actionable performance data to guide strategic planning. Such data would allow evidence-based resource allocation decisions that can be made and justified, and ensure that universities that are especially effective in turning inputs into noteworthy research discoveries are widely recognised."[23] As with Snowball, this suggests that the optimal solution to the challenge of measuring performance would be a bottom-up collaborative approach[24] that allows universities to identify those indicators that best align with their institutional mission, rather than a top-down or government-mandated approach. In moving toward this, it will be important for institutional managers to ensure that this bottom-up approach is done transparently within the institution and with the involvement of academic staff.

---

[22]Ibid. p11.

[23]Ibid. p5.

[24]This is the U-Multirank approach which uses 'like with like' comparisons. However, as institutions are required to opt in and supply data, many missing institutions are not featured which reduces utility. In the 30 March 2015 data it was reported that only 12 UK HEIs 'fully participated'; see www.universityworldnews.com/article.php?story=2015033009083650. Retrieved 1 June 2015.

# SEVEN

## CULTURES OF COUNTING

## CHAPTER CONTENTS

"A decision made by the numbers (or by explicit rules of some other sort) has at least the appearance of being fair and impersonal. Scientific objectivity thus provides an answer to a moral demand for impartiality and fairness. Quantification is a way of making decisions without seeming to decide. Objectivity lends authority to officials who have very little of their own."

Theodore M. Porter[1]

Across the higher education sector, quantitative data is now used far more widely as a management aid, reflecting developments in the private sector over recent decades. As described in the previous chapter, most universities now plan resource allocation centrally, often drawing on the advice of dedicated intelligence and analysis units that

---

[1]Porter, T. M. (1995) *Trust in Numbers: The Pursuit of Objectivity in Science and Public Life.* Princeton University Press.

gather information from departments and faculties. The use of such systems has helped universities to strengthen their reputation as responsible, well-managed institutions. The relatively robust financial position of the sector, and the continued trust placed in universities by public funders to manage their own affairs, is in part founded on such perceptions of sound financial governance.

The extent to which management systems in HEIs help or hinder institutional success is of course contested. On the positive side, such systems have helped to make decision making fairer and more transparent, and allowed institutions to tackle genuine cases of underperformance. At the same time, many within academia resist moves towards greater quantification of performance management on the grounds that these will erode academic freedoms and the traditional values of universities. There is of course a proper place for competition in academic life, but there are also growing concerns about an expansion in the number and reach of managers, and the distortions that can be created by systems of institutionalized audit.

In the research arena, this debate often focuses on finding an appropriate balance between curiosity-driven and more directly applied forms of investigation. Linked to this, the impact agenda – both prospectively, as a part of research grant applications, and retrospectively, in the form of the impact case studies that were introduced to the REF in 2014 – is perceived by some as incentivising more applied research, even though this is not the stated intention of research funders.

Uneasiness over the growth of audit, quantification and competition within higher education is reflected in recent high-profile contributions by scholars such as Stefan Collini and Thomas Docherty.[2] We have also seen the emergence of grassroots groups, such as the Council for the Defence of British Universities and the Campaign for the Public University, arguing for the continued autonomy of HEIs and a halt to a perceived drift towards instrumentalism and marketisation. Further critique has focused on the REF, initially around the introduction of its assessment of impact, but more recently around the continued validity of the broader exercise.[3] One prominent voice in this discussion is Derek Sayer, whose polemic *Rank Hypocrisies: The Insult of the REF* has stimulated debate.[4] Related concerns are expressed in a number of the responses to our call for evidence.[5]

---

[2]See Collini, S. (2012). *What are Universities For?* London: Penguin; and Docherty, T. (2014). *Universities at War.* London: SAGE.

[3]See, for example, a letter to the Times Higher Education from Lord Stern of Brentford and Sir Paul Nurse. https://www.timeshighereducation.co.uk/comment/letters/its-our-duty-to-assess-the-costs-of-the-ref/2017479.article?storyCode=2017479

[4]Sayer, D. (2015) *Rank Hypocrisies: The Insult of the REF.* London: SAGE.

[5]E.g. Meera Sabaratnam and Paul Kirby's response: http://thedisorderofthings.com/2014/06/16/why-metrics-cannot-measure-research-quality-a-response-to-the-hefce-consultation/. Retrieved 28 June 2015.

A recurrent concern is that research managers can become over-reliant on indicators that are widely felt to be problematic or not properly understood (e.g. JIFs), or on indicators that may be used insensitively or inappropriately (e.g. research income targets), and these are driving managerial approaches in a way that does not fully recognise the diverse contributions of individual researchers to the overall institutional mission or the wider public good. Prominent examples include widespread suspicions (and some anecdotal reports) that research managers made decisions about which papers to include in the institution's REF submission on the basis of the JIF metric alone.

In this case, a reliance on JIFs by decision-makers might be reinforced by the attitudes and behaviours of academics themselves, but irrespective of this point, the primary issue remains: metrics are widely seen as absolving research managers of the responsibility for making assessments based on more accurate and complete information, and as contributing to mistrust of research management more generally.

It is beyond the scope of this report to resolve all of these issues; they cut across broader aspects of higher education policy and culture, and there are enough counter-examples of the positive use of metrics-informed decision-making to argue for a more evidence-based approach. However, perceived shifts within the sector towards greater accountability for public funding, the closer alignment of research strategies and institutional competitiveness, and the broader emergence of market forces in research and education, must be taken into account in any assessment of the broader consequences for academic culture of relying on particular indicators.

Some of the disquiet over these developments is reflected in the findings of the Best University Workplace Survey 2015. This reveals a gulf between the views of academics and administrators, and reports that many academics feel overworked and taken advantage of.[6] Indeed, the experience of many academics might most neatly be characterised by a quote from one physicist in Australia: "The metrics have gone absolutely berserk...."[7]

This chapter takes a closer look at these issues and how they relate to individual researchers, beginning with an overview of what is known about the effects of evaluative metrics in research practices, including strategic behaviour and goal displacement, task reduction, and potential biases against interdisciplinarity. This is followed by a discussion of empirical research on institutional responses to metrics-based assessments, and the relationship between indicators and knowledge production. Lastly, we consider the equality and diversity implications of an increasing reliance on metrics for research management, assessment and decision-making.

---

[6]Parr, C. (2015). Best University Workplace Survey 2015: Results and analysis. The Times Higher Education, 5 February 2015. www.timeshighereducation.co.uk/features/best-university-workplace-survey-2015-results-and-analysis/2018272.article.

[7]Quoted in Gill, J. (2015). Measure still for measure? The Times Higher Education, 5 February 2015. www.timeshighereducation.co.uk/comment/leader/measure-still-for-measure/2018343.article

## 7.1 GAMES WITHOUT FRONTIERS?

"The use of indicators will inevitably have effects on the systems measured, signalling desired outcomes and producing behaviours, whether intended or otherwise, and making a difference to lives and careers."

Ismael Rafols, Sussex workshop[8]

No research assessment regime is completely benign; there will always be the potential for strategic behaviours and gaming.[9] Researchers are not passive recipients of research evaluation but play an active role in assessment contexts.[10] Therefore any system used to assess research, whether peer review or indicator-based, that affects money or reputation will tend to influence researchers' behaviour in two ways.[11]

The first is goal displacement: high scores in the measures become the goal rather than a means of measuring whether an objective (or performance level) has been attained.[12] The second is a change in the research process itself in response to assessment criteria, which may be more difficult to recognise, for instance through a shift towards more mainstream, less risky research topics.[13]

Goal displacement has been highlighted by studies that looked at the effects of funding and evaluation regimes on the production of scholarly publications. For instance, Butler analysed the introduction of quantitative performance indicators in Australian research funding allocation.[14] She shows that there is a sharp rise in ISI-ranked publications in all university fields (but not in other branches of research where this type of funding allocation is not present) when funding is linked to publications.[15] Since the

---

[8]Rafols' slides are available at **www.hefce.ac.uk/media/hefce/content/news/Events/2014/ Metrics,we,trust/Ismael%20Rafols%20Slides-%20In%20Metrics%20we%20Trust.pdf**

[9]cf. MacRoberts, M.H., and MacRoberts, B.R. (1989). Problems of citation analysis: A critical review. *Journal of the American Society for Information Science*, 40(5): 342–349.

[10]cf. Aksnes, D. W., and Rip, A. (2009). Researchers' perceptions of citations. *Research Policy*, 38(6): 895–905; Van Noorden, R. (2010). Metrics: A profusion of measures. *Nature*, 465(7300): 864–866.

[11]Butler, L. (2007). Assessing university research: a plea for a balanced approach. *Science and Public Policy*, 34(8): 565–574. DOI:10.3152/030234207X254404.

[12]Council of Canadian Academies (2012). *Informing Research Choices: Indicators and Judgment. Report of the Expert Panel on Science Performance and Research Funding.* Ottawa: CCA, p27.

[13]Butler, L. (2007). p572 (see Footnote 11 above).

[14]Butler, L. (2003). Explaining Australia's increased share of ISI publications – the effects of a funding formula based on publication counts. *Research Policy*, 32(1): 143–155; Butler, L. (2005). What happens when funding is linked to publication counts? in Moed, H., Glänzel, W., and Schmoch, U. (Eds.), *Handbook of Quantitative Science and Technology Research*. Dordrecht: Springer. p389–405.

[15]Butler, L. (2005). (see Footnote 14 above).

Australian evaluation system did not differentiate between publications (besides being peer-reviewed or not), the number of publications especially rose in journals that are easier to get published in. Earlier research by Butler shows that while the relative global share of Australian publications rose as a result of this strategy, their academic impact (measured in citations) declined during the same period.[16]

The Council of Canadian Academies study concludes that linking funding explicitly to research output (in terms of the number of publications) may lead researchers to produce a higher quantity of publications at the expense of quality.[17] Similar effects of the use of bibliometrics on the quantities of publications have been found in Spain,[18] Sweden,[19] Denmark[20] and Norway.[21]

UK publication patterns between 1985 and 2003 suggest that specific publication patterns emerged in the years before three RAEs in that period (1992, 1996, 2001), depending on whether the RAE limited the number of publications submitted per academic FTE. In the UK, accounts of "playing the RAE game"[22] in this way are numerous.[23] Another study of the RAE shows that the cumulative research productivity of individuals increased over time, but the effects differed across departments and individuals. Where researchers in higher-ranked programmes increased their output in higher-quality journals, researchers

---

[16]Butler, L. (2003). (see Footnote 14 on the previous page).

[17]Council of Canadian Academies (2012). p26. (see Footnote 12 above).

[18]Jiménez-Contreras, E., de Moya Anegón, F. and López-Cózar, E. D. (2003). The evolution of research activity in Spain: The impact of the National Commission for the Evaluation of Research Activity (CNEAI). *Research Policy*, 32(1): 123–142.

[19]Hammarfelt, B., and de Rijcke, S. (2015). Accountability in context: Effects of research evaluation systems on publication practices, disciplinary norms and individual working routines in the faculty of Arts at Uppsala University, *Research Evaluation*, 24: 63–77.

[20]Ingwersen, P. and Larsen, B. (2014). Influence of a performance indicator on Danish research production and citation impact 2000–12. *Scientometrics*, 101(12): 1325–1344.

[21]Ossenblok, T. L., Engels, T. C., and Sivertsen, G. (2012). The representation of the social sciences and humanities in the Web of Science—a comparison of publication patterns and incentive structures in Flanders and Norway (2005–2009). *Research Evaluation*, 21(4): 280–290.

[22]Harley, S. (2002). The impact of research selectivity on academic work and identity in UK universities. *Studies in Higher Education*, 27(2): 187–205.

[23]Hare, P. G. (2003). The United Kingdom's Research Assessment Exercise: impact on institutions, departments, individuals. *Higher Education Management and Policy*, 15: 43–62; Keenoy, T. (2005). Facing Inwards and Outwards at Once: The liminal temporalities of academic performativity. *Time & Society*, 14(2–3): 303–321; Alldred, P., and Miller, T. (2007). Measuring what's valued or valuing what's measured? Knowledge production and the Research Assessment Exercise, in Gillies, V., and Lucey, H. (eds.) *Power, Knowledge and the Academy: The Institutional Is Political*. Basingstoke: Palgrave. p147–167.; Sousa, S. B., and Brennan, J. L. (2014). The UK Research Excellence Framework and the Transformation of Research Production, in Musselin, C., and Teixeira, P. (eds.), *Reforming Higher Education*. Dordrecht: Springer. p65–80.

in lower-ranked departments aimed at increasing their publications in outlets considered as less prestigious.[24] A survey among journal editors conducted at the end of the 1990s also showed that the RAE influenced where authors published. Indeed, research shows that the status of a journal is crucial for academics' submission decisions.[25] The fear that the RAE would lead to salami-slicing of research outputs into "least publishable units"[26] was not confirmed.[27]

However, it isn't always entirely evident what distinguishes gaming from strategising.[28] Partly for this reason, the evidence base on gaming specific indicators remains fairly undeveloped.[29] It is of course possible, indeed common, for strategic research management to be genuinely constructive. For example, one outcome of REF2014 is likely to be, in many institutions, the introduction of new measures to improve the quality of the research environment by providing better research facilities, freeing up researchers' time, and supporting career development in a variety of ways.

## 7.2 BIASES AGAINST INTERDISCIPLINARITY

A related concern is the potential influence of research assessment on interdisciplinary research. An early survey of the impact of the 1996 RAE reported evidence of negative effects for interdisciplinary work. Nearly half of those in management positions felt the RAE "had hindered" interdisciplinarity.[30] These effects differ by discipline: for example,

---

[24]Moore, W. J., Newman, R. J., Sloane, P. J., and Steely, J. D. (2002). *Productivity Effects of Research Assessment Exercises*. University of Aberdeen, Department of Economics.

[25]Harley, D., Acord, S. K., Earl-Novell, S., Lawrence, S., and King, C. J. (2010). Assessing the future landscape of scholarly communication: An exploration of faculty values and needs in seven disciplines. Center for Studies in Higher Education. https://escholarship.org/uc/item/15x7385g Retrieved 29 November 2014.; Chew, M., Villanueva, E. V., and Van Der Weyden, M. B. (2007). Life and times of the impact factor: retrospective analysis of trends for seven medical journals (1994–2005) and their Editors' views. *Journal of the Royal Society of Medicine*, 100(3): 142–150.

[26]cf. Huth, E. J. (1986). Irresponsible authorship and wasteful publication. *Annals of Internal Medicine*, 104(2): 257–259.

[27]Georghiou, L., et al. (2000). Impact of the Research Assessment Exercise and the Future of Quality Assurance in the Light of Changes in the Research Landscape. Manchester: Policy Research in Engineering, Science and Technology. https://research.mbs.ac.uk/INNOVATION/Portals/0/docs/raec.pdf. Retrieved 29 November 2014.

[28]McRae, A. (2015). What's the difference between 'game-playing' and 'strategizing'? More on the REF. https://headofdepartmentblog.wordpress.com/2015/02/24/whats-the-difference-between-game-playing-and-strategizing-more-on-the-ref/

[29]Such matters were discussed at a conference, 'Weighed and measured: how metrics shape publication (mis)behaviour', http://publicationethics.org/cope-european-seminar-and-workshop-2015

[30]Mcnay, I. (1998). The Research Assessment Exercise (RAE) and after: "You never know how it will all turn out." *Perspectives: Policy and Practice in Higher Education*, 2(1): 19–22.

one survey of demographers showed no tendency to focus on monodisciplinary research in terms of reading or publishing activity.[31] In economics and business studies, however, publication strategies have been strongly stimulated by the ubiquitous use of journal rankings, such as the one produced annually by the Chartered Association of Business Schools.[32] These lists are not based on citations but on a qualitative consensus about the 'top' journals. A comparative analysis by Rafols et al. of the effect of these rankings in business and innovation studies found them to be biased against interdisciplinary work.[33] That study concludes that citation indicators may be more suitable than peer review for interdisciplinary work because criteria of excellence are too tightly based on narrow disciplinary standards.

Pontille and Torny analysed three journal lists in the humanities and social sciences, produced by the Australian Research Council (ARC), the European Science Foundation (ESF), and the French Agency for Evaluation Research and Higher Education (AERES).[34] They found that the production of journal ratings is a highly political task, and not merely a matter of inventory-making. The modalities that were selected produced very different effects in terms of which academic communities were involved, how boundaries were drawn around disciplines, and the ways in which revision processes adopted criticism from the fields involved.[35] The ARC decided to drop journal rankings from its assessment system when research managers began to set publication targets on the basis of the two top categories in its list.[36]

## 7.3 TASK REDUCTION

Another concern is that researchers respond to assessment criteria by focusing tasks and narrowing their types of publication. There has been some analysis of this issue in relation to the Australian ERA initiative.[37] In around half of the disciplines studied, the

---

[31]Van Dalen, H. P., and Henkens, K. (2012). Intended and unintended consequences of a publish-or-perish culture: A worldwide survey. *Journal of the American Society for Information Science and Technology*, 63(7): 1282–1293.

[32]http://charteredabs.org/academic-journal-guide-2015/. Retrieved 28 June 2015.

[33]Rafols, I., Leydesdorff, L., O'Hare, A., Nightingale, P., and Stirling, A. (2012). How journal rankings can suppress interdisciplinary research: A comparison between innovation studies and business & management. *Research Policy*, 41(7): 1262–1282.

[34]Pontille, D., and Torny, D. (2010). The controversial policies of journal ratings: Evaluating social sciences and humanities. *Research Evaluation*, 19(5): 347–360.

[35]See also Jensen, C. B. (2011). Making lists, enlisting scientists. *Science Studies*, 24(2): 64–84.

[36]Council of Canadian Academies (2012). *Informing Research Choices: Indicators and Judgment. Report of the Expert Panel on Science Performance and Research Funding*. Ottawa: CCA, p56.

[37]Laudel, G., and Gläser, J. (2006). Tensions between evaluations and communication practices. *Journal of Higher Education Policy and Management*, 28(3): 289–295.

four publication types used in ERA were not identical to the four publication types that researchers found most important. As one historian expressed it: "The way we are funded now by the government, by the faculty, by the university, we are severely discouraged from writing book reviews, we are severely discouraged from writing reference articles, encyclopedia articles. I mean, if somebody asked me to do that now, I always say no."[38] The study concludes that arts and humanities are more affected by prescriptive modes of assessment, as more journal-oriented disciplines serve as the archetype for evaluations.

Task reduction has also been reported in the social sciences. The survey of demographers (discussed in the previous section) reports that traditional scholarly tasks – such as writing referee reports or translating research outcomes for policymakers – are negatively affected by a drive for individual productivity.[39] A study of the RAE in 1996 similarly found that publication in professional journals was "actively discouraged" by some managers.[40] Hoecht argues that audit-based quality control has replaced trust-based form of control in UK academia, which may negatively affect innovative teaching and research practices.[41] Similarly, Willmott argues that audit mechanisms push academics towards mainstream topics that have the highest chance of being published in top-ranked journals.[42]

An exploratory study of UK university education departments shows that the use of performance indicators in evaluation is perceived as rewarding specific forms of academic involvement – research and publications – that sit in tension with more public roles, including applied research, writing professional publications, or teaching.[43]

## 7.4 EFFECTS ON INSTITUTIONS AND THEIR EMPLOYEES

The use of metrics in research assessment has also affected institutional arrangements, and the relationship between higher education and government.[44] For example, the

---

[38]Ibid. p294.

[39]Van Dalen, H. P. and Henkens, K. (2012). (see Footnote 31 on the previous page).

[40]Mcnay, I. (1998). p22. (see Footnote 30 on the previous page).

[41]Hoecht, A. (2006). Quality assurance in UK higher education: Issues of trust, control, professional autonomy and accountability. *Higher Education*, 51(4): 541–563.

[42]Willmott, H. (2011). Journal list fetishism and the perversion of scholarship: reactivity and the ABS list. *Organization*, 18(4): 429–442.

[43]Wilson, M., and Holligan, C. (2013). Performativity, work-related emotions and collective research identities in UK university education departments: an exploratory study. *Cambridge Journal of Education*, 43(2): 223–241.

[44]Martin, B., and Whitley, R. (2010). The UK Research Assessment Exercise: a case of regulatory capture, in Whitley, R., Gläser, J., and Engwall, L. (eds.), *Reconfiguring Knowledge Production: Changing Authority Relationships in the Sciences and their Consequences for Intellectual Innovation*. Oxford: Oxford University Press. p51–80.

REF, like the RAE before it, encourages more of a 'transfer market' for academic faculty in the UK. Some see this outcome as 'unintentional', others as desirable, in that it has increased the mobility of researchers between institutions in positive ways.[45] Some universities have focused on hiring early-career staff with research potential, while others have taken a more conservative approach and focused on "well-established researchers."[46]

In Australia, there is evidence that universities responded to formula-based funding by more or less mirroring this practice at an institutional level.[47] Wouters hypothesises that such mirroring may be a more general phenomenon, related to the way universities tend to transfer responsibility upwards and downwards.[48] Such strategic behaviour may have long-lasting effects on research agendas.

The demands of formal evaluation according to broadly standardised criteria are likely to focus the attention system of organisations on satisfying them, and give rise to local lock-in mechanisms.[49] But the extent to which mechanisms like evaluation actually control and steer loosely coupled systems of academic knowledge is still poorly understood.[50]

Evidence of the performativity of quantitative data – their capacity to influence the activities they are supposed merely to indicate – suggests that the availability of metrics creates a demand for such information.[51] Such information-generating functions carry authority

---

[45]Council of Canadian Academies (2012) *Informing Research Choices: Indicators and Judgment. Report of the Expert Panel on Science Performance and Research Funding*. Ottawa: CCA.; See also Elton, L. (2000). The UK research assessment exercise: unintended consequences. *Higher Education Quarterly*, 54(3): 274–283.

[46]Ibid. p27–28.

[47]Gläser, J., Laudel, G., Hinze, S. and Butler, L. (2002). *Impact of Evaluation-Based Funding on the Production of Scientific Knowledge: What to Worry About, and How to Find Out*. Report for the German Ministry for Education and Research. www.laudel.info/wp-content/uploads/2013/pdf/research%20papers/02expertiseglaelauhinbut.pdf. Retrieved 29 November 2014. p17.

[48]Wouters, P. (2014). The Citation: From Culture to Infrastructure, in Cronin, B., and Sugimoto, C.R. (eds.), *Beyond Bibliometrics: Harnessing Multidimensional Indicators of Scholarly Impact*. Cambridge MA: MIT press. p47–66.

[49]cf. Van der Meulen, B. (2007). Interfering Governance and Emerging Centres of Control: University research evaluation in the Netherlands, in Whitley, R. and Gläser, J. (eds.), *The Changing Governance of the Sciences*. Dordrecht: Springer. p191–203.

[50]Gläser, J. (2013). *How does Governance Change Research Content? On the Possibility of a Sociological Middle-Range Theory Linking Science Policy Studies to the Sociology of Scientific Knowledge*. Berlin: The Technical University Technology Studies Working Papers.

[51]Porter, T. (1995). *Trust in Numbers: The Pursuit of Objectivity in Science and Public Life*. Princeton, NY: Princeton University Press.

even if their limitations are known.[52] Organisations cannot resist the temptation to collect such information because it is considered strategically useful in managing and improving organisational performance. The fact that competitors collect similar information for strategic purposes makes the prospect of opting out or ignoring such information perilous.[53] This tendency explains in part the lure of university league tables, JIFs and, indeed, strategic approaches to the REF. The legitimacy of such indicators does not rest exclusively on their first-order accuracy, but also on the fact that they are assumed to carry authority within the institutional environments with which organisations strategically engage.

Conversely, empirical work on university rankings shows how, in complex academic settings, performance metrics are not tightly coupled with actions across the entire organisation.[54] Broader changes in the character of universities as independent and critical institutions,[55] as well as increased levels of stress and anxiety among academics, are also reported in interview-based analyses.[56] Burrows argues that performance-based control mechanisms are increasingly used outside their original context of evaluation, contributing to feelings of powerlessness among academics, and leading to an inappropriate emphasis on individual measures such as the h-index.[57] The use of metrics in decision-making contexts cannot be explained simply as explicit responses to top-down commands.

---

[52]Dahler-Larsen, P. (2012). *The Evaluation Society.* Stanford, CA: Stanford Business Books.

[53]See also Espeland, W. N., and Sauder, M. (2007). Rankings and Reactivity: How Public Measures Recreate Social Worlds. *American Journal of Sociology*, 113(1): 1–40.

[54]cf. De Rijcke, S., Wallenburg, I., Bal, R. and Wouters, P. (forthcoming). Comparing Comparisons. On Rankings and Accounting in Hospitals and Universities, in Guggenheim, M., Deville, J., and Hrdlickova, Z. (eds.) *Practising Comparison: Logics, Relations, Collaborations.* Manchester: Mattering Press.

[55]Shore, C. (2008). Audit culture and illiberal governance: Universities and the politics of accountability. *Anthropological Theory*, 8(3): 278–298; Shore, C. (2010). Beyond the multiversity: neoliberalism and the rise of the schizophrenic university. *Social Anthropology*, 18(1): 15–29; Craig, R., Amernic, J., and Tourish, D. (2014). Perverse audit culture and accountability of the modern public university. *Financial Accountability & Management*, 30(1): 1–24.

[56]Chandler, J., Barry, J. and Clark, H. (2002). Stressing academe: The wear and tear of the new public management. *Human Relations*, 55(9): 1051–1069; Gill, R. (2009). Breaking the silence: The hidden injuries of neo-liberal academia, in R. Gill (Eds.) *Secrecy and Silence in the Research Process: Feminist Reflections.* London: Routledge, p228–244; Sá, C. M., Kretz, A., and Sigurdson, K. (2013). Accountability, performance assessment, and evaluation: Policy pressures and responses from research councils. *Research Evaluation*, 22(2): 105–117. University and College Union (2014) *UCU Survey of Workplace Stress* www.ucu.org.uk/media/pdf/t/a/ucu_stress survey14_summary.pdf. Retrieved 28 June 2015.

[57]Burrows, R. (2012). Living with the h-index? Metric assemblages in the contemporary academy. *The Sociological Review*, 60(2): 355–372.

To some extent, metrics seem to transform more fundamentally 'what can be talked about' and how valuations are made.[58]

## 7.5 EFFECTS ON KNOWLEDGE PRODUCTION

Emerging evidence suggests that performance-informed research assessment does indeed increase the pressure on researchers and institutions to meet performance criteria, irrespective of whether these are based on peer review or metrics. In part, these effects are intended: performance indicators became more prominent in the governance of research explicitly to change production dynamics and to align them with policy priorities.[59] That the research community and other stakeholders respond strategically may in turn have unintended effects: either through the mechanism of goal displacement or through more structural changes in research priorities, publication activities, research capacity and organisation.

Yet the evidence remains fragmented and sometimes contradictory. Systems that link performance to funding have been studied in greatest detail, but whether a direct link is necessary for unintended effects to occur is debatable. More influential than the amount of funding linked to performance differences is the effect that it has on researcher reputations.[60] Systems where performance is publicly reported, but not directly linked to funding, may lead to comparable or identical effects.

As Butler notes, the conservatism of metrics users is a long-standing problem, creating a preference for established or user-friendly measurements over more sophisticated or diverse metrics. Researchers in the scientometric field are also increasingly concerned about the unintended effects that some metrics are having in an era of expanding academic audit.[61] For instance, in 2012, one of the leading journals – *Scientometrics* – produced

---

[58]cf. Espeland, W. N., and Stevens, M. L. (1998). Commensuration as a social process. *Annual Review of Sociology*, 24: 313–343; Lamont, M. (2012). Toward a Comparative Sociology of Valuation and Evaluation. *Annual Review of Sociology*, 38: 201–221.

[59]Whitley, R., and Gläser, J. (eds.) (2007). 'The changing governance of the sciences. The advert of research evaluation systems.' *Sociology of the Sciences Yearbook*. Springer: Dordrecht.

[60]Hicks, D. (2012). Performance-based university research funding systems. *Research Policy*, 41(2): 251–261.

[61]Van Dalen, H. P., and Henkens, K. (2012) (see Footnote 31 on p.89). Garfield, E. (1996) How can impact factors be improved? *BMJ*. 313(7054): 411–3; Garfield, E. (2006). The history and meaning of the journal impact factor. *JAMA*, 295(1): 90–93; Weingart, P. (2005). Impact of bibliometrics upon the science system: Inadvertent consequences? *Scientometrics*, 62(1): 117–131. Hicks, D., Wouters, P., Waltman, L., de Rijcke, S., and Rafols, I. (2015). Bibliometrics: The Leiden Manifesto for research metrics. *Nature*, 520: 429–431.

a special issue concentrating on the uses and misuses of JIFs.[62] Arguments against JIFs often cite their technical shortcomings,[63] and susceptibility to "manipulation by journal editors and misuse by uncritical parties".[64]

Emerging empirical evidence paints a more complex picture of how certain metrics, including JIFs, become reified in research management, as both formal and informal standards against which to assess the value and usefulness of research.[65] Firstly, such metrics are used to reinforce deep-seated, firmly established mechanisms to build reputation and to hire, select and promote staff (including publishing in high-JIF journals). Secondly, the responsibility for applying certain bibliometric indicators is spread across many stakeholders in the current "citation infrastructure"[66] – including scientometricians, publishers, librarians, policymakers, evaluators, research managers, consultancies, researchers, and other users.[67] As a result, reforming systems of research assessment is a distributed and complex task.[68]

---

[62]Braun, T. (2012). Editorial. *Scientometrics*, 92(2): 207–208.

[63]cf. Moed, H. F., and Van Leeuwen, T. N. (1996). Impact factors can mislead. *Nature*, 381: 186; Buela-Casal, G., and Zych, I. (2012). What do the scientists think about the impact factor? *Scientometrics*, 92(2): 281–292.; Seglen, P. O. (1992). The skewness of science. *Journal of the American Society for Information Science*, 43(9): 628–638.l; Seglen, P. O. (1994). Causal relationship between article citedness and journal impact. *Journal of the American Society for Information Science*, 45(1): 1–11; Seglen, P. O. (1997). Why the impact factor of journals should not be used for evaluating research. *British Medical Journal*, 314(7079): 498–502.; Simons, K. (2008). The misused impact factor. *Science*, 322(5899): 165.

[64]Archambault, É., and Larivière, V. (2009). History of the journal impact factor: Contingencies and consequences. *Scientometrics*, 79(3): 635–649.

[65]Aksnes, D. W., and Rip, A. (2009). Researchers' perceptions of citations. *Research Policy*, 38(6): 895–905.; Buela-Casal, G., and Zych, I. (2012). How to measure the internationality of scientific publications. *Psicothema* 24(3): 435–441. Derrick, G., and Gillespie, J. (2013) "A number you just can't get away from": Characteristics of Adoption and the Social Construction of Metric Use by Researchers. STI 18th International Conference on Science and Technology Indicators. Berlin; Sá, C. M., Kretz, A., and Sigurdson, K. (2013); Stephan, P.E. (2012). *How Economics Shapes Science*. Cambridge, MA: Harvard University Press.

[66]Wouters, P. (2014). (see Footnote 48 on p.91).

[67]De Rijcke, S. and Rushforth, A.D. (2015). To intervene, or not to intervene, is that the question? On the role of scientometrics in research evaluation. *Journal of the Association for Information Science and Technology*, Article first published online: 13 May 2015, DOI: 10.1002/asi.23382.

[68]cf. Boltanski, L., and Thévenot, L. (2006). *On Justification: Economies of Worth*. Princeton, NJ: Princeton University Press; Linkova, M. (2014). Unable to resist: Researchers' responses to research assessment in the Czech Republic. *Human Affairs*, 24(1): 78–88; Stöckelová, T. (2014). Power at the interfaces: The contested orderings of academic presents and Futures in a social science department. *Higher Education Policy*, 27(4): 435–451.

An exploratory study in Dutch biomedicine[69] details the multiple ways that performance metrics affect knowledge-production processes.[70] The authors found that academic prestige was tightly coupled with citation counts and indicators like JIFs and the h-index, in targeting specific publication outlets, referencing 'hot' papers, and negotiation of authorship priority. Quantitative indicators were also observed to feed into quite routine knowledge-producing activities, for example, discussions over whom to collaborate with and how much additional time to spend in the laboratory producing data. JIFs in particular functioned on occasions as screening devices for selecting useful information from the overwhelming amounts of literature researchers could potentially read.

Generally speaking, the function of bibliometrics in 'reducing complexity' is frequently cited as a reason for their ongoing appeal among research policymakers and managers.[71] In evaluation contexts, ranking tools like the JIF help to render the prestige from publishing in one journal comparable with another.[72] Many researchers are willing to wait longer on editorial decisions when the JIF is higher, which shows the clogging effects JIFs can have on scholarly communication.[73]

Empirical research does however reveal a discrepancy between the importance of indicators in evaluation practices and researchers' own judgement of their accuracy.[74] According to Hargens and Schuman,[75] researchers often have an ambivalent attitude with respect to citation indicators. Citations are sought-after because they are part of the reward system and can be drawn upon in competitive struggles, while at the same time they are criticised for not reflecting the actual contribution to research.[76] Such 'folk

[69]Rushforth, A. and De Rijcke, S. (2015). Accounting for impact? The journal impact factor and the making of biomedical research in the Netherlands. *Minerva*, 53: 117–139.

[70]Colyvas, J. A. (2012). Performance metrics as formal structures and through the lens of social mechanisms: When do they work and how do they influence? *American Journal of Education*, 118(2): 167–197.

[71]Cronin, B. and Sugimoto, C. R. (eds.). (2014). *Beyond Bibliometrics: Harnessing Multidimensional Indicators of Scholarly Impact*. Cambridge, MA: MIT Press; Woelert, P. (2013). The 'Economy of Memory': Publications, citations, and the paradox of effective research governance. *Minerva*, 51(3): 341–362.

[72]Espeland, W. N., and Stevens, M. L. (1998).

[73]Rousseau, S., and Rousseau, R. (2012). Interactions between journal attributes and authors' willingness to wait for editorial decisions. *Journal of the American Society for Information Science and Technology*, 63(6): 1213–1225.

[74]Buela-Casal, G. and Zych, I. (2012). How to measure the internationality of scientific publications. *Psicothema* 24(3): 435–441.

[75]Hargens, L. L., and Schuman, H. (1990). Citation counts and social comparisons: Scientists' use and evaluation of citation index data. *Social Science Research*, 19(3): 205–221.

[76]Aksnes, D. W. and Rip, A. (2009). Researchers' perceptions of citations. *Research Policy*, 38(6): 895–905.

citation theories' do not have to be consistent in order to be mobilised by researchers as explanatory devices in their competition for reputation. However, the sophistication and complexity of researchers' interpretations of citation should not be underestimated.[77]

## 7.6 EQUALITY AND DIVERSITY CONCERNS

In considering how metrics can affect research cultures, one important concern is that women, early-career researchers and other groups with protected characteristics (as defined in the Equality Act 2010[78]), might be negatively affected by an emphasis on particular indicators. Twenty-four of the responses to our call for evidence highlighted concerns in this area. Respondents also noted that any system of assessment based on total citation numbers (such as an h-index) was likely to favour more established researchers, as they would have had more time to produce articles and other outputs. A handful of responses pointed out that the predominance of English-language publications in most academic fields meant that those publishing in non-English outlets would be disadvantaged in terms of citations.

A recent study by the Nuffield Council on Bioethics on the culture of scientific research has underlined some of these concerns.[79] To explore these issues in greater depth, the review made equality and diversity the focus of a one-day workshop on 'Metrics for All?' at the University of Sheffield in December 2014.[80] This drew contributions from 45 people, from across the academic community, learned societies, research offices, sector bodies, equality and diversity officers and data providers.

Points made at the Sheffield workshop included:

- The need to humanise the metrics debate, and consider the likely effects of different indicators and assessment structures on the diverse groups of people involved;
- Metrics used to assess and measure higher education should examine a range of levels and scales, whether institutions, departments or individuals;
- Context is paramount – methodologies and ethical considerations should be adapted to suit the scale of enquiry;
- Attention should be paid to implicit biases, and further research on such biases and their effects needs to be done;
- Due consideration should be paid to the possible unintended consequences of research assessment regimes, in terms of the potential to change behaviours across different academic populations and scales of enquiry;

---

[77]Ibid. p904.

[78]https://www.gov.uk/equality-act-2010-guidance. Retrieved 28 June 2015.

[79]Nuffield Council on Bioethics. (2014). *The culture of scientific research in the UK.* http://nuffieldbioethics.org/wp-content/uploads/Nuffield_research_culture_full_report_web.pdf

[80]www.hefce.ac.uk/news/Events/Name,101078,en.html. Retrieved 28 June 2015.

- Particularly for early-career researchers, metrics can shape the character of academic practice.

With regard to gender bias, there is a growing volume of evidence to underpin these concerns.[81] As a recent *Nature* paper by Sugimoto and colleagues observes, problems of gender inequality are still widespread across the research community, whether in respect to hiring, earning, funding, satisfaction or patenting.[82] There has been considerable discussion of the 'productivity puzzle', whereby men publish more papers on average than women, but debate continues as to whether this is caused by gender bias, childbearing and caring responsibilities, other variables – or a combination of these.[83]

Sugimoto et al. present a global and cross-disciplinary bibliometric analysis of the relationship between gender and research output across 5,483,841 research papers and articles with 27,329,915 authorships. They find that "in the most productive countries, all articles with women in dominant author positions receive fewer citations than those with men in the same positions. And this citation disadvantage is accentuated by the fact that women's publication portfolios are more domestic than their male colleagues – they profit less from the extra citations that international collaborations accrue. Given that citations now play a central part in the evaluation of researchers, this situation can only worsen gender disparities."[84]

Others studies suggest women are less likely to engage in self-citation. One recent study by Bergstrom et al. analysed 1.6 million papers with 40 million citations, of which one million were from scholars referring to their own work. They found that men were 56% more likely to cite their own work. In some male-heavy fields, the gender gap was even more pronounced, for example mathematics, where men were 84% more likely than women to self-cite.[85]

A widely discussed paper by Moss-Racusin et al. suggests that subtle gender biases may play a significant role. Based on a nationwide sample of 127 biology, chemistry

---

[81]Savonick, D and Davidson, C. N. (2015) *Gender Bias in Academe: An Annotated Bibliography of Important Recent Studies*. HASTAC Futures Initiative. www.hastac.org/blogs/superadmin/2015/01/26/gender-bias-academe-annotated-bibliography-important-recent-studies. Retrieved 28 June 2015.

[82]Sugimoto, C. et al. (2013). 'Global gender disparities in science'. *Nature*, 504: 211–213. www.nature.com/news/bibliometrics-global-gender-disparities-in-science-1.14321. Retrieved 28 June 2015.

[83]Leahey, E. (2007). Not by productivity alone: How visibility and specialization contribute to academic earnings. *American Sociological Review*, 72. See also: https://www.timeshighereducation.co.uk/news/sexist-peer-review-causes-storm-online/2020001.article

[84]Sugimoto, C. et al. (2013). 'Global gender disparities in science'. *Nature*, 504: 211–213. www.nature.com/news/bibliometrics-global-gender-disparities-in-science-1.14321. Retrieved 28 June 2015.

[85]www.the-scientist.com/?articles.view/articleNo/39450/title/Self-Citation-Gender-Gap/

and physics professors, who were asked to evaluate the application materials of an undergraduate science student, the study found that "both male and female faculty judged a female student to be less competent and less worthy of being hired than an identical male student, and also offered her a smaller starting salary and less career mentoring."[86]

Early career researchers can feel particular pressure to perform well against certain indicators. The Nuffield Council on Bioethics noted in its study of research culture that, "Throughout… we heard repeatedly that publishing in high impact factor journals is still thought to be the most important element in determining whether researchers gain funding, jobs and promotions, along with article-level metrics such as citation numbers."[87] Another recent study of almost 200 early career researchers in the UK found that a focus on "REFable publications" had created "a huge amount of pressure and anxiety, which impacts particularly on those at the bottom rung of the career ladder" and contributed to a "two-tier hierarchy" between teaching and research staff.[88]

Linked to this is the extent to which typical academic career trajectories vary between disciplines. For instance, in many arts and humanities subjects, academics are often employed on teaching-only contracts prior to achieving tenure; the recent AHRC/BA Oakleigh Report on research careers in the arts and humanities provides some useful insights on this point.[89]

There is also considerable variation between disciplines in terms of the relationship between expected achievement and academic age. It is also important to consider which academics are more likely to get involved with inter- or multidisciplinary projects, and what their associated outputs might look like. We need to consider the sort of indicators or metrics that could be used to assist rather than obstruct interdisciplinary working, and the kinds of equality and diversity issues that might be faced. Some areas of research seldom make it into the top journals and this could have knock-on effects for equality and diversity that also need to be borne in mind.

It is also worth emphasising that in some contexts, metrics can be used to support greater equality and diversity. For example, McMaster University recently used a quantitative analysis of its pay structures to discover the extent of gender inequality, leading to a decision

---

[86]Moss-Racusin, C. A., Dovidio, J. F., Brescoli, V. L., Graham, M. J. and Handelsman, J. (2012). 'Science faculty's subtle gender biases favor male students'. *PNAS*, 109(41): 16474–16479. www.pnas.org/content/109/41/16474.full.pdf. Retrieved 28 June 2015.

[87]Nuffield Council on Bioethics. (2014). The Culture of Scientific Research in the UK. London: Nuffield Council on Bioethics, p25.

[88]https://www.timeshighereducation.co.uk/news/ref-is-a-misery-for-early-career-researchers-survey-finds/2019941.article; https://charlottemathieson.wordpress.com/2015/04/24/a-culture-of-publish-or-perish-the-impact-of-the-ref-on-ecrs/. Retrieved 28 June 2015.

[89]Details of this project can be accessed at: www.ahrc.ac.uk/What-We-Do/Research-careers-and-training/Pages/Oakleigh-Report.aspx. Retrieved 1 March 2015.

to increase the annual salary of all its female academics by C$3,500 (£1,900).[90] Academic Analytics presented examples at our Sheffield workshop of how metrics-based analysis could be used by university managers to identify promising early-career researchers, whose potential might otherwise be missed, and use this for targeted career development.

In respect of equality and diversity concerns, several ways forward were suggested by participants at our Sheffield workshop:

- **'Baskets' of indicators:** If metrics are used, 'baskets' of indicators should be developed. These should include qualitative and quantitative measures, crafted to suit the contexts under scrutiny. In choosing a 'diversity of metrics', biases should be explored and particular care taken to avoid selections that are biased in similar directions;
- **Embedding equality, diversity and inclusivity:** Within HEIs, equality and diversity considerations are often linked more closely to HR rather than research; equality and diversity should be better embedded within research (integrity), processes and policy, which academics are more likely to understand and embrace with ease;
- **Early-career researchers:** Greater efforts could be made to develop metrics that might more readily identify the contributions of early-career researchers, whether assessing the value, quality and significance of work they've undertaken to date, or to better indicate future potential success;
- **Weighting by age:** Some asked whether metrics could be weighted by academic age to mitigate for potential effects and biases (for example, for research income accrued);
- **Involving the sector:** Any decisions about the potential use of metrics should be made with the involvement of representatives from the sector and with a keen eye on equality and diversity concerns;
- **Guidance:** Lessons can be learnt from REF2014, where clear equality and diversity guidance benefited (early-career) researchers and those with complex circumstances;
- **Training:** Training should be provided to assessors and researchers, adapted appropriately to fit career level. This would help everyone to gain an understanding of the equality and diversity implications involved. There is evidently a place for organisations such as the Equality Challenge Unit and Vitae to assist with this, but across the higher education sector, leadership and support at the highest levels is crucial for these matters to be taken seriously.

Related points are made by the Australian biologist Jenny Martin in two recent blogposts on metrics and research culture.[91] Martin argues that the academic community needs to identify and adopt alternative metrics to support equality, diversity and improved work-life balance.

---

[90]Discussed in www.timeshighereducation.co.uk/comment/opinion/why-mcmaster-university-gave-its-female-academics-a-pay-rise/2020176.article. Retrieved 1 May 2015.

[91]https://cubistcrystal.wordpress.com/2015/01/12/imagine-theres-new-metrics-its-easy-if-you-try/; https://cubistcrystal.wordpress.com/2015/06/06/merit-and-demerit/. Retrieved 28 June 2015.

## 7.7 CULTURES OF RESPONSIBILITY

The various relationships between metrics, institutional strategy setting and the management of research – and the resultant effects on academic culture and practice – are complex, but a few distinct themes have emerged. Quantitative indicators clearly have a place in institutional performance management and can in some cases lead to significant positive outcomes for institutions and their staff. However, assessing performance is a very difficult and complex task, and so even where the means of quantitative assessment are fallible, people tend to gravitate towards them, with variable consequences for institutional strategy and for individuals. In this way, metrics can become unhelpfully institutionalised. Administrators and employers should therefore give due attention to the need to use them sensitively, transparently, and with the full input and co-operation of their staff. Wherever possible, damaging effects of quantitative indicators should be identified and addressed before use.

In considering how the use of quantitative indicators affects research behaviour, a number of distinct patterns and trends emerge around interdisciplinarity, task reduction and the effects of metrics on knowledge production more broadly. Policymakers and institutional managers would benefit from more input from the scientometrics community to suggest how quantitative indicators can influence the culture and practice of research in positive ways.

To that end, it is incumbent on research policymakers, the wider academic community, institutions, funders and government to promote decent and fair standards of behaviour in the use of metrics. DORA offers one set of guidelines for reducing damaging uses of JIFs in assessing individuals' research. We set out our own framework for 'responsible metrics' in Chapter 10.

# EIGHT

## SCIENCES IN TRANSITION

### CHAPTER CONTENTS

"Not everything that can be counted counts, and not everything that counts can be counted."

William Bruce Cameron[1]

The two previous chapters have explored the changing roles of data, indicators and performance measures in the culture and management of HEIs. Here we want to look at how other significant players in the research system are responding to these changes, and experimenting in various ways with new uses of quantitative indicators. This chapter looks first at developments within the UK Research Councils, then at research charities such as the Wellcome Trust, and the national academies. It then turns to

-------------------

[1]Cameron, W. (1963). *Informal Sociology: A Casual Introduction to Sociological Thinking.* Random House.

developments at the European level, as reflected in the European Commission's recent Science 2.0 White Paper. Finally, it considers how government could make greater use of quantitative data sources to inform horizon scanning and policies for research and innovation.

This is by no means an exhaustive survey of what all research funders are doing in this arena. But it does provide a variety of lenses through which to view developments in the UK system, and to highlight efforts to improve indicators, data infrastructure and interoperability.

## 8.1 THE RESEARCH FUNDING ECOSYSTEM

UK research benefits from a variety of funding sources. The Office for National Statistics estimates that in 2013, £28.9 billion was spent on research and development in the UK, as displayed in Figure 3 below.

UK universities benefitted from £7.6 billion of external funding for research (26% of GERD) in 2013, including; £2.1 billion from the Research Councils, £2.3 billion from the Funding Councils, £1 billion from UK charities, £1.2 billion from overseas sources and £300 million from business. What is often referred to as the 'dual support' system for University research describes the twin routes of: i) institutional block grants from the Funding Councils based on periodic quality assessment exercises; and ii) funding won

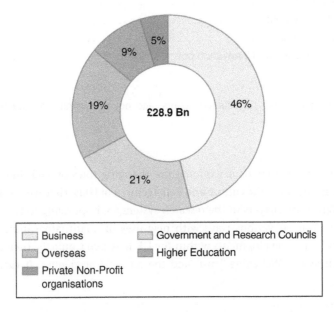

Figure 3   Composition of UK Gross Expenditure on R&D (GERD) by funding sector, 2013[2]

---

[2]ONS data available at: www.ons.gov.uk/ons/dcp171778_398876.pdf. Retrieved 1 June 2015.

in peer-reviewed competition from the Research Councils. Elements of the dual support system are outlined below.[3]

---

## THE DUAL SUPPORT SYSTEM

**HEFCE quality-related research funding (QR) (~£1.6 billion in England 2014–15) enables:**

- Stability and long-term planning
- Capacity building
- Freedom and flexibility for universities

*Rewards retrospectively*

**Research Council funding (~£2.6 billion in the UK 2014-15) enables:**

- Targeted, strategic funding
- Investigator-led initiatives
- Maintenance of excellence and value for money through short-term competition

*Rewards prospectively*

---

## 8.2 RESEARCH COUNCILS[4]

Each year, the seven UK Research Councils[5] invest around £3 billion in research covering the full spectrum of academic disciplines from the medical and biological sciences to astronomy, physics, chemistry and engineering, social sciences, economics, environmental sciences and the arts and humanities. The Research Councils' shared ambition, under the banner of 'Research Councils UK' (RCUK), is to ensure that the UK remains the best place in the world to do research, innovate and grow business. Research Council funding is allocated via individual grants for specific projects, programmes and infrastructure, via the Research Councils' own units, institutes and centres, and to national research facilities such as the UK synchrotron, Diamond Light Source.

---

[3]Taken from 'Impact and the importance of the dual support system' a presentation by Philip Nelson (EPSRC), given at the HEFCE 'REFlections 25 March 2015' event, and redrawn. Available at www.hefce.ac.uk/news/Events/Name,101448,en.html

[4]Particular thanks to Dr Ian Viney, MRC Director of Strategic Evaluation and Impact (and steering group member) for his contributions to this section. RCUK also contributed to the Review's Call for Evidence.

[5]Research Councils UK (RCUK) is the strategic partnership of all seven UK Research Councils, details about the work of RCUK and the Research Councils can be found at www.rcuk.ac.uk

The Research Councils report that they are committed to strengthening the evidence base for the assessment of research. RCUK works with other organisations to better understand the relationship between research and the subsequent impact of that research, and to improve the quantitative and qualitative description of research progress, productivity and quality. The Research Councils' stated policy on metrics is:

- Metrics will always require expert review to ensure appropriate interpretation and moderation, so metrics-based approaches should be developed within the broader context of peer or expert review, and not as a substitute for it;
- Ideally metrics should challenge assumptions made in peer review and stimulate informed debate about research quality and impact.

In this section, we outline RCUK's approaches to the application of metrics in research assessment, before summarising approaches towards the collection of information on impacts.

### 8.2.1 Application of metrics in research assessment

RCUK highlighted in its submission to the review[6] that, as with any metrics, those based on publication and citation data (bibliometrics) are limited in the breadth of their applicability. Research Councils recognise the well-documented concerns about the use of bibliometrics as the basis for a standardised approach to research assessment across all research disciplines; for instance, such issues have been explored in detail by the ESRC and AHRC.[7]

ESRC has refrained from the extensive use of metrics in research assessment[8], but also acknowledges that recent advancement in metrics, particularly in certain disciplines, may have begun to provide ways to adjust for and/or overcome these issues. AHRC recognise that there are currently no reliable or commonly accepted metric indicators available for the majority of research outputs from the arts and humanities.[9]

The Research Councils work in partnership with leading experts (such as CWTS[10], Science-Metrix[11], and Evidence Ltd.[12]) to ensure that the bibliometrics they use for

---

[6]www.rcuk.ac.uk/RCUK-prod/assets/documents/submissions/HEFCEMETRICSFINAL RCUK.pdf

[7]www.esrc.ac.uk/research/evaluation-impact/research-evaluation/bibliometrics.aspx. Retrieved 1 June 2015.

[8]www.esrc.ac.uk/research/evaluation-impact/. Retrieved 1 June 2015.

[9]Montgomery, L. (2013). Metrics challenges for monographs. www.knowledgeunlatched.org/2013/04/metrics-challenges-for-monographs/. Retrieved 1 June 2015.

[10]Centre for Science and Technology Studies (CWTS), Netherlands www.cwts.nl/Home

[11]http://science-metrix.com

[12]Now part of Thomson Reuters Ltd. http://researchanalytics.thomsonreuters.com/

evaluation of the outcomes of funding awards, primarily in the science, technology, engineering and medicine disciplines, are robust and appropriate.[13] Care is taken to ensure that bibliometric data is normalised by academic field, and year, as far as is currently possible. The source of the data, and known limitations of the normalisation and coverage are made clear in analysis. Inconsistent metrics or over-simplifications such as JIFs or h-indexes are avoided. RCUK noted that the science of this kind of analysis is still (60 years from its inception) an emerging field, and unfortunately, is a field in which the UK has limited established research capacity.

As noted above, RCUK also exercise care when considering the use of new metrics (such as download statistics, analysis of social media) to avoid inconsistencies, biases, over-simplification, lack of normalisation, and other statistical pitfalls.[14] RCUK recognise that while the data from social media provides attractive statistics, there is a lot of work to do in order to understand what contribution this is making to accelerating translation or realising/widening impact. The extent of participation by the academic community in these conversations, the accuracy of the data, how to distinguish between positive and negative attention etc, are all documented challenges to using social media as an alternative indicator of research impact.

Similarly, RCUK recognise that developments in information management technologies such as text mining, network and cluster analysis and visualisation software, coupled with the significant increase in the availability of digitalised data, offer opportunities for exploring and developing new metrics. However, until any new metrics are better understood they advocate that these should be used with care. They also state that increasing the availability of full-text, openly accessible publications, and encouraging other research outputs to also be openly accessible will clearly increase the opportunity to link information about funding inputs and identified researchers as contributors to particular research outcomes.[15]

RCUK highlight the importance of recognising that research assessment is used for different purposes and at different levels – it is important to be clear on the context when considering the role of metrics. For example, the Research Councils use *ex ante* research assessment to allocate funding at the level of individual projects: where the primary consideration is the quality of the proposed research. Research Councils argue that there is no substitute for expert peer review for this assessment. Metrics as a proxy for peer review assessment based on quality judgements are not used by Research Councils to allocate funding. However, metrics may be used as part of the information on the previous track

---

[13]EPSRC 2009 citations study https://www.epsrc.ac.uk/newsevents/pubs/epsrc-citations-study-2009/, Baseline bibliometric analyses of NERC funded research 2003–2010 www.nerc.ac.uk/about/perform/evaluation/evaluationreports/citations-study-2012/. Bibliometric study of India's research output and international collaboration www.rcuk.ac.uk/international/offices/india/landscape/bibliometric/

[14]See for example the NISO White Paper on Alternative metrics which has launched a consultation on standards for 'alternative metrics' www.niso.org/apps/group_public/download.php/13295/niso_altmetrics_white_paper_draft_v4.pdf. Retrieved 1 June 2015.

[15]www.rcuk.ac.uk/research/openaccess/

record of applicants, as an input to peer review. For example, Research Councils will be exploring the use of previously gathered output information to inform the assessment of future research applications.

The Research Councils also undertake *ex post* assessment of research programmes and/ or groups of research projects according to the high-level principles set out in the Treasury 'Green'[16] and 'Magenta'[17] books. Often metrics are used within this context as an input to the evaluation. For example, the 2012 Impact Review of the RCUK Digital Economy Programme provides a useful framework of evidence-based metrics.[18] Research Councils also use metrics (e.g. bibliometrics such as citation impact analyses) to benchmark the research they have funded, against other research nationally and internationally.

NERC last year evaluated the research excellence and impact of five of its Research Centres using slightly modified REF methodology.[19] The resulting REF-style excellence and impact profiles will be one of the sources of evidence used by NERC when making strategic decisions.

The Research Councils use a range of metrics within performance monitoring and reporting, which include aspects of research assessment. For example, Research Councils use input and output information to report on progress against their delivery plans and strategic plans, and on a regular basis for reporting to BIS.[20] The type of information used includes: the volume of publications, numbers of postgraduates supported, the extent of collaboration with industry, funding leveraged and further funding attracted, patents, licenses, creative outputs and spinouts as well as large numbers of useful case studies.[21]

The MRC is beginning to use bibliometric and other metrics drawn from the Researchfish system to complement its annual assurance processes for its units, university units and institutes. Evidenced outputs and outcomes are used to summarise

---

[16]HMT (2011). *Appraisal and Evaluation in Central Government 'The Green Book'* https://www.gov.uk/government/uploads/system/uploads/attachment_data/file/220541/green_book_complete.pdf. Retrieved 1 June 2015.

[17]HMT (2011). *Guidance for evaluation 'The Magenta Book'.* https://www.gov.uk/government/uploads/system/uploads/attachment_data/file/220542/magenta_book_combined.pdf. Retrieved 1 June 2015.

[18]www.rcuk.ac.uk/RCUK-prod/assets/documents/documents/RCUKDEconReport.pdf. Retrieved 1 June 2015.

[19]www.nerc.ac.uk/latest/news/nerc/centre-eval/. Retrieved 1 June 2015.

[20]For instance: BIS (2014). *Trends in Inputs, Outputs and Outcomes.* https://www.gov.uk/government/uploads/system/uploads/attachment_data/file/301473/bis-14-654-research-council-impact-reports-2013-trends-in-inputs-outputs-and-outcomes_formatedit.pdf. Retrieved 1 March 2015. Also, see the following article which notes how Research Councils are under pressure to measure themselves against metrics: Else, H. (2014). Research councils 'should develop metrics' to measure success. www.timeshighereducation.co.uk/news/research-councils-should-develop-metrics-to-measure-success/2012814.article. Retrieved 1 June 2015.

[21]The RCUK 2014 impact report, and also individual research council impact reports can be found at www.rcuk.ac.uk/publications/reports/rcuk-impact-report-2014/

achievements in a format more easily compared across research organisations. MRC Units will be expected to re-use this information in their quinquennial reviews. The Research Councils undertake and support studies to better understand the factors that lead to impact, although as noted above, their view is that the UK is not internationally competitive in this field. RCUK therefore advocate that improving the UK capacity to carry out high quality 'science of science policy' research should be a shared concern across all UK funding agencies.

From a more strategic perspective, RCUK's view is that metrics are more effective when used in combination as individual metrics tend to give at best a very partial picture. RCUK also suggest that the use of multiple metrics (quantitative and qualitative) with expert moderation/interpretation will help to reduce the risk of researchers, research managers and publishers 'gaming' the system.

RCUK has no evidence, through Researchfish, that users are trying to game the system; the main issue is under-reporting of eligible outputs, not over-reporting, or inaccurate reporting. The re-use of output data in research applications, publication of outputs, outcomes and impacts, as well as streamlining reporting requirements, will support and encourage researchers in providing accurate, consistent and complete data. If output information is used in a variety of ways – e.g. to communicate research progress to the public and other stakeholders (including via the RCUK Gateway to Research), to complete applications for funding (which are scrutinised by peers), and wherever possible re-used in other repositories (e.g. Researchfish grant-paper linkages are added to Europe PubMed Central) – then it becomes difficult to game the system.

## 8.2.2 Evaluation of impact

RCUK recognise that the 'research to impact' process is impossible to describe using a small set of indicators, given that it may extend over a long time period, involve many individuals, organisations, and funding inputs, and encompass complex and varied activities. They also emphasise the message that this process is not linear,[22] and agree

---

[22]Recent thinking on innovation portrays research as a 'chain-linked' model. "The linear perspective has been challenged not least by modern innovation theorising and empirical research." In the words of Kline and Rosenberg "innovation is neither smooth nor linear, nor often well behaved." Kline, S. and Rosenberg, N. (1986). An overview of innovation, in Landau, R. and Rosenberg. N. (eds.) *The Positive Sum Strategy: Harnessing Technology for Economic Growth.* Washington, DC: National Academy Press. p285. Their chain-linked model is an influential and widely cited focusing device for making sense of the complex structure and diversity of patterns of the innovation process. The non-linear nature of translation has also been emphasised in the widely used Donovan and Hanney 'Payback Framework' which provides a multidimensional categorisation of benefits from research, starting with more traditional academic benefits of knowledge production and research capacity-building, and then extending to wider benefits to society. Donovan, C. and Hanney, S. (2011). The 'Payback Framework' explained, *Research Evaluation*, 20(3): 181–183. DOI: 10.3152/095820211X13118583635756 http://rev.oxfordjournals.org/content/20/3/181.short

with concerns that there are currently few well-defined markers of progress, with work on the 'measurement' of research and research impact tending to focus on publication and citation data (particularly of journal articles) and patenting of intellectual property, as proxies for progress, productivity and quality of research. Comprehensive and structured information about other aspects of the research to impact process has been lacking.

One aim of the Research Councils in using the Researchfish approach is to develop improved quantitative and qualitative information collection for other research activities such as the establishment and maintenance of productive academic and user community collaborations, the dissemination of results to the public and policymakers, the development of new products and processes, and the sharing of research methods/tools and databases. Structured and comprehensive feedback on these activities are needed to provide a more holistic picture of research. Although metrics may be developed for some of these activities and outputs, there is a danger of over-simplification through the use of numbers, for example, counting the size of an audience for dissemination does not capture the extent to which the knowledge/ideas have really had an impact on that audience.

The RCUK's typology and approach to impact draws on the work of Martin and Tang who outlined a series of 'exploitation channels' from research to economic impact, emphasising a variety of pathways:[23]

A   Increasing the stock of useful knowledge
B   Training skilled graduates
C   Creating new instrumentation and methodologies
D   Forming networks and stimulating social interaction
E   Increasing the capacity for technological problem-solving
F   Creating new firms
G   Provision of social knowledge

This approach underlines the fact that reliance on just a few metrics or indicators will fail to adequately capture the full breadth of routes to impact, and therefore miss important aspects of eventual impact. Accordingly, a suggested high level typology of impact is as depicted in Figure 4 below.

The Research Councils have also developed and tested an approach for capturing output information closely tied to these activities in a systematic and standardised way. Using feedback from researchers and users, the Research Councils are gathering data to connect the steps between the research they fund and its subsequent impacts (see Figure 5 below).

Using a common system (currently Researchfish[24]) RCUK gathers data across a range of outcomes (including publications, collaborations, measures of esteem, further funding, commercialisation etc); 2014 saw the first large-scale, cross-disciplinary implementation of

---

[23]Martin, B. and Tang, P. (2007). *The Benefits of Publicly Funded Research*. SPRU Electronic Working Paper Series no.161. https://www.sussex.ac.uk/webteam/gateway/file.php?name=sewp161.pdf&site=25

[24]www.researchfish.com

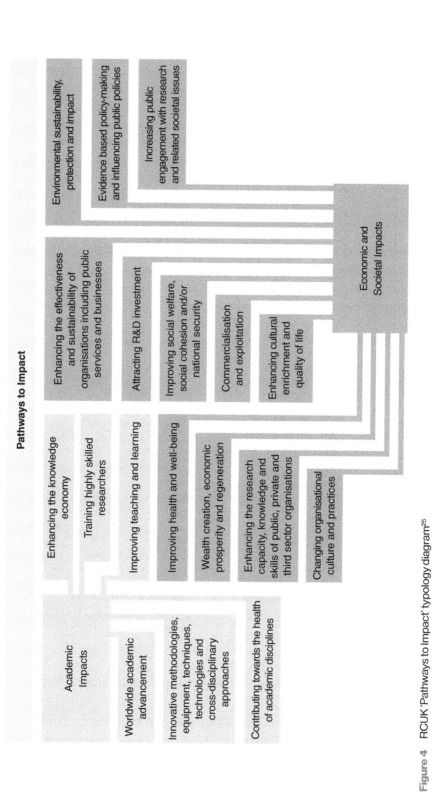

**Figure 4** RCUK 'Pathways to Impact' typology diagram[25]

[25] Available at: www.rcuk.ac.uk/RCUK-prod/assets/documents/impacts/RCUKtypologydiagram.pdf

such an approach with researchers providing feedback on over £16 billion of RCUK funding activity since 2006. RCUK will use the data collected to enable the further development of metrics associated with outcomes and impacts. Some metrics may be potential indicators of progress (e.g. technology-readiness levels for product development, involvement in policy-setting processes), and some may be helpful to indicate the extent of impact (wide-scale adoption of new products and interventions, or uptake of new policies).

Comprehensive output information will allow modelling and hypothesis building regarding the most effective ways to support research, and is already proving to be a rapid way of identifying relevant case studies[26] and setting these in the context of total output. As the data collected by Researchfish is federated across all subscribing funders it is straightforward for organisations to share data for joint analysis. At the start of 2015 the UK Researchfish dataset contained information on over £40 billion of research investment and over 1.1 million reports of output linked to this. The majority of the RCUK output information is made publicly available via the RCUK Gateway to Research (GtR) within a few months of it being submitted to Research Councils, with the RCUK GtR offering a free API for users to work with the data.

RCUK suggest that one important area needing further development is the tracking of training and career development. The training and movement of skilled people is one of the most impactful routes of knowledge exchange.[27] The strengths of the first

| Input | Outputs/Outcomes | Impacts (Academic/Economic/Social) |
|---|---|---|
| Funding for Research and Training | Generation of new knowledge/ publication | Improvements to health (living longer and with better quality of life) |
| | Trained people | Academic impact (effects on further research including other disciplines) |
| | Development of collaborative networks | Improving the performance of existing businesses |
| | Intellectual property/ licensing | Creating new businesses (that contribute to economic growth and further R&D) |
| | Research materials/ technologies | Delivering highly skilled people to the labour market |
| | Influences on policy & practice | Attracting R&D investment (from global business and non-UK funding sources) |
| | Development of new products/processes | Improving public policy and public services (including the NHS) |
| | Dissemination of research | Engaging public support for medical research |

Figure 5    Inputs/Outputs and Impacts (MRC, 2011)

*Source:* Medical Research Council (2012). Outputs, outcomes and impact of MRC research: 2012 report.

---

[26]For example see MRC's 2012 report on research output at www.mrc.ac.uk/research/achievements/outputs-report/

[27]For example see the analysis of 'brain circulation' presented in Elsevier (2013). https://www.gov.uk/government/uploads/system/uploads/attachment_data/file/263729/bis-13-1297-international-comparative-performance-of-the-UK-research-base-2013.pdf

phase of the US NIH/NSF STAR METRICs project (see Section 2.6.6) was that it provided a process to capture comprehensive statistics about the research workforce from universities, and the linkage of this data to other records. Such an approach may not be practical in the UK, but there may be ways in which HESA data can be extended to provide more helpful information in this area. Over the long-term the ORCID (see Section 2.5.1) initiative will assist in the unambiguous identification of researchers and thereby the linkage of a researcher's output to their career record, as they move from organisation to organisation.

RCUK is supporting several pieces of work to support greater inter-operability between key systems which will be of practical importance to the use of metrics. Two examples are:

- **Overview of System Interoperability Project** (OSIP), supported by RCUK, Jisc and ARMA,[28] which will look at the interface between: Researchfish and university systems, the RCUK grant management system and university systems, RCUK Gateway to Research and third party systems, and data on research students in higher education. OSIP will also examine the main ways in which data on people, projects, locations and other objects are uniquely identified in these systems, with a view to recommending how this could be better managed in future;
- **Researchfish interoperability pilot**, supported by RCUK and Researchfish. This work aims to examine the process of exchanging publication information between Researchfish and university systems, and the main changes that are required to make this feasible. RCUK have recently published an update to this work pointing out that linking grant references to research outputs is a pre-requisite for being able to exchange data between HEIs and funder systems.[29]

RCUK priorities for the future[30] include:

- **The continued development of the Researchfish approach**. This will ensure that entering data is made as simple as possible, that exchange of data with other systems is increased, and that use of the information to support evaluation and strategy development is maximised;
- **Further studies to better understand the link between research and impact** in collaboration with other funders (funding councils, charities and government), either by commissioning new work or via strategic or response-mode funding.

---

[28]http://orcidpilot.jiscinvolve.org/wp/files/2014/05/presentation.pptx. Retrieved 1 June 2015.

[29]www.rcuk.ac.uk/research/researchoutcomes/future/

[30]Individual research council evaluation strategies and policies can be found at www.ahrc.ac.uk/What-We-Do/Build-the-evidence-base/Pages/Build-the-evidence-base.aspx (AHRC); www.bbsrc.ac.uk/about/policies/reviews/funded-science/ (BBSRC); https://www.epsrc.ac.uk/about/plans/evaluation/ (EPSRC); www.esrc.ac.uk/research/evaluation-impact/ (ESRC); www.mrc.ac.uk/research/achievements/evaluation-programme/ (MRC); www.nerc.ac.uk/about/perform/evaluation/(NERC); www.stfc.ac.uk/files/stfc-impact-framework-evaluation-strategy/ (STFC).

## 8.3 CHARITY FUNDERS

Given the high number and diversity of charities funding research within the UK higher education sector,[31] we do not provide an exhaustive description of systems and approaches to pre- or post-award research assessment within this report, but make some overall observations and then focus on the Wellcome Trust in more detail as a case study example.

### 8.3.1 Pre-award processes of assessment

HESA datasets, which capture details of charitable research income awarded to Higher Education Providers (HEPs), indicate that the majority of charitable funding is allocated following an open competition process. For instance, scrutiny of HESA datasets for 2013–14 informs us that £901 million of funding was allocated through the open competition route versus £94 million of charitable income awarded through other means.

The guidance provided by HESA on what is deemed to constitute allocation of funds through open competition underlines the importance of peer review and/or external expert advice implemented within rigorous processes.[32]

Moreover, if we look at a few of the bigger UK charities funding higher education research (see links provided below), it is also apparent that most allocate funding primarily on the basis of peer review and/or, to a lesser degree, tap into other forms of expert external advice.

| Name of charity | Weblink to details of pre-assessment processes |
| --- | --- |
| British Heart Foundation | https://www.bhf.org.uk/research/information-for-researchers/how-we-award |
| Cancer Research UK | www.cancerresearchuk.org/funding-for-researchers/applying-for-funding/funding-committees<br>www.cancerresearchuk.org/prod_consump/groups/cr_common/@fre/@gen/documents/generalcontent/funding-terms-of-reference.pdf |
| Leverhulme Trust | www.leverhulme.ac.uk/funding/choosing-a-referee.cfm |
| Nuffield Foundation | www.nuffieldfoundation.org/how-apply |
| Wellcome Trust | www.wellcome.ac.uk/Funding/Biomedical-science/Application-information/WTD004051.htm |

[31]For instance, the Association of Medical Research Charities alone involves 136 members.

[32]See paras 4–7 of the guidance listed at https://www.hesa.ac.uk/index.php?option=com_studrec&task=show_file&mnl=13031&href=income_from_charities.html. Retrieved 15 March 2015.

However, organisations within the charity sector, like government funders, have been working to enhance their capacity to assess grants and monitor and evaluate the research and activity they support; the challenge is to keep it simple, proportionate and palatable where donor funding is predominantly provided to address a specific cause or medical condition. The Association of Medical Research Charities (AMRC)[33] advocates five principles of peer review to its members: accountability, balance, independent decision making, rotation and impartiality. AMRC assesses charities' peer review when members apply to become a member and conducts audits of all members every five years. AMRC also makes a direct link between universities, government and funding bodies' use of AMRC membership as a 'hallmark of quality' on the basis of these processes.[34]

## 8.3.2 Post-award processes of assessment: the Wellcome Trust's approach[35]

Approaches to research assessment post-award across charities vary and are largely determined by the budget and skills available and adhering to the principles of proportionality. The Wellcome Trust, currently the largest medical research charity in the UK, has developed a practical approach to post-award monitoring and evaluation which other charities have drawn upon. The Wellcome Trust currently spends around £700 million per year on biomedical research and related activities. Understanding the impacts of research, what works and what doesn't, is an important requirement to support Wellcome's vision:

"To improve health by supporting bright minds in science, the humanities and social sciences, and public engagement."[36]

Since 2005, the Trust has established and evolved a set of outcomes which it would like its funding to deliver and alongside these outcomes, a set of 'indicators of progress' which are used to guide information-capture to demonstrate how far the Trust is making a difference and to build the evidence base on where and when the Trust's funding is being particularly effective. Table 1 sets out the key indicators of progress used to guide information-capture and analysis. The Trust has deliberately used the terms 'indicators' and 'progress' to realistically represent the facts that (1) most of the information used to demonstrate academic advancements are not objective or quantifiable proofs but are proximate 'measures' at best, and (2) research and knowledge does not have defined, absolute or 'success' end points so progress is a more helpful concept.

---

[33]www.amrc.org.uk

[34]www.amrc.org.uk/publications/principles-peer-review provides further information on AMRC's principles of peer review. Retrieved 1 June 2014.

[35]Particular thanks to Dr Liz Allen, Head of Evaluation at the Wellcome Trust (and steering group member) for her contributions to this section. The Wellcome Trust also contributed to the review's call for evidence.

[36]www.wellcome.ac.uk/our-vision/

However, the Wellcome Trust recognises that the major challenge in setting up frameworks to support impact assessment is in the availability of the types of information that can be used to describe progress (and impact); put simply, most of the data we would like to be able to bring together to understand impact are not easily available or accessible. In the field of research assessment more broadly, there has been a large tendency to rely on more quantitative types of information (e.g. counts of publication outputs and bibliometrics) as indicators of impact rather than appreciating that the outputs of research are broad ranging and not always easily quantified.

The Wellcome Trust has therefore evolved a pragmatic approach to monitoring and evaluating the impacts of research it has supported by bringing together a range of information – both quantitative and qualitative – that shows whether things are pointing in the right (or wrong) direction. It is also exploring ways to enhance the infrastructure to support grant progress monitoring through initiatives like FundRef, and ORCID (see Section 2.5.1 for further information: Wellcome is a founder member of this initiative). From August 2015, all lead applicants to the Wellcome Trust will be required to have an ORCID iD to proceed with a grant application. Wellcome is keen to use tools like ORCID to help easily connect researchers to their research works and career status, to support easy impact and career tracking and also to reduce researcher burdens in adding the same information across multiple systems.

The Trust has set in place a number of systematic approaches to capturing the more 'quantitative' data on:

- Published research outputs directly though web-based platforms such as PubMed, EPMC, WoS, Scopus, F1000, Impact Story and Altmetric;
- Broader research outcomes and impacts, through an online grant progress reporting platform (WT e-Val) and career choices, through a career tracking tool (Career Tracker).[37]

To complement the more quantitative data on research progress which is increasingly being pulled from source systems, the Trust also produces a set of between 30 and 50 'stories of impact' (case studies) each year. These stories, while not necessarily representative of the whole portfolio of Wellcome Trust funding, do bring breakthroughs and progress to life and are used to support various reviews, evaluation, stakeholder engagement and advocacy. The stories are selected by the Trust's scientific staff and validated by peer experts and the researchers, and the narrative is supported by metadata (e.g. grant details; characteristics of the research/team; location; HEI) and made available as a searchable resource.

Once a year, a digest of progress, major outputs and achievements in relation to the Trust's outcome goals is presented to the Board of Trustees, staff and stakeholder community. The information is also used to support organisation learning and dissemination of – and engagement with – the findings and impact of Trust funded research and is published on its website.[38]

---

[37] www.wellcome.ac.uk/Funding/Biomedical-science/Career-tracker/index.htm

[38] www.wellcome.ac.uk/About-us/Publications/Reports/Biomedical-science/WTVM 054494.htm

Table 1    Wellcome Trust Outcomes and Indicators of Progress

| Outcomes (what the Wellcome Trust wants to achieve) | Indicators of progress |
|---|---|
| Discoveries | The generation of significant new knowledge and understanding. Contributions to discoveries with tangible impacts on health. |
| Applications of Research | Contributions to the development of enabling technologies, products and devices. Uptake of research into policy and practice. |
| Engagement | Enhanced level of informed debate on biomedical science issues. Significant engagement of key audiences in biomedical science and increased audience reach. |
| Research Leaders | Development of a cadre of research leaders. Evidence of significant career progression among those supported by the Wellcome Trust. |
| Research Environment | Key contributions to the creation, development and maintenance of major research resources. Contributions to the growth of centres of excellence. |
| Influence | Significant impact on science funding and policy developments. Significant impact on global research priorities. |

## 8.4 NATIONAL ACADEMIES

This section is based on information received from the British Academy (BA)[39] and Royal Society (RS),[40] both of which use peer review as the primary basis of pre-award research assessment.[41]

The RS makes limited use of research metrics in its work. In its publishing activities, ever since it signed DORA, the RS has removed the JIF from its journal home pages and marketing materials, and no longer uses them as part of its publishing strategy. As authors still frequently ask about JIFs, however, the RS does provide them, but only as one of a number of metrics (including EigenFactor, SCImago journal rank etc). The RS also offers article-level metrics tools (such as article downloads and the altmetrics donut) on all its journals, and it tracks total downloads at the journal level.

---

[39]Roger Kain, Vice-President of the British Academy, is a member of the review's steering group. www.britac.ac.uk/funding/peer-review.cfm

[40]https://royalsociety.org/grants/applications/

[41]The Royal Society and British Academy are taken here as illustrative of wider developments across the national academies, and separate details have not been included on the Academy of Medical Sciences or Royal Academy of Engineering.

In assessing and awarding grants, the RS does not use metrics as part of the grant assessment process. Decisions to award grants are based on peer review. The RS is currently updating its guidance to panels and, following DORA guidelines, it will ensure that committee members are aware that it does not take account of metrics in assessment of grants. The RS does use metrics (together with qualitative measures) to evaluate programmes and demonstrate the impact of programmes funded via its BIS grant. This is retrospective and plays no part in the awarding of grants.

In its policy work, the RS engages in debates over the use of metrics in research assessment and how these shape the research landscape. Examples include the Society's involvement in the recent Nuffield Council on Bioethics report *The Culture of Scientific research in the UK* and its engagement with HEFCE on the design and evaluation of the REF. The report *Knowledge, Networks and Nations* is the only recent RS policy study to make extensive use of bibliometrics, although they are used in other policy contexts to demonstrate or support specific points.

The BA is also a signatory to DORA and takes no account of metrics when assessing grant applications. It asks assessors primarily to focus on the quality of the proposed research, the ability of the applicant(s) to carry it out successfully and the feasibility of methodology and timescale. In its assessment processes, scores provided by assessors at the first assessment stage enable the Academy to make an evaluation of their overall relative quality, as marginal, unfundable or fundable. This information is useful for internal purposes, and can be used to offer feedback to Fellows and universities on the overall quality of the applications they receive.

For the BA's main early-career Postdoctoral Fellowships scheme, assessors are asked to consider an applicant's publication record, but in terms of whether the applicant has demonstrated the capacity to make a significant contribution to their chosen field through their work to date, whether their publication record is appropriate to their current career development stage, and whether the proposed outputs from the Fellowship, if awarded, are appropriate. The BA does not seek to mandate what those outputs should be, or limit consideration to academic publications.

As with the RS, the BA does use some metrics (including citations and leverage) when evaluating programmes and demonstrating to BIS the value of BA funding, though this is retrospective and does not influence the decision to fund.[42]

## 8.5 EUROPEAN FUNDING

For 30 years, the European Commission's framework programmes have been providing funding to support research and technology development across Europe. The latest multi-year framework programme, Horizon2020 (H2020) has the ambition to provide €80 billion to research over seven years (2014 to 2020), including €13 billion for the European Research Council (ERC). ERC funding schemes are open to researchers of any nationality or age who wish to carry out their frontier research in the 28 EU member

---

[42]www.britac.ac.uk/funding/monitoring.cfm

states or associated countries.[43] ERC funding is based on international peer review[44] with "excellence as the sole criteria". The evaluation of Horizon2020 proposals is also founded on principles of expert review, guided by the principles of: excellence; transparency; fairness and impartiality; efficiency and speed; ethics; and security.[45]

As noted in Section 1.1, the European Commission's 'Science 2.0: Science in Transition' agenda is highly relevant to this review.[46] Carlos Moedas, Commissioner for Research, Science and Innovation, signalled recently that his priorities in office will be "open innovation, open science and openness to the world", and further proposals to advance this agenda are expected in the second half of 2015.[47] Responses to the Science 2.0 consultation reflect a diversity of opinions, but it appears likely that recommendations may include calls to review quality assessment and evaluation criteria for research proposals, with potential impacts on H2020 and beyond.[48] The consultation document also notes that "research funding organisations may need to improve the communication of research data from the projects that they fund by recognising those who can maximise usability and good communication of their data."[49]

The European parliament in its oversight of funding and science policy in Europe has examined the issue of measuring scientific performance[50] and recognised the importance of good, standardised and open information about science and technology to strengthen the European Research Area (ERA). The EC has also recently launched a €20 million Policy Support Facility (PSF). The PSF is a new instrument to give EU member state governments practical support to identify, implement and evaluate those reforms needed to enhance the quality of their public funding, such as opening up public funding to competition and introducing performance assessments of universities, or stimulating co-operation between academia and business. It supports government officials from

---

[43]http://erc.europa.eu/funding-and-grants/funding-schemes

[44]http://erc.europa.eu/evaluation-panels

[45]http://ec.europa.eu/research/participants/data/ref/h2020/grants_manual/pse/h2020-guide-pse_en.pdf; http://ec.europa.eu/programmes/horizon2020/en/how-get-funding; http://ec.europa.eu/programmes/horizon2020/en/experts

[46]The background document to the Science 2.0 consultation can be found at: http://ec.europa.eu/research/consultations/science-2.0/background.pdf. Retrieved 1 June 2015.

[47]Moedas, C. (2015) Open Innovation, Open Science, Open to the World. Speech to the 'New ERA of Innovation' conference, 22 June 2015 http://europa.eu/rapid/press-release_SPEECH-15-5243_en.htm Retrieved 28 June 2015.

[48]There are diverse views in relation to different elements of the consultation, for instance for the potential involvement of altmetrics. https://scienceintransition.files.wordpress.com/2014/10/draft-policy-brief-science-2-0-workshop-madrid-04-december-2014.pdf. Retrieved 1 June 2015.

[49]Ibid. p11.

[50]Technopolis and European Parliament STDA (2014). Measuring scientific performance for improved policy making. Summary of a study. Available at: http://www.europarl.europa.eu/RegData/etudes/join/2014/527383/IPOL_JOIN_ET(2014)527383(SUM01)_EN.pdf

other countries to peer review the effectiveness of research and innovation policies and provides access to independent high-level expertise and analysis. The first member states to take up the services of the PSF are Hungary and Bulgaria.[51]

Further relevant initiatives include the following:

- UK funders such as the Research Councils note the results of studies using international data. Bibliometrics are often used to compare research output across nations,[52] and many countries and regions have published studies to identify strengths, gaps and opportunities in their research base.[53] The World Health Organisation is promoting efforts to combine data on global health research investments in a single 'health research observatory' which would allow analysis of international investments in research.[54] However, information on research portfolios is rarely complete at a national level, let alone in a consistent format internationally.
- Science Europe and some European member state funding agencies are exploring the use of metrics in relation to humanities research as part of campaigns to make humanities research more 'visible'. Previous attempts – such as the European Reference Index for the Humanities (ERIH)[55] have highlighted how difficult it is to establish a comprehensive database for the humanities.[56]
- The European Science Foundation supported networking between evaluation teams across Europe from 2007 to 2011, and the member organisation forum for the evaluation of publicly funded research published several summaries of international evaluation practices.[57] A consistent theme was the need for a 'common language' for describing research progress across the European Research Area to allow comparison, benchmarking and aggregation of research output.

---

[51]Rabesandratana, T. (2015). Bulgaria and Hungary volunteer for E.U. scrutiny of their research systems, March 2015. *Science*. http://news.sciencemag.org/europe/2015/03/bulgaria-and-hungary-volunteer-e-u-scrutiny-their-research-systems. Retrieved 1 June 2015.

[52]Elsevier (2014). Response to HEFCE's call for evidence: independent review of the role of metrics in research assessment. Available at: https://www.elsevier.com/research-intelligence/resource-library/response-to-hefces

[53]Science-Metrix. (2014). *The UK's Performance in Physics Research: National and International Perspectives*. www.iop.org/publications/iop/2014/file_63082.pdf. Retrieved 1 June 2015; Science-Metrix (2013). *Intra-European Co-operation Compared to International Collaboration of the ERA Countries*. http://ec.europa.eu/research/innovation-union/pdf/intra-european_intern_collab.pdf#view=fit&pagemode=none. Retrieved 1 June 2015.

[54]WHO (2013). A global health R&D observatory. WHO draft working paper, May 2013. www.who.int/phi/documents/dwp1_global_health_rd_observatory_16May13.pdf. Retrieved 1 June.

[55]www.esf.org/index.php?id=4813. Retrieved 1 June.

[56]https://globalhighered.files.wordpress.com/2010/07/esf_report_final_100309.pdf. Retrieved 1 June.

[57]www.esf.org/coordinating-research/mo-fora/evaluation-of-publicly-funded-research.html. Retrieved 1 June.

## 8.6 SMARTER SCIENCE AND INNOVATION POLICY

As noted above, various efforts have been made by funders and sponsors to progress more sophisticated research assessment and management methodologies within the UK and beyond. Many funders, including RCUK and Wellcome, are vocal advocates for greater investment in more 'science of science policy' research. If this field develops, as we recommend in Chapter 10, further positive strides will be made. In addition, we applaud many of the various efforts being made to improve data infrastructure within the UK and beyond.

However, much more could still be done to improve transparency and openness. Too often, it is difficult or impossible for those outside an organisation to find and understand the terms and approaches to research assessment being employed. Moreover, there are poor levels of interoperability across the system, as many of the funders and other organisations involved in research assessment and management operate in silos.

These problems extend beyond the main actors within the research system, and to the government departments and agencies that try to shape the overall policy framework for research and for wider aspects of the innovation system. As Stian Westlake, Director of Research and Policy at Nesta,[58] has noted: "There are plenty of *intelligent* people making innovation policy, both in the UK and the rest of the world. But there is a shortage of *intelligence*. Too often, policymakers lack basic data...".

For effective management of the research system, the quality of information-flows matters hugely. But at the moment, government gets relatively little value from the enormous amount of effort that goes into gathering information for research management and assessment, across both sides of the dual support system.

Nesta has argued that sources of data within government bodies, such as Innovate UK's database of grants, or the Intellectual Property Office's information on UK patents, are underexploited as tools for policymaking. The same applies to information captured by HEFCE, the Research Councils, HESA and individual HEIs.

As real-time data on the performance and impacts of the higher education and research system increases in volume and sophistication, it can be analysed and used in new, interconnected ways. HESA and Jisc are exploring future possibilities in this area through the Higher Education Data and Information Improvement Programme (HEDIIP), which aims to integrate and simplify processes of data capture, reporting and analysis.[59] HESA and Jisc are also leading the development of a next-generation Higher Education Information Database for Institutions (HEIDI), which aims "to ease the burden for users in higher education providers of accessing, extracting and manipulating data for essential planning and reporting."[60] Both HEDIIP and HEIDI are focused on the teaching side of the higher education system, where data has in large part been managed separately from the research side,

---

[58]Nesta is "an innovation charity with a mission to help people and organisations bring great ideas to life". www.nesta.org.uk/

[59]www.hediip.ac.uk

[60]See www.business-intelligence.ac.uk for details of the HEIDI project.

but with discussions now underway at a policy level about the introduction of a 'teaching excellence framework' (which may include its own outcome-focused metrics),[61] the scope for sensitive integration of processes across the system as a whole is likely to increase. Related scoping work on the next generation of 'national performance indicators' is underway, led by HEFCE and HESA.[62]

At a national level, policies for higher education, research and the wider innovation system can be made more robust if they are supported and informed by high quality data from within the research system. Currently, links between 'micro' data and indicators, as captured by the REF, Researchfish and Gateway to Research, and 'macro' policies and strategies set by HM Treasury, BIS, Research Councils and Innovate UK are underdeveloped. This also applies at the international level, for example in the uses that bodies like the OECD make of micro-level research data to inform the measurement and benchmarking of national research and innovation systems.

Some countries are beginning to draw on scientometric mapping and analysis in more creative and strategic ways to shape technology and innovation policies,[63] to determine funding priorities and manage portfolios,[64] to measure the wider impacts of research,[65] or to support wider approaches to foresight and horizon scanning.[66] In line with the wider drive to open up and derive greater value from public sector data[67], further work should be done across the UK research system to link different datasets, so that connections, interdependencies and trade-offs between different parts of the research system can be more readily identified and fed back into policymaking. BIS, Cabinet Office (in terms of links to the open data agenda) and Government Office for Science (in terms of links to Foresight and horizon scanning) are best placed to coordinate these efforts, with input from HEFCE, HESA, Jisc, Research Councils, Innovate UK and HEIs. These broader opportunities to connect research data to policy should also form part of the remit of a new Forum for Responsible Metrics (see Chapter 10).

---

[61]https://www.timeshighereducation.co.uk/news/johnson-tef-offer-universities-financial-incentives

[62]See www.hes.ac.uk/pis for details of the most recent review of national performance indicators.

[63]Rotolo, D., Rafols, I., Hopkins, M. and Leydesdorff, L. (2014). *Scientometric Mapping as a Strategic Intelligence Tool for the Governance of Emerging Technologies.* SPRU Working Paper Series 2014–10.

[64]Wallace, M. L. and Rafols, S. (2015). Research portfolio analysis in science policy: Moving from financial returns to societal benefits. *Minerva*, 53(2): 89–115.

[65]Small Advanced Economies Initiative (2014). *Broadening the Scope of Impact: Defining, assessing and measuring impact of major public research programmes, with lessons from 6 small advanced economies.* SAEI. www.smalladvancedeconomies.org/wp-content/uploads/SAEI_Impact-Framework_Feb_2015_Issue2.pdf Retrieved 1 July 2015.

[66]Ciarli, T., Coad, A and Rafols, I. (2013). *Quantitative Analysis of Technology Futures. Part 1: Techniques, Context, and Organizations.* Nesta Working Paper No. 13/08.

[67]See e.g. HM Government (2012). *Open Data White Paper: Unleashing the Potential.* Cabinet Office/HM Stationery Office, June 2012.

# NINE

## REFLECTIONS ON REF

### CHAPTER CONTENTS

"I tell American colleagues bemused by the UK's dual-support system of research funding that, for all the gripes, it is better than the US system, where state-university professors must hustle for grants to meet even basic academic needs. If we want to retain dual support in a larger and more diverse university system, a mechanism such as the Research Excellence Framework is a necessary evil."

Martin Rees[1]

While the terms of reference for this review (Section 1.1) are to consider the use of quantitative information for research assessment broadly, the role of metrics in future national-scale research assessments, such as the REF, was an important part of our deliberations. Much of the evidence that the panel received, both in response to our written call for evidence and at the workshops that we organised, has been concerned with the potential benefits and challenges associated with increased use of quantitative data in the REF.

---

[1]Rees, M. (2015). The importance – and limits – of the Haldane Principle. *Research Fortnight*, 24 June 2015.

In this chapter, we consider this evidence, together with the outcomes of the literature review (Supplementary Report I) and analysis of REF2014 outcomes (Supplementary Report II), and draw conclusions that the four UK higher education Funding Bodies should consider as they develop future national assessment exercises. The findings in this chapter will also be of interest outside the UK, where more or less quantitative approaches to national research assessment are already being used, or being considered.[2]

The REF fulfils a number of policy objectives. The exercise provides both information about research quality that is used by the UK HE Funding Bodies to distribute funding for research, and accountability for public research investment. The research quality assessments also provide valuable information that allows institutions to benchmark their performance against others in the UK. And this, in turn, allows the identification of strengths and weaknesses that provide both incentives for improvement and the information needed to target actions to achieve that improvement. Not all the written evidence about the REF we received acknowledged the diversity of purposes of the REF, and there are clearly differences of opinion about the relative importance of the purposes. It is not surprising, therefore, that there are equally different views on how and whether quantitative indicators of research quality should feature in the assessment.

The UK has a 30-year history of research assessment, and there is good and varied evidence that the overall quality of UK research has improved over that period. While it is not possible to ascribe any causal link, it is the case that research assessment has strongly shaped the environment within which quality has improved.

While research assessment in general, and the REF in particular, bring benefits, this is not without cost. A recurring theme in much of the evidence we received was the burden, both perceived and actual, of the REF and opportunity costs associated with the exercise. For many who argued in favour of increased use of metrics and indicators in future assessments, the reduction in burden was seen as the major reason, perhaps the sole reason, for pursuing this approach. Many of these advocates for metrics appeared to consider their use as essentially cost-free, a point we will return to later in the chapter.

It is also the case that there is evidence that the opportunities to gather quantitative data about research are increasing. As set out in the literature review (Supplementary Report I), and Chapter 3, the repertoire of metrics that can be attached to research outputs is increasing. As well as a growing suite of bibliometric indicators, the range of disciplines to which those indicators can be applied is also rising. Bookmarking services like Academia.edu, Mendeley and ResearchGate offer the prospect of the earlier prediction of papers that will become highly cited, and the measurement of social media sharing, and other online mentions of research, raises the possibility of quantitative data that provides some evidence for the impact of research beyond its value in academia.

At its heart, the REF is a process built on expert and peer review. While peer review is used across the global research system, and is widely accepted as the 'gold standard' of assessment, it is not without its problems and challenges. These are discussed in Chapter 5 of this report (and the literature review, Supplementary Report I), and include numerous

---

[2] Please see Chapter 2 for a discussion of the international landscape.

ways in which peer review may be biased, leading to outcomes that are related to factors other than the merit of the object reviewed. The scope of this review does not extend to a detailed critique of the use of peer review. However, we note that in considering the replacement or augmentation of peer review with approaches based on the use of quantitative data and indicators, we also need to acknowledge that peer review itself may not always deliver an accurate outcome.

The submissions made to our call for evidence were largely sceptical about the enhanced (and in some cases, current) use of metrics for research assessment. The majority suggested that peer review should remain central to the process. However, there was some support for the additional use of quantitative data in the REF. This was primarily raised as a potential means by which the burden of the exercise could be reduced.[3]

It was also suggested that quantitative data could be used alongside peer review to enhance, and perhaps simplify, the assessment process:

"There are many new (and old) sources of data that will be valuable in providing quantitative and qualitative evidence in supporting evaluative and resource allocation decisions associated with research assessment."

PLOS response[4]

A significant concern for many respondents to our call for evidence was the potential that some types of quantitative data could encourage particular behaviours that were not necessarily positive. Examples ranged from the use of 'citation clubs' to boost citations, to major distortions in the research endeavour, downplaying whole disciplinary areas.

This chapter will summarise and synthesise the evidence we have reviewed that is pertinent to consideration of future iterations of the REF. In this discussion we have opted to follow the structure of the REF2014, considering the use of quantitative data in the assessment of research outputs, impact and environment in turn. In Chapter 10 of this report, where we make a series of recommendations, we will discuss whether the use of quantitative data could support a national research assessment process with a radically different structure.

## 9.1 QUANTITATIVE DATA AND THE ASSESSMENT OF RESEARCH OUTPUTS

### 9.1.1 Guidance and process for outputs in REF2014

The assessment of research outputs formed a significant part of REF2014. This element of the REF accounted for 65% of the overall assessment, and submitting institutions were required to include up to four outputs listed against each member of staff entered in the

[3]www.hefce.ac.uk/rsrch/REFreview/feedback/

[4]All responses can be downloaded from www.hefce.ac.uk/media/hefce,2014/content/research/research,metrics/responses_to_metrics_review_call_for_evidence.pdf

exercise. There were few limits imposed on the nature of research outputs that could be submitted to the REF.[5]

Provisions were made for staff with individual staff circumstances who, depending on the nature of their circumstances, had the option to provide fewer than four outputs. Circumstances include early-career researchers, staff who had taken career breaks (including maternity or paternity leave), and staff with illnesses or disabilities.[6]

There were also provisions for the submission of double-weighted outputs where a case could be made that the output was of considerable 'scale and scope'.[7] The sub-panels were required to judge whether these criteria were met, and for each double-weighted output a reserve could also be submitted. The reserve was assessed when the sub-panel did not accept the argument for double weighting.

Outputs were assessed by expert review carried out by sub-panel members. Outputs were assessed against criteria for originality, rigour and significance, with the interpretation of these criteria being carried out in a disciplinary context by sub-panels.

Following the bibliometrics pilot carried out in 2008–09,[8] REF sub-panels were permitted to use citation data to inform their peer review judgements. Citation data were sourced centrally by the REF team from the Scopus database. Citation data were only provided for journal articles and conference proceedings that were available in the database, and raw citation counts for each output were provided, together with contextual information to aid the interpretation of the data.[9]

General guidance on how citation data were to be used for REF2014 was as follows:[10]

- The number of times that an output was cited was provided as additional information about the academic significance of submitted outputs. However, assessors were advised to continue relying on expert review as the primary means of assessing outputs, in order to reach rounded judgements about the full range of assessment criteria ('originality, significance and rigour');

---

[5]REF2014: Assessment framework and guidance on submissions, p23, para 118 www.ref.ac.uk/pubs/2011-02/

[6]Ibid. paras 64–91.

[7]Ibid. para 123.

[8]Details of the past pilot exercise can be found at www.ref.ac.uk/about/background/bibliometrics/

[9]Sub-panel 11 Computer Science and Informatics, had originally indicated that in addition to the Scopus citation data provided by the REF team, this sub-panel intended to make use of Google Scholar as a further source of citation information. However, this did not transpire as it was not possible to agree a suitable process for bulk access to their citation information due to Google Scholar's arrangements with publishers.

[10]Ibid. However, more detailed specific guidance was also provided at the panel level as well. Guidance for Main Panel A, B and C was provided at www.ref.ac.uk/pubs/2012-01/#d.en.69569. It should be noted that citation data was only utilised in some Main Panel A, B and C units of assessment, and not at all in Main Panel D.

- They were advised to also recognise the significance of outputs beyond academia wherever appropriate, and assess all outputs on an equal basis, regardless of whether or not citation data is available for them;
- In using citation data, panels were asked to recognise the limited value of citation data for recently published outputs, the variable citation patterns for different fields of research, the possibility of 'negative citations', and the limitations of such data for outputs in languages other than English;
- The sub-panels also received discipline-specific contextual information about citation rates for each year of the assessment period to inform, if appropriate, the interpretation of citation data;
- Panels were also instructed to have due regard to the potential equality implications of using citation data as additional information, and were referred to *Analysis of data from the pilot exercise to develop bibliometric indicators for the REF: The effect of using normalised citation scores for particular staff characteristics;*[11]
- Sub-panels were explicitly instructed **not** to refer to any additional sources of bibliometric analysis, such as JIFs, or other journal-level metrics in their assessments.

### 9.1.2 Assessment of outputs REF2014 in practice

Over 190,000 outputs were submitted for assessment in REF2014. As in previous exercises the range of outputs submitted was diverse, although the majority were identified as journal articles (80%), books (8%) or book chapters (7%). A significant number (2,254) of double-weighted outputs were submitted, the majority, but by no means all, of which were books that were submitted to UOAs in arts and humanities disciplines.

In all sub-panels outputs were allocated to members for assessment with generally at least two members assessing each output. Outputs were scored on a five-point scale,[12] with a discussion between panel members, and sometimes the whole sub-panel, used where necessary to agree a consensus score. Citation data was requested by 11 of the 36 sub-panels, mostly in the life- and physical-science areas, as listed in the 'Annex of tables' (Table 6).

The outcome of the assessment reflected the generally strong performance of the UK research base, and the highly selective nature of the outputs submitted to the exercise. Of the outputs submitted, 22% were assessed to be of 4-star quality (world-leading) with a further 50% assessed as 3-star (internationally excellent). This represents an increase compared to the 2008 RAE, and REF-team analysis has shown that the increase is similar to the increasing volume of UK highly-cited journal articles over the

---

[11]HEFCE 2011/03. www.hefce.ac.uk/pubs/year/2011/201103/. Retrieved 1 June 2015.

[12]In addition to 4-star ratings, outputs could also be graded 'unclassified', defined as "Quality that falls below the standard of nationally recognised work. Or work which does not meet the published definition of research for the purposes of this assessment", see www.ref.ac.uk/panels/assessmentcriteriaandleveldefinitions. Retrieved 1 June 2015.

same period.[13] However, an alternative analytical approach, using a different source of citation data, has produced results that suggest some difference in the relationship between citation measures and grade boundaries across the exercises (Jonathan Grant, personal communication). Similar comparisons were also made in the panel overview reports; for example Sub-panel 7 (earth and environmental sciences) commented:

> "The overall assessment of the quality of research within the UOA 7 submissions is consistent with recent metrics analysis showing the high international standing of UK Environmental Sciences (see: 'International Comparative Performance of the UK Research Base – 2013: A report prepared by Elsevier for the UK's Department of Business, Innovation and Skills (BIS)'). This study shows that UK Environmental Sciences has the highest field-weighted citation impact of all the sub-disciplines considered, and that it has strengthened significantly between 2008 and 2012."[14]

In their overview reports those sub-panels that used citation data reported that the data was useful in informing peer review judgements, although Main Panel B (physical sciences and engineering) reported variability in the quality and usefulness of citation data. The one sub-panel under Main Panel C that used citation data (18: economics and econometrics) reported that the data had informed 'marginal judgements', but that few scores had been influenced.

The use of citation data in marginal judgements or to resolve disagreement appears to have been commonplace. In the Main Panel A overview report it states that:

> "Citation data were only used where these provided a positive indicator of academic uptake (typically if there was any disagreement between those assessing the output)."[15]

In our discussions with members from sub-panels that had used citation data, this point was repeatedly emphasised. While the citation data was useful, we heard that it was used in borderline cases and so had had a limited impact on overall scoring patterns. It was also clear that members of sub-panels that had used citation data were aware of, and had taken into account, the data limitations. In particular, the importance of time since publication in interpreting citation numbers, and the possibility of articles that are considered to contain errors being highly cited were discussed in the focus groups.

Our discussions with members of sub-panels that did not opt to use citation data focused on the limitations of citation-based metrics in research assessment, with a general feeling

---

[13]www.ref.ac.uk/pubs/refmanagersreport/

[14]REF2014: Overview report by Main Panel B and Sub-panels 7 to 15. www.ref.ac.uk/media/ref/content/expanel/member/Main%20Panel%20B%20overview%20report.pdf, para 10. Retrieved 1 June 2015.

[15]REF2014: Overview report by Main Panel A and Sub-panels 1 to 6. www.ref.ac.uk/media/ref/content/expanel/member/Main%20Panel%20A%20overview%20report.pdf, para 39. Retrieved 1 June 2015.

that these limitations were likely to be material for at least the medium term and possibly longer. The limitations reflected those discussed in the literature review (Supplementary Report I), but the (lack of) utility for many disciplines or types of research was emphasised (see also Chapter 4). For example, it was pointed out that citation may not be a useful proxy for quality in more applied research in disciplines like engineering, or for whole fields of study:

> "What would [bibliometrics'] use be for poetry, drama, and how would they be useful where the key output is the book, or where academics for a particular subject published through a range of different output types?"

Concerns about the impact of extensive use of citation data on under-represented groups and early-career researchers were also raised repeatedly, and the potential negative behavioural consequences if the focus of assessment was on a small number of specific metrics was mentioned as a concern.

### 9.1.3 Further evidence on the assessment of outputs

The literature review that we commissioned (Supplementary Report I) summarises the scholarly literature on the use of bibliometric indicators in contexts including national research assessments systems. The general conclusions from the literature can be summarised as follows and are also discussed in Section 3.

Firstly, the disciplinary coverage of citation databases and the diversity of publication practices mean that bibliometric indicators cannot be considered to be equally applicable across all disciplines. Secondly, there are significant limitations of bibliometric indicators that have implications for their use in national research assessment systems. Thirdly, the choice of indicators may have behavioural consequences on institutions or researchers, at least some of which are not aligned with policy objectives. Fourthly, while there are correlations between metrics and peer review-based assessments, they vary by indicator, by field and by level of aggregation (see Chapter 5). Some fields show strong correlations, but many fields have moderate to weak correlations between metrics and peer ratings. In particular, the evidence suggests that the power of bibliometric indicators to predict the outcomes of peer review (and *vice versa*) is rather limited. Fifthly, the existence of strong correlations is a necessary but not a sufficient condition to replace peer review by bibliometric indicators, since the role of national research assessments does not limit itself to the distribution of research funds. The literature review (in Section 3) also examined the potential of new 'alternative metrics' for the assessment of outputs and concluded that they did not appear to add any additional information for the assessment of outputs, and can also be susceptible to biases, gaming and difficulties of interpretation.

The biases of bibliometric indicators and the risk of promoting undesirable behaviours featured prominently in the evidence that we received both in response to our call for written evidence, and in contributions at the workshops we held, as discussed elsewhere in this report.

We considered in detail the issue of the consistency of peer review and quantitative indicators as applied to research outputs, and also commissioned analysis from HEFCE of the REF2014 outcomes (see Supplementary Report II). Evidence from the scholarly literature on this point (Supplementary Report I, Section 2.2) suggests that peer review judgements and quantitative indicators correlate, but only weakly. A similar conclusion emerges from the bibliometrics pilot that HEFCE conducted in 2009, which tested a number of options for the use of bibliometric indicators.

Based on her analysis of psychology and physics departments, Dorothy Bishop argued at our Sussex workshop in favour of using the departmental h-index as an alternative to peer review evaluation for the allocation of research funding.[16] This work seems to demonstrate a high correlation between the department h-index and UK research funding allocations, at least for the discipline of psychology. More recently, the utility of the departmental h-index as a predictor of the outcomes of REF2014 has been tested for a range of disciplines.[17] This work concluded that these h-indices do indeed correlate with REF outcomes, but the relationship is not strong enough to justify the use of the departmental h-index as a replacement for peer review.

All the studies examining the relationship between bibliometric indicators and the outcomes of peer review in the RAE and REF have been carried out at the level of the scores given to whole submissions to the exercise, grouping together outputs from, typically, a university department. In our more detailed analysis (see Supplementary Report II), we asked HEFCE to examine the relationship between a suite of bibliometric and other indicators and peer review scoring at the level of individual outputs.

The HEFCE analysis considered the coverage, correlation and predictive qualities of 15 metrics to REF2014 output scores across all units of assessment. This analysis used anonymised REF scores at the output-by-author level and linked these to a selection of bibliometric and altmetric indicators. This approach differs from other analyses, such as that recently undertaken by Elsevier, which tend to compare REF scores with metrics at more aggregated levels.[18] In our view, HEFCE's analysis is superior to Elsevier's, as looking very closely at output-level scores and metrics allows for a more robust judgement to be made about any correlative link between the REF peer review process and various metrics at the level of the individual research contribution.

Coverage of the outputs by the metrics used was generally poor for units of assessment in Main Panels C and D, while those UOAs in Main Panels A and B had over 90% coverage. This meant that the findings from the analysis were more applicable to Main Panels A and B, however UOAs in the other panel groups were included in the analysis and significant findings reported.

The initial analysis considered metrics as possible predictive indicators of outputs achieving a 4-star score. Generally, this found that correlation between the metric indicator and

---

[16]Bishop discusses this further in a blog post: http://deevybee.blogspot.co.uk/2013/01/an-alternative-to-ref2014.html

[17]For predictions see Mryglod et al. (2014). *Scientometrics,* 102: 2165–2180. http://arxiv.org/abs/1411.1996. Retrieved 9 March 2015; also http://arxiv.org/pdf/1501.07857v1.pdf. Retrieved 9 March 2015.

[18]Details of the Elsevier analysis can be found here: https://www.timeshighereducation.co.uk/can-the-research-excellence-framework-ref-run-on-metrics

those achieving 4-star was low (less than 0.5), indicating that individual metrics do not provide a like-for-like replacement for REF peer review. However, this varied by UOA and the analysis indicated that the following UOAs had relatively good correlation with some of the associated metrics: clinical medicine; biological sciences; chemistry; physics; economics and econometrics. For all metrics, except mentions on Twitter, correlations were much weaker for articles published more recently.

The relative relationships between the metrics, achieving 4-star in REF and additional characteristics were considered using regression models. The additional characteristics considered were year of publication, unit of assessment or main panel, early-career researcher status and sex of author. The modelling helped identify those metrics most influential in explaining the variation in achieving the 4-star threshold. This identified Scopus full text clicks, number of authors, number of times cited on Google Scholar, SJR, source normalised impact per paper, tweets and Science Direct downloads as influential in predicting REF score.

The addition of output and author characteristics showed that there was a significant year-of-publication effect. Of those with low metrics scores, more recent publications were more likely to get a 4-star rating; this could be because the metrics have not had time to reach their final magnitude or have not yet been calculated. Papers submitted by early-career researchers in Main Panel C were significantly less likely to achieve a 4-star rating than those by non-early-career researchers with the same metrics ratings. Female authors in Main Panel B were significantly less likely to achieve a 4-star rating than male authors with the same metrics ratings.

## 9.2 QUANTITATIVE DATA AND THE ASSESSMENT OF IMPACT

### 9.2.1 Guidance and process for impact in REF2014

The assessment of the economic and societal impact of research was a new element added to the UK's national research assessment for the first time in REF2014, and accounted for 20% of the overall quality profile. Following considerable debate, and an extensive pilot exercise carried out in 2010,[19] the impact element of REF2014 consisted of two components:[20]

- Assessment of information on how impact is supported (the 'impact template');
- Assessment of case studies describing impact.

For the purposes of the REF, a broad definition of impact was adopted, and panels made their assessments on the basis of two criteria: reach and significance. As with the assessment of outputs, the sub-panels themselves provided a discipline-specific interpretation

---

[19]Details of HEFCE's REF pilot impact exercise are available at: www.ref.ac.uk/pubs/refimpact-pilotexercisefindingsoftheexpertpanels/. Retrieved 1 June 2015.

[20]Decisions relating to assessing research impact are available at: www.ref.ac.uk/pubs/2011-01/. Retrieved 1 June 2015.

of both the definition and assessment criteria. The impact assessment was made by a process of expert review, with users of research from outside of academia playing an important role. In contrast with the assessment of outputs, no systematic gathering or use of quantitative data on impact was carried out to support the assessment.

### 9.2.2 Assessment of impact in REF2014

There were 6,975 case studies and 1,911 impact templates submitted for assessment in REF2014. Overall, the sub-panels identified a significant proportion of research impact to be 4-star (44%) or 3-star (40%), although there was variation in the quality assessment across submissions. In their overview reports, main panels and sub-panel reflected positively, on the scale, breadth and quality of impact assessed, and on the process of the assessment.

Because of its novelty, HEFCE and the other UK HE Funding Bodies commissioned RAND Europe to undertake detailed evaluations of the impact element.[21] These examined both the costs and benefits to HEIs of preparing for the impact element and the experiences of panel members of the assessment. The impact element also featured significantly in the feedback that HEIs provided directly to HEFCE[22] and was also discussed by Technopolis in their report on the administrative burden of the REF.[23] Synthesising these sources of evidence we conclude as follows. For HEIs, preparing for the impact element brought benefits in terms of better understanding their impact, and providing strategic insight into the maximal delivery of impact from research. There were, however, concerns raised about the burden of preparing the submission, and the cost of this part of the exercise alone is estimated to be £55 million across the whole sector.[24] As with the REF more broadly it was suggested by some that increased use of quantitative indicators or metrics could reduce this burden. The feedback from panel members on the process of assessment is also positive, although a number of potential points for improvement for future assessments were noted.[25]

A common theme in both the experience of HEIs in preparing submissions to the impact element, and the experience of panel members in the assessment, were the challenges of evidencing impact. These concerns were related to specific types of impact, or concerned with the timescales over which impact occurred. For panel members, in particular, there were challenges in making assessments of corroborating evidence, especially where this was qualitative in nature.

---

[21]Manville, C., Guthrie, S., Henham, M., Garrod, B., Sousa, S., Kirtley, A., Castle-Clark, S. and Ling, T. (2015). Assessing impact submissions for REF 2014. An evaluation. Cambridge: RAND Europe.

[22]www.hefce.ac.uk/rsrch/REFreview/feedback/

[23]Technopolis, *REF Accountability Review: Costs, benefits and burden.* (Available at: http://www.tech nopolis-group.com/wp-content/uploads/2015/11/REF_costs_review_July_2015.pdf). (2015).

[24]Manville, C., Guthrie, S., Henham, M., Garrod, B., Sousa, S., Kirtley, A., Castle-Clark, S. and Ling, T. (2015). Assessing impact submissions for REF 2014. An evaluation. Cambridge: RAND Europe.

[25]Manville, C., Guthrie, S., Henham, M., Garrod, B., Sousa, S., Kirtley, A., Castle-Clark, S. and Ling, T. (2015). Assessing impact submissions for REF 2014. An evaluation. Cambridge: RAND Europe.

### 9.2.3 Further evidence on the assessment of impact

Compared to bibliometrics, where their use for the analysis of the academic impact of journal articles has a long history, the use of quantitative data for the assessment of broader impact is a newer phenomenon (see Chapter 3). A number of metrics have been proposed for the assessment of impact, including those related to patents (and their citations) and other documentation relating to intellectual property rights, social media dissemination and discussion, or weblinks and traffic. All of these indicators are in an early stage of development, and have not been extensively analysed or validated (see discussion in the literature review (Supplementary Report I), section 3). It is also the case that most, if not all, of the quantitative indicators proposed are highly specific to particular types of research impact. For example, while patent numbers or citations may be relevant for some impacts that arise from research commercialisation, they are of no value in measuring policy impact.

In the Australian ERA, some quantitative measures of broader impact are assessed, namely patents, plant breeders' rights, registered designs and research commercialisation income. We heard evidence that there are concerns with this approach, related to the implied narrow definition of societal impact and the potential that focusing on a small number of metrics might significantly skew behaviour.[26]

Despite the challenges, in response to our call for evidence some expressed a hope that more quantitative data might help with the assessment of impact. It was also suggested that analysis for the case studies submitted to REF2014:

> "might present a picture of whether there are in fact a set of metrics which could be applied to impact; nevertheless whether these could be collected in a way which is any less time consuming than preparing a case study it is clearly too early to say."
>
> University of Hertfordshire response

As noted in Chapter 3, a recent study undertaken by King's College London and Digital Science indicates that this is not currently feasible. However, more work could be done to identify quantitative data or indicators that could be used as supporting evidence for specific types of impact.

## 9.3 QUANTITATIVE DATA AND THE ASSESSMENT OF RESEARCH ENVIRONMENT

### 9.3.1 Guidance and process for environment in REF2014

The third element of REF2014 is the assessment of the research environment, which accounts for 15% of the overall assessment. This element is based on a combination of

---

[26]Donovan, C. (2011). State of the Art in Assessing Research Impact: Introduction to a special issue. *Research Evaluation*, 3: 175–179; Presentation to the review steering group available at www.hefce.ac.uk/media/hefce/content/What,we,do/Research/How,we,fund,research/Metrics/Donovan%20HEFCE%2027%20May%202014.pdf

narrative and quantitative information, the former supplied by the HEIs and the latter extracted from data collected by HESA.[27] Three items of quantitative data were collected for all UOAs:

- Research doctoral degrees awarded;
- Research income;
- Research income in-kind.

These measures were linked to submitted units by HEIs, and reflected the activity of the whole unit, not just those staff who were entered into the REF.

Sub-panels assessed the environment element by a process of expert review, against the criteria of vitality and sustainability, with a discipline-specific interpretation of these criteria being provided by the sub-panels themselves.

### 9.3.2 Assessment of environment in REF2014 in practice

Based on the panel overview reports, and on the feedback collected from panel members by HEFCE, we conclude that, in terms of the provision of quantitative data, environment was the least successful element of REF2014. The element is an improvement on the equivalent component of the RAE, with panel members being positive about the more structured approach, and HEIs welcoming the use of data that were already collected. However, panel members expressed concerns that the narrative elements were hard to assess, with difficulties in separating quality in research environment from quality in writing about it. There were also issues with the quantitative data, which panels found difficult to interpret without knowing the overall scale of the unit under assessment, or how the data related to the staff selected for submission. For example, Main Panel C commented in their overview report that:

> "The sub-panels found that these data could not be used in any sort of mechanistic fashion, since they [...] relate to all the staff in a given unit, rather than relating only to those staff submitted."[28]

Similar concerns were raised by other sub-panels.

In our discussions with REF panel members it was often suggested that the assessment of research environment would benefit from extended use of appropriate, and appropriately contextualised, quantitative data. Indeed this is the only aspect of the REF where we encountered general enthusiasm for a strongly quantitative approach. In contrast, this area of the REF received little mention in our call for evidence, and was not discussed at the workshops we convened.

---

[27] www.ref.ac.uk/subguide/ref4environmentdata/

[28] REF2014: Overview report by Main Panel C and Sub-panels 16 to 26 www.ref.ac.uk/media/ref/content/expanel/member/Main%20Panel%20C%20overview%20report.pdf, para 116.

## 9.4 COST OF METRICS-BASED RESEARCH ASSESSMENT

As discussed earlier, a significant driver for those in favour of increased use of metrics was the potential to reduce the cost and burden of the national research assessment. This assertion is based on an assumption that a metrics-based exercise would indeed cost less. The collection of quantitative data and its processing to produce metrics and indicators is not itself cost free, so it is important to accompany any consideration of the increased use of quantitative data with a robust estimate of the associated costs.

If quantitative data are already collected, readily available and do not require significant further validation or checking then the cost of their use will be low. However, experience from REF2014 suggests this is not always the case, even with relatively straightforward data sources. For example, HEIs report that considerable effort was required to validate, and sometimes correct both citation data and HESA statistics used in REF2014. We also note the commentary in the review of the costs of the REF[29] that the use of a citation data in REF2014 encouraged HEIs to use this information in their preparations for the exercise, which resulted in additional costs locally. Furthermore, as set out in Chapter 3, considerable challenges remain due to the nature of the data infrastructure.

It is also important to remember that some costs of assessment are related to the structure, rather than the mechanism of assessment. For example, significant costs to HEIs are associated with selecting staff or outputs to be submitted for assessment.[30] If these features remain, the reduction in cost that resulted in using bibliometrics to assess outputs might be rather modest.

## 9.5 CONCLUSIONS

### 9.5.1 Research outputs in the REF

On the basis of the evidence we have considered, we conclude that it is not currently feasible to assess the quality of research outputs using quantitative indicators alone.

For published scholarly work, there are some robust data sources that can be used to derive 'indicators', though caution needs to be exercised when considering all disciplines via existing bibliographic databases. Nevertheless, citations of a published output – in some form or another – remain a useful indicator of knowledge production, use and re-use – among the academic community at the very least. While there has been some improvement in the disciplinary coverage of citation databases (e.g. WoS; Scopus) since HEFCE's previous work on this issue,[31] at this time the coverage of many

---

[29]Technopolis, *REF Accountability Review: Costs, benefits and burden.* (Available at: http://www.tech nopolis-group.com/wp-content/uploads/2015/11/REF_costs_review_July_2015.pdf). (2015).

[30]Ibid.

[31]www.ref.ac.uk/about/background/bibliometrics/

arts and humanities fields remains limited. Additionally, where the published research output is not a peer-reviewed journal article, the ability to systematically capture bibliographic data on the outputs and any data on use and re-use among the academic or other community is more limited – though there are indications that some of the larger information providers are exploring this space.

For these reasons of coverage and for limitations in the conclusions that can be made alone via citation and use and re-use metrics, those nations that use quantitative indicators in their national research assessments generally adopt a dual approach and use peer review for disciplines outside of the natural sciences; this is the case with the Australian and Italian systems, discussed in Chapter 2.

Other issues with the use of quantitative indicators to assess research outputs include concerns over gender bias in citation practices and resultant effects on equality and diversity. Even if these technical problems of coverage and bias can be overcome, we are not convinced that the quantitative indicators currently available, even including new 'alternative metrics', could be used, alone, as a robust indicator of quality across all disciplines. No set of numbers, however broad, is likely to be able to capture the multifaceted and nuanced judgements on the quality of research outputs that the REF process currently provides.

Notwithstanding these challenges, we also conclude that more quantitative data – particularly around published outputs (both scholarly and other) – do continue to have a place in complementing expert/peer review judgements of research quality, excellence and impact. This approach has been used relatively successfully in REF2014, and we recommend that it be continued and enhanced in future exercises.

### 9.5.2 Research impact in the REF

On the basis of the evidence considered, we have concluded that it is not feasible to assess the quality of research impact using quantitative indicators alone.

The impact case studies are necessarily narrative and describe a range of self-selected impacts associated with HEI submissions. Research impact in the REF is broadly defined and we believe this is the right approach. On the other hand, quantitative data and indicators are highly specific to the types of impact concerned. We are keen that impact does not become narrow and specifically defined. For an exercise such as the REF where HEIs are effectively competing for funds, narrowly defining impact is likely to constrain thinking around which impact case studies should be submitted, and certain types of research are therefore likely to gain greater currency than others. Moreover, as described in early chapters, we should avoid creating perverse incentives within the research ecosystem. It is also the case that quantitative data about impact will need to be seen in context, and providing that context is likely to continue to require a narrative element.

Nevertheless, we conclude that there is considerable potential to enhance and streamline the use of quantitative data as supporting evidence within a narrative case-study-based approach to impact assessment; more quantitative data can help to illustrate magnitude and specifics and help bring impacts to life. We recommend that the UK HE Funding Bodies build on the analysis of the impact case studies from REF2014 to develop a set of guidelines on the use of quantitative evidence of impact. While not being prescriptive, these guidelines should provide suggested data to evidence specific types of impact and should also include standards for the collection of metadata to ensure the characteristics of the research being described by the submitting HEIs are captured systematically.

### 9.5.3 Research environment in the REF

We advocate the need and value of structured and consistent 'input' data for each submission to the REF. We also conclude that there is scope for enhancing the use of quantitative data for the assessment of the research environment, but that these data need to be provided with sufficient context to enable their interpretation. As a minimum this needs to include information on the total size of the unit to which the data refers, and in some cases the collection of data specifically relating to staff submitted to the exercise may be preferable, albeit more costly.

We also emphasise the enormous potential value of building the research information infrastructure to support REF in the future. If HEIs were to establish a platform of research identifiers for all their researchers (and researchers could be encouraged to link their career path and research works to these identifiers through various systems) then it would be easier to draw data together and reduce the burden on researchers in future REF exercises when delivering their submissions. Further, unique identifiers for research inputs, outputs and other entities such as organisations, and the ability to semantically link these to researchers, would enable more robust assessment and analysis.

# TEN

## RESPONSIBLE METRICS

## CHAPTER CONTENTS

"We need new metrics... To move forward, we need to challenge the current norms; define merit much more broadly; measure qualities we value in people but which are hard to measure... This way we can bequeath new models of success and leadership to the next generation to help fix the problems we have inherited from the past."

Jenny Martin[1]

Over the past five years, there has been an increasingly sophisticated debate in the UK, across Europe and internationally about the governance of research and innovation – and the need for better evidence and intelligence to underpin policies in this area. The concept of 'responsible research and innovation' (RRI) has gained currency as a framework for research governance within the European Commission, UK Research Councils,[2] and research funders in the Netherlands, Germany, the US and Japan. At its simplest, RRI can be defined as "taking care of the future through collective stewardship of science and innovation in the present". It brings to research policy a focus on questions

---

[1]Martin, J. (2015). Merit and demerit. Blogpost, 6 June 2015. https://cubistcrystal.wordpress. com/2015/01/12/imagine-theres-new-metrics-its-easy-if-you-try/. Retrieved 20 June 2015.

[2]Such as EPSRC; see https://www.epsrc.ac.uk/research/framework/. Retrieved 1 June 2015.

of anticipation, reflexivity, deliberation, inclusiveness and responsiveness.[3] But we also need robust evidence to underpin this shift and to validate expert opinion.

Drawing on discussions over RRI, we propose the notion of **responsible metrics** as a way of framing appropriate uses of quantitative indicators in the governance, management and assessment of research. The notion of responsible metrics distils the essence of other important contributions to these debates, including the Leiden Manifesto and DORA. Responsible metrics can be understood in terms of a number of dimensions:

- **Robustness**: basing metrics on the best possible data in terms of accuracy and scope;
- **Humility**: recognising that quantitative evaluation should support – but not supplant – qualitative, expert assessment;
- **Transparency**: keeping data collection and analytical processes open and transparent, so that those being evaluated can test and verify the results;
- **Diversity**: accounting for variation by field, and using a range of indicators to reflect and support a plurality of research and researcher career paths across the system;
- **Reflexivity**: recognising and anticipating the systemic and potential effects of indicators, and updating them in response.

As stated in the Leiden Manifesto,[4] "research metrics can provide crucial information that would be difficult to gather or understand by means of individual expertise. But this quantitative information must not be allowed to morph from an instrument into the goal."

Everyone can agree that one of the primary aims of research policy at all levels should be to recognise, promote and nurture 'excellence'. The promise of metrics is that they can make the identification of research excellence more straightforward and more objective – and cheaper and easier to administer. When one designs a metric for research excellence, one also implicitly constructs a definition of excellence, and locks that definition in place. But excellence in research is multidimensional and, crucially, it changes over time. Within this multidimensionality, there are elements that relate to the advancement of knowledge, and elements that relate to benefits beyond the academy ('impact'). The relationship between these is complex. Research that delivers impact doesn't necessarily always advance fundamental knowledge, but evidence from REF2014 does suggest that, by-and-large, they are inextricably intertwined.

Because of this, we need to think very clearly about what we are assessing, and select methods and metrics appropriate to our needs. As new research fields develop, definitions of what constitutes excellent research evolve. Interdisciplinary and multidisciplinary

---

[3]Stilgoe, J., Owen, R. and Macnaghten, P. (2013). Developing a framework for responsible innovation. *Research Policy*, 42: 1568–1580; Valdivia, W. and Guston, D. (2015). *Responsible Innovation: A Primer for Policymakers*, Centre for Technology Innovation, Brookings Institution, May 2015. www.brookings.edu/research/papers/2015/05/05-responsible-innovation-valdivia-guston. Retrieved 1 June 2015.

[4]www.leidenmanifesto.org

research creates new kinds of excellence that don't necessarily correspond to the definitions appropriate for the component disciplines from which new fields emerge.

Scientometric data are fairly well developed, and can be used to indicate knowledge progression and use and re-use among academic audiences (particularly in the sciences/biosciences but increasingly across different disciplines). However the danger of thoughtless over-reliance on metrics to evaluate research quality is that they can lock in place backward-looking definitions of what constitutes research excellence. A focus on responsible metrics is designed to avoid these pitfalls and ensure that quantitative indicators are used in appropriate, ethical ways.

## 10.1 HEADLINE FINDINGS

- **There are powerful currents whipping up the metric tide.** These include: growing pressures for audit and evaluation of public spending on higher education and research; demands by policymakers for more strategic intelligence on research quality and impact; the need for institutions to manage and develop their strategies for research; competition within and between institutions for prestige, students, staff and resources; and increases in the availability of real-time 'big data' on research uptake. Consequently the number and range of tools to identify, analyse and assess research information is increasing. This is a fast moving area, but many approaches are still in the early stages of development and will take time to mature. There is a danger in rushing to over-interpret the available data.

- **Across the research community, the description, production and consumption of metrics remains contested and open to misunderstandings.** In a positive sense, wider use of quantitative indicators, and the emergence of alternative metrics for societal impact, form part of the transition to a more open, accountable and outward-facing research system. But this has been accompanied by a backlash against the inappropriate weight being placed on particular indicators – such as JIFs – within the research system, as reflected by DORA, which now has over 570 organisational and 12,300 individual signatories.[5] Responses to this review reflect this division of opinion. The majority of those who submitted evidence, or engaged with the review in other ways, are sceptical about any moves to increase the role of metrics in research management. However, a significant minority are enthusiastic about metrics, particularly if appropriate care is exercised in their design and application, and data infrastructure can be improved.

- **There is significant interest in online platforms and tools that can enhance access to and visibility of research** including Twitter, Facebook, blogs and sector-specific sites like Academia.edu, Mendeley, and ResearchGate. Evidence on whether and how these may relate to research quality is very limited. But over time, they might be

---

[5] www.ascb.org/dora. As of July 2015, only three UK universities are DORA signatories: the Universities of Manchester, Sussex and UCL.

developed to provide indicators of research progression and impact, or act as early pointers towards indicators more closely correlated with quality, such as citations.

- **Peer review, despite its flaws and limitations, continues to command widespread support across disciplines.** Metrics should support, not supplant, expert judgement. Peer review is not perfect, but it is the least worst form of academic governance we have, and should continue to be the primary basis for assessing research papers, proposals and individuals, and for national assessments like the REF. However, carefully selected and applied quantitative indicators can be a useful complement to other forms of decision-making.

- **One size is unlikely to fit all: a mature research system needs a variable geometry of expert judgement, quantitative and qualitative measures.** Research assessment needs to be undertaken with due regard for research diversity: the nature of research varies, as does its domain (by discipline and context) and the form of its outputs – from academic papers in journals, through single and jointly authored books, to performances and practices. We need greater clarity as to which indicators are most useful – or not – for specific disciplines and contexts, and why. The assessment of academic quality is highly context-specific, and it is sensible to think in terms of research *qualities,* rather than striving for a single definition or measure of quality.

- **Indicators can only meet their potential if they are underpinned by an open, transparent and coherent data infrastructure.** How underlying data are collected and processed – and the extent to which they remain open to interrogation – is crucial. If we want agreed, standardised indicators, we need to develop and promote: unique, unambiguous, persistent, verified, open, global identifiers; agreed standard data formats; and agreed standard data semantics. Without this holy trinity of identifiers, standards and semantics, we risk developing metrics that are not robust, trustworthy or properly understood.

- **Common data standards are needed to support interoperability.** The reliable identification and effective authentication of information is a prerequisite for producing and maintaining trustworthy metrics. The different systems operated by HEIs, funders and publishers need to interoperate and to import and exchange data more efficiently and effectively; also definitions of research-related concepts need to be harmonised across the systems. An obvious example is the overlap between HEI institutional uses of CRISs for research management and RCUK's requirement that researchers use Researchfish for reporting, which is creating a need for the same information to be entered twice, into different systems.

- **There are growing opportunities for sharing data across platforms.** The drive for transparency in all aspects of research and associated activities, including metrics, has increased the pressures for data-sharing and interoperability. Fundamental information about funding inputs remains fragmented, despite the improvements brought by RCUK's Gateway to Research, and initiatives such as Europe PubMed grant lookup, and even commercial efforts such as UberResearch's Dimensions system. It is not possible to easily generate a UK view of public and charitable funding in many areas. As described in Chapter 2, the development and uptake of unique identifiers associated with individuals and their research works (e.g. ORCID and DOIs) will present the research community with an opportunity to connect existing and future information about research as never before, improving the robustness of metrics, and reducing administrative burden.

- **Inappropriate indicators create perverse incentives**. Across the community, there is legitimate concern that some of the quantitative indicators already being used to support decisions around research excellence and quality can be gamed and can lead to unintended consequences. The worst example of this is the widespread use of JIFs, where group (journal-level) metrics are ascribed to its non-homogenous constituents (articles) as a proxy for quality. There is also a very real possibility of existing or emergent indicators being gamed (for example through 'citation clubs', salami-slicing of papers to increase citation counts, and battles over author positioning). These consequences need to be identified, acknowledged and addressed.

- **There is a need for greater transparency in the construction and use of indicators**. Actors within research assessment and management systems should behave responsibly, considering and pre-empting negative consequences wherever possible, for instance in relation to considerations of researcher equality and diversity, and the use of league tables in institutional management. The development of more transparent processes and open data systems should help to improve the situation and reduce the potential for abusive practices.

- **At present, further use of quantitative indicators in research assessment and management cannot be relied on to reduce costs or administrative burden**. Unless existing processes (such as peer review) are reduced when additional metrics are added, there will inevitably be an overall increase in burden. However, as the underlying data infrastructure is improved and metrics become more robust and trusted by the community, it is likely that the additional burden of collecting and assessing metrics could be outweighed by the reduction of peer review effort in some areas – and indeed by other uses for the data.

- **Our correlation analysis of the REF2014 results at output-by-author level (Supplementary Report II) has shown that individual metrics give significantly different outcomes from the REF peer review process, and therefore cannot provide a like-for-like replacement for REF peer review**. Publication year was a significant factor in the calculation of correlation with REF scores, with all but two metrics showing significant decreases in correlation for more recent outputs. There is large variation in the coverage of metrics across the REF submission, with particular issues with coverage in units of assessment (UOAs) in REF Main Panel D (mainly arts and humanities). There is also evidence to suggest statistically significant differences in the correlation with REF scores for early-career researchers and women in a small number of UOAs.

- **Within the REF, it is not currently feasible to assess the quality of UOAs using quantitative indicators alone**. In REF2014, while some indicators (citation counts, and supporting text to highlight significance or quality in other ways) were supplied to some panels to help inform their judgements, caution needs to be exercised when considering all disciplines with existing bibliographic databases. Even if technical problems of coverage and bias can be overcome, no set of numbers, however broad, is likely to be able to capture the multifaceted and nuanced judgements on the quality of research outputs that the REF process currently provides.

- **Similarly, for the impact component of the REF, it is not currently feasible to use quantitative indicators in place of narrative impact case studies, or the impact template.** There is a danger that the concept of impact might narrow and become too specifically defined by the ready availability of indicators for some types of impact and not for others. For an exercise like the REF, where HEIs are effectively competing for funds, defining impact by indicators is likely to constrain thinking around which impact stories have greatest currency and should be submitted, potentially limiting the overall diversity of the UK's research base.

- **For the environment component of the REF, there is scope to enhance the use of quantitative indicators in the next assessment cycle,** provided they are used with sufficient context to enable their interpretation.

- **There is a need for more research on research.** The study of research systems – sometimes called the 'science of science policy' – is poorly funded in the UK. The evidence base to address the questions that we have been exploring throughout this review is very limited; however the questions being asked of funders and HEIs – *'What should we fund?' 'How best should we fund?' 'Who should we hire/promote/invest in?'* – are far from new. BIS has commissioned work in this area,[6] mainly focused on innovation and economic impact, and the MRC's 'research impact' initiative has committed £1 million to seven studies now under way to better understand the link between publicly funded research and economic/societal impact.[7] But more funding is needed as part of a coordinated UK effort to improve the evidence base in this area. Connected to this, there is potential for the scientometrics community to more actively communicate how quantitative indicators are used.

## THREE SCENARIOS FOR THE NEXT REF

For the next REF cycle (currently expected to conclude in 2020), the review considered three ways in which greater use of quantitative data could enable national assessments on a different basis to REF2014 (these are also illustrated in Figure 6):

- **Option A: incremental addition of quantitative data.** This would involve retaining the basic structural framework and peer-review-based approach of REF2014, with the

[6]See: BIS (2014). *BIS research strategy 2014/15.* https://www.gov.uk/government/uploads/system/uploads/attachment_data/file/357021/BIS_14_1065_BIS_Research_Strategy_2014-2015.pdf

[7]www.mrc.ac.uk/funding/how-we-fund-research/highlight-notices/economic-impact-[] highlight-notice/. Retrieved 1 June 2015.

additional use of quantitative data to inform peer review judgements. We analysed the potential for this option in Chapter 9, and recommend that it be explored. Over time, the incremental addition of more quantitative information to the assessment is likely to enrich the exercise; in the longer term, as the quality and quantity of reliable quantitative data increase, it leaves open more radical options such as Option C below.

- **Option B: metrics only.** Here the present system would be replaced by one based wholly on a set of quantitative metrics. There could be flexibility on how these measures were combined and weighted to deliver an overall 'score', so that the present tripartite structure of the REF would no longer be needed. This type of approach is in use in Australia and Italy, for example, although in both cases it is not linked directly to funding allocations and is used only for the natural sciences, with other disciplines still assessed by peer review. Our assessment of the evidence leads us to conclude that this approach is not sufficiently robust, defensible or desirable. Many sources of quantitative data have issues of coverage and bias, and there are significant behavioural implications that would result from a focus on a set of quantitative indicators – particularly where there is a link to research funding. There are also limits to the availability of quantitative indicators for the assessment of the broader impacts of research, which were captured for the first time in REF2014. Losing the impact element of the REF would be a retrograde step that should be avoided.

- **Option C: interim or sampled evaluations.** An alternative might be to conduct interim assessments using quantitative data more often (perhaps annually) with full peer-review-based assessments occurring less frequently (perhaps every ten years). A similar idea would be to assess a representative sample of research outputs, without the wide coverage achieved by the REF. Both options would have the advantage of reducing costs and administrative burden. The aim here would be to identify changes in research performance, rather than measuring absolute performance levels, which would be reserved for the full peer-review-based exercises. However, the same concerns over coverage and bias would apply as in Option B, and it is questionable whether this approach would command sufficient confidence to support adjustments in funding. Given the limited ability at this stage of quantitative indicators to predict peer review outcomes (cf. Supplementary Reports I and II), it is possible that any changes reflected in interim or sampled assessments would be related to the differences in assessment approach rather than underlying research quality. As a result, we cannot recommend this approach.

## 10.2 RECOMMENDATIONS

This review has identified a number of specific recommendations for further work and action on the part of key actors in the UK research system. These draw on the evidence we have gathered, and should be seen as part of broader attempts to strengthen research governance, management and assessment which have been gathering momentum, and

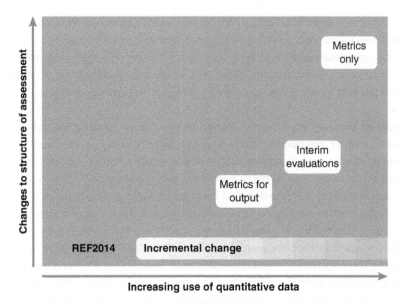

**Figure 6**   Options for the greater use of quantitative data in national assessments

where the UK is well positioned to play a leading role internationally. We have grouped the recommendations under a number of thematic headings, as follows:

* Supporting the effective leadership, governance and management of research cultures;
* Improving the data infrastructure that supports research information management;
* Increasing the usefulness of existing data and information sources;
* Using metrics in the next REF;
* Coordinating activity and building evidence.

At the end of each recommendation, we list the people, organisations and roles that we see as being best placed to act upon it. In all cases, we hope that these recommendations can be adopted and taken forward in the spirit of positive and constructive engagement that has underpinned this review.

### 10.2.1  Supporting the effective leadership, governance and management of research cultures

1 **The research community should develop a more sophisticated and nuanced approach to the contribution and limitations of quantitative indicators.** Greater care with language and terminology is needed. The term 'metrics' is often unhelpful; the preferred term 'indicators' reflects a recognition that data may lack specific relevance, even if they are useful overall. *(HEIs, funders, managers, researchers)*
2 **At an institutional level, HEI leaders should develop a clear statement of principles on their approach to research management and assessment, including**

**the role of quantitative indicators.** On the basis of these principles, they should carefully select quantitative indicators that are appropriate to their institutional context. Where institutions are making use of league tables and ranking measures, they should explain why they are using these as a means to achieve particular ends. Where possible, alternative indicators that support equality and diversity should be identified and included. Clear communication of the rationale for selecting particular indicators, and how they will be used as a management tool, is paramount. As part of this process, HEIs should consider signing up to DORA, or drawing on its principles and tailoring them to their institutional contexts. *(Heads of institutions, heads of research, HEI governors)*

3 **Research managers and administrators should champion these principles and the use of responsible metrics within their institutions.** They should pay due attention to the equality and diversity implications of research assessment choices; engage with external experts such as those at the Equality Challenge Unit; help to facilitate a more open and transparent data infrastructure; advocate the use of unique identifiers such as ORCID iDs; work with funders and publishers on data interoperability; explore indicators for aspects of research that they wish to assess rather than using existing indicators because they are readily available; advise senior leaders on metrics that are meaningful for their institutional or departmental context; and exchange best practice through sector bodies such as ARMA. *(Managers, research administrators, ARMA)*

4 **HR managers and recruitment or promotion panels in HEIs should be explicit about the criteria used for academic appointment and promotion decisions.** These criteria should be founded in expert judgement and may reflect both the academic quality of outputs and wider contributions to policy, industry or society. Judgements may sometimes usefully be guided by metrics, if they are relevant to the criteria in question and used responsibly; article-level citation metrics, for instance, might be useful indicators of academic impact, as long as they are interpreted in the light of disciplinary norms and with due regard to their limitations. Journal-level metrics, such as the JIF, should not be used. *(HR managers, recruitment and promotion panels, UUK)*

5 **Individual researchers should be mindful of the limitations of particular indicators** in the way they present their own CVs and evaluate the work of colleagues. When standard indicators are inadequate, individual researchers should look for a range of data sources to document and support claims about the impact of their work. *(All researchers)*

6 **Like HEIs, research funders should develop their own context-specific principles for the use of quantitative indicators in research assessment and management** and ensure that these are well communicated, and easy to locate and understand. They should pursue approaches to data collection that are transparent, accessible, and allow for greater interoperability across a diversity of platforms. *(UK HE Funding Bodies, Research Councils, other research funders)*

7 **Data providers, analysts and producers of university rankings and league tables should strive for greater transparency and interoperability between different measurement systems.** Some, such as Times Higher Education, have

taken commendable steps to be more open about their choice of indicators and the weightings given to these, but other rankings remain opaque and 'black-boxed'. *(Data providers, analysts and producers of university rankings and league tables)*

8 **Publishers should reduce emphasis on journal impact factors as a promotional tool, and only use them in the context of a variety of journal-based metrics that provide a richer view of performance.** As suggested by DORA, this broader indicator set could include 5-year impact factor, EigenFactor, SCImago, editorial and publication times. Publishers, with the aid of the Committee on Publication Ethics (COPE), should encourage responsible authorship practices and the provision of more detailed information about the specific contributions of each author. Publishers should also make available a range of article-level metrics to encourage a shift toward assessment based on the academic quality of an article rather than JIFs. *(Publishers)*

## 10.2.2 Improving the data infrastructure that supports research information management

9 **There is a need for greater transparency and openness in research data infra-structure. A set of principles should be developed for technologies, practices and cultures that can support open, trustworthy research information management.** These principles should be adopted by funders, data providers, administrators and researchers as a foundation for further work. *(UK HE Funding Bodies, RCUK, Jisc, data providers, managers, administrators)*

10 **The UK research system should take full advantage of ORCID as its preferred system of unique identifiers. ORCID iDs should be mandatory for all researchers in the next REF.** Funders and HEIs should utilise ORCID for grant applications, management and reporting platforms, and the benefits of ORCID need to be better communicated to researchers. *(HEIs, UK HE Funding Bodies, funders, managers, UUK, HESA)*

11 **Identifiers are also needed for institutions, and the most likely candidate for a global solution is the ISNI, which already has good coverage of publishers, funders and research organisations.** The use of ISNIs should therefore be extended to cover all institutions referenced in future REF submissions, and used more widely in internal HEI- and funder-management processes. One component of the solution will be to map the various organisational identifier systems against ISNI to allow the various existing systems to interoperate. *(UK HE Funding Bodies, HEIs, funders, publishers, UUK, HESA)*

12 **Publishers should mandate ORCIDs and ISNIs and funder grant references for article submission, and retain this metadata throughout the publication lifecy-cle.** This will facilitate exchange of information on research activity, and help deliver data and metrics at minimal burden to researchers and administrators. *(Publishers and data providers)*

13 **The use of DOIs should be extended to cover all research outputs.** This should include all outputs submitted to a future REF for which DOIs are suitable, and DOIs should also be more widely adopted in internal HEI and research funder processes.

DOIs already predominate in the journal publishing sphere – they should be extended to cover other outputs where no identifier system exists, such as book chapters and datasets. *(UK HE Funding Bodies, HEIs, funders, UUK)*

14 **Further investment in research information infrastructure is required.** Funders and Jisc should explore opportunities for additional strategic investments, particularly to improve the interoperability of research management systems. *(HMT, BIS, RCUK, UK HE Funding Bodies, Jisc, ARMA)*

### 10.2.3 Increasing the usefulness of existing data and information sources

15 **HEFCE, funders, HEIs and Jisc should explore how to leverage data held in existing platforms to support the REF process, and vice versa.** Further debate is also required about the merits of local collection within HEIs and data collection at the national level. *(HEFCE, RCUK, HEIs, Jisc, HESA, ARMA)*

16 **BIS should identify ways of linking data gathered from research-related platforms (including Gateway to Research, Researchfish and the REF) more directly to policy processes in BIS and other departments,** especially around foresight, horizon scanning and research prioritisation. *(BIS, other government departments, UK HE Funding Bodies, RCUK)*

### 10.2.4 Using metrics in the next REF

17 For the next REF cycle, we make some specific recommendations to HEFCE and the other UK HE Funding Bodies, as follows. *(UK HE Funding Bodies)*

    a   **In assessing outputs, we recommend that quantitative data – particularly around published outputs – continue to have a place in informing peer review judgements of research quality.** This approach has been used successfully in REF2014, and we recommend that it be continued and enhanced in future exercises.

    b   **In assessing impact, we recommend that HEFCE and the UK HE Funding Bodies build on the analysis of the impact case studies from REF2014 to develop clear guidelines for the use of quantitative indicators in future impact case studies.** While not being prescriptive, these guidelines should provide suggested data to evidence specific types of impact. They should include standards for the collection of metadata to ensure the characteristics of the research being described are captured systematically; for example, by using consistent monetary units.

    c   **In assessing the research environment, we recommend that there is scope for enhancing the use of quantitative data, but that these data need to be provided with sufficient context to enable their interpretation.** At a minimum this needs to include information on the total size of the unit to which the data refer. In some cases, the collection of data specifically relating to staff submitted to the exercise may be preferable, albeit more costly. In addition, data on the structure and use of digital information systems to support research (or research and teaching) may be crucial to further develop excellent research environments.

### 10.2.4 Coordinating activity and building evidence

18 **The UK research community needs a mechanism to carry forward the agenda set out in this report. We propose the establishment of a Forum for Responsible Metrics, which would bring together research funders, HEIs and their representative bodies, publishers, data providers and others to work on issues of data standards, interoperability, openness and transparency.** UK HE Funding Bodies, UUK and Jisc should coordinate this forum, drawing in support and expertise from other funders and sector bodies as appropriate. The forum should have preparations for the future REF within its remit, but should also look more broadly at the use of metrics in HEI management and by other funders. This forum might also seek to coordinate UK responses to the many initiatives in this area across Europe and internationally – and those that may yet emerge – around research metrics, standards and data infrastructure.[8] It can ensure that the UK system stays ahead of the curve and continues to make real progress on this issue, supporting research in the most intelligent and coordinated way, influencing debates in Europe and the standards that other countries will eventually follow. *(UK HE Funding Bodies, UUK, Jisc, ARMA)*

19 **Research funders need to increase investment in the science of science policy.** There is a need for greater research and innovation in this area, to develop and apply insights from computing, statistics, social science and economics to better understand the relationship between research, its qualities and wider impacts. *(Research funders)*

20 **One positive aspect of this review has been the debate it has generated. As a legacy initiative, the steering group is setting up a blog (www.ResponsibleMetrics. org) as a forum for ongoing discussion of the issues raised by this report.** The site will celebrate responsible practices, but also name and shame bad practices when they occur. Researchers will be encouraged to send in examples of good or bad design, or application of metrics and indicators across the research system. Adapting the approach taken by the Literary Review's "Bad Sex in Fiction" award, every year we will award a "Bad Metric" prize to the most egregious example of an inappropriate use of quantitative indicators in research management. *(Review steering group)*

---

[8]For example, www.niso.org/topics/tl/altmetrics_initiative/

# ANNEX OF TABLES

# CHAPTER 1

Table 1　Independent Metrics Review Workshops

| Topic, host and date | Roundtable with London-based HEIs. UCL, 15 July 2014 | In Metrics We Trust? Prospects and pitfalls of new research metrics. University of Sussex, 7 October 2014 | Metrics for All? University of Sheffield, 2 December 2014 | REF panel focus groups. Royal Academy of Engineering, 28 November 2014 | Arts and Humanities workshop. University of Warwick, 16 January 2015 | Roundtable with Scottish-based HEIs. Scottish Funding Council, Edinburgh, 30 March 2015 |
|---|---|---|---|---|---|---|
| Description | Participants discussed a range of issues including: The purpose of research assessment; Variations between elements of assessment and disciplines; Developments in metrics; Enabling new approaches in future REF exercises; Consequences of metrics use; Using metrics for assessment of research impact. | A broad range of speakers introduced and encouraged debate on some of the key issues pertinent to the project. The workshop was organised into three thematic plenary panels: (1) The changing landscape for research metrics; (2) The darker side of metrics; (3) Towards responsible uses of metrics. A 'metrics bazaar' also provided attendees with an interactive opportunity to explore metric tools and platforms with providers. | Focused on equality and diversity related issues, with themed sessions, as follows: (1) Metrics of success: how to ensure metrics support early-career researchers? (2) Metrics and bias: how to ensure that metrics support gender equality? (3) Metrics for all? How to ensure that metrics support the broader diversity agenda in research. | Five hour-long focus groups were held with academics involved with the REF process as follows: The key aim of the focus groups was to seek feedback on the (potential) use of metrics within the REF2014 process, and future research assessment exercises. Questions probed on the (potential) use of metrics in relation to the assessment of: (1) Outputs; (2) Environment; and (3) Impact. Groups were facilitated by members of the Steering Group. Chatham House rules were employed to encourage honest and full discussion. | The three aims of the workshop were to: (1) Offer a clear overview of the progress to date in the development of metrics of relevance to arts and humanities to date and persisting challenges; (2) Explore the potential benefits and drawbacks of metrics use in research assessment and management from the perspective of disciplines within the arts and humanities; (3) Generate evidence, insights and concrete recommendations that can inform the final report of the independent metrics review. | Participants drawn from across the Scottish HE system discussed a range of issues relevant to the review. |

| | | | | | | |
|---|---|---|---|---|---|---|
| **Audience** | c.40 pro-vice chancellors, deans and departments heads from across London HEIs. | Over 150 delegates attended the event including members of the metrics review panel, researchers, university managers, metrics developers and a range of providers and a range of stakeholders from the research and higher education community. | 45 people attended this event including representatives from the academic community, learned societies, research offices, sector bodies, equality and diversity offices, sector press and data providers. | Focus Group 1: reps from sub-panels under Main Panel (MP) A; Focus Group 2: reps from sub-panels under MP B; Focus Group 3: reps from sub-panels under MP C; Focus Group 4: reps from sub-panels under MP D; Focus Group 5: reps from all MPs. | 50 people attended this event including representatives from the academic community, learned societies, research offices, sector bodies, sector press, publishers and data providers. | Representatives from Scottish-based HEIs and organisations |
| **Web link** | www.hefce.ac.uk/media/hefce/content/What,we,do/Research/How,we,fund,research/Metrics/Paper%2018%2014%20Summary%20of%20UCL%20roundtable.pdf | www.hefce.ac.uk/news/Events/Name,101079,en.html | www.hefce.ac.uk/news/Events/Name,101078,en.html | No link available | www.hefce.ac.uk/news/Events/Name,101073,en.html | No link available |

Table 2  Sector consultation/engagement activities

| Date | Event | Location |
|---|---|---|
| 12 May 2014 | Scientometrics workshop | Paris |
| 9–11 June 2014 | ARMA Conference | Blackpool |
| 26 June 2014 | Roundtable with Minister for Universities and Science | London |
| 10–13 August 2014 | National Council of University Research Administrators (NCURA) (USA) | Washington DC |
| 15 August 2014 | Roundtable at Melbourne University | Melbourne |
| 3–5 September 2014 | Science and Information Technology meeting | Leiden |
| 8–9 September 2014 | Higher Education Institutional Research Conference | Oxford |
| 9–10 September 2014 | Vitae Researcher Development International Conference | Manchester |
| 25–26 September 2014 | Wellcome Trust altmetrics conference | London |
| 18–22 October 2014 | Society of Research Administrators International (SRA) 47th Annual Meeting | San Diego |
| 30 October 2014 | Russell Group meeting | London |
| 30 October 2014 | HEPI dinner | London |
| 6 November 2014 | Science 2.0 – Science in Transition event | London |
| 14 November 2014 | SpotOn London event | London |
| 21 November 2014 | UKSG 2014 Forum | London |
| 21 November 2014 | British Sociological Association event | London |

| Date | Event | Location |
| --- | --- | --- |
| 26 January 2015 | Vitae Every Researcher Counts conference | London |
| 2 February 2015 | Heads of Chemistry UK, REF 2014 Review Meeting | London |
| 23–24 February 2015 | Middle East and North Africa (MENA) Summit | Doha |
| 9 March 2015 | The Political Studies Association and British International Studies Association REF meeting | London |
| 10 March 2015 | Humanities and Social Sciences Learned Societies and Subject Associations Network Meeting | London |
| 25 March 2015 | HEFCE REFlections conference | London |
| 30 March 2015 | UKSG conference | Glasgow |
| 31 March 2015 | HEPI-Elsevier Annual Research Conference 'Reflections on REF 2014 – Where Next?' | London |
| 23 April 2015 | Westminster Higher Education Forum on 'The Future of the REF' | London |
| 6 May 2015 | 'In Metrics We Trust? Impact, indicators and the prospect for social sciences' Oxford Impact seminar series | Oxford |
| 18–19 May 2015 | ORCID–CASRAI joint conference | Barcelona |
| 1–3 June 2015 | ARMA conference | Brighton |
| 7 June 2015 | Consortium of Humanities Centers and Institutes annual meeting | Madison, U.S. |
| 10 June 2015 | 'Approaches to Facilitating Research Impact', Oxford Impact seminar series | Oxford |
| 11 June 2015 | IREG Forum on university performance | Aalborg, Denmark |
| 22–23 June 2015 | European Commission conference on 'A new start for Europe: opening up to an ERA of innovation' | Brussels |
| 24 June 2015 | Thomson Reuters 3rd Annual Research Symposium | Tokyo |
| 28 June–1 July 2015 | EARMA conference: Global Outreach: Enabling Cultures and Diversity in Research Management and Administration | Leiden, South Holland |

# CHAPTER 3

Table 3   Summary of alternative indicators

| Object | Indicator | Impact type | Evidence of value | Possible to spam? | Method of collection for large sets |
|---|---|---|---|---|---|
| Academics | Academic website followers | Scholarly | Correlations with h-index | Yes | Manual |
| Articles, papers | Downloads or views | Scholarly | Correlations with citations | Yes | From publishers? or sites such as Academia.edu or ResearchGate |
| Books | Google Books Citations | Scholarly; educational; cultural | Correlations with citations | Yes? | Automatic collection via API |
| Books | Library holdings = Libcitations | Scholarly; educational; cultural | Correlations with citations | No? | Automatic collection via API |
| Books | Reviews | Scholarly; public | Correlations with citations | Yes (web); No (mag.) | Automatic from web, manual from magazines? |
| Data-sets | Web of Science citations | Scholarly or public | None | No | From Web of Science in the future |
| Images | Views, copies, tags | Scholarly; educational; cultural | None | Yes | Automatic collection via API in some cases, TinEye/Google image searches |
| All pubs. | Blog citations | Scholarly; educational; public | Correlations with citations | Yes | Commercial altmetric provider |
| All pubs. | Downloads or views in social websites | Scholarly | | Yes | Manual or from site owner? |
| All pubs. | Forum citations | Scholarly; educational; public | Weak associations with citations | Yes | Commercial altmetric provider |

| Object | Indicator | Impact type | Evidence of value | Possible to spam? | Method of collection for large sets |
|---|---|---|---|---|---|
| All pubs. | Google Scholar citations | Scholarly | Correlations with Web of Science and Scopus citations | Yes | Publish or Perish software for individual cases; manual |
| All pubs. | Mendeley bookmarks | Scholarly; educational? | Correlations with citations | Yes | Automatic collection via API |
| All pubs. | Other bookmarks | Scholarly; educational? | | | Manual |
| All pubs. | Patents (Google patent search) | Commercial | | No | Manual |
| All pubs. | Tweets | Mainly scholarly | Very weak association with citations | Yes | Buy from altmetrics providers; limited free API access |
| All pubs. | Web or URL citations | Educational; scholarly | Correlations with citations | Yes | Automatic collection via Bing API |
| All pubs. | Web presentation mentions | Educational; scholarly | Correlations with citations | Yes | Automatic collection via Bing API |
| All pubs. | Web syllabus mentions | Educational | Correlations with citations | Yes? | Automatic collection via Bing API |
| Software | Web of Science citations | Scholarly | None | | Web of Science |
| Videos | Views, comments, sentiment | Scholarly; educational; cultural | None | Yes | Automatic collection via API in some cases |

## CHAPTER 4

Table 4   Output types submitted to the REF across the 36 units of assessment

| UOA | Name | Authored book | Edited book | Chapter in book | Journal article | Conference contribution | Patent/published patent application | Software | Website content | Performance | Composition | Design | Artefact | Exhibition | Research report for external body | Devices and products | Digital or visual media | Scholarly edition | Research datasets and databases | Other form of assessable output | Working paper | Total |
|---|---|---|---|---|---|---|---|---|---|---|---|---|---|---|---|---|---|---|---|---|---|---|
| 1 | Clinical Medicine | 5 | | | 13382 | 7 | 10 | | | | | | | | 1 | | | | | | | 13400 |
| 2 | Public Health, Health Services and Primary Care | | | | 4861 | 4 | | | | | | | | | 11 | | | | | | | 4881 |
| 3 | Allied Health Professions, Dentistry, Nursing and Pharmacy | 12 | 6 | 25 | 10249 | 14 | 15 | | | | | | | | 36 | 1 | | | | | | 10358 |
| 4 | Psychology, Psychiatry and Neuroscience | 10 | 1 | 16 | 9086 | 4 | | | 4 | | | | | | 1 | | | | | 1 | 3 | 9126 |
| 5 | Biological Sciences | 11 | | 6 | 8582 | 4 | 3 | 1 | | | | | | | | | | 1 | | | | 8608 |
| 6 | Agriculture, Veterinary and Food Science | 1 | | 8 | 3884 | 7 | | | | | | | | | 8 | | | | | 11 | | 3919 |
| 7 | Earth Systems and Environmental Sciences | 14 | 4 | 22 | 5200 | 4 | 3 | 4 | | | | | | | 2 | | | | | | | 5249 |
| 8 | Chemistry | | | 1 | 4688 | 2 | 3 | | | | | | | | | | | | | | | 4698 |
| 9 | Physics | 1 | 2 | 1 | 6376 | 18 | 6 | | | | | | | | 4 | | | | | | 38 | 6446 |

| UOA | Name | Authored book | Edited book | Chapter in book | Journal article | Conference contribution | Patent/published patent application | Software | Website content | Performance | Composition | Design | Artefact | Exhibition | Research report for external body | Devices and products | Digital or visual media | Scholarly edition | Research datasets and databases | Other form of assessable output | Working paper | Total |
|---|---|---|---|---|---|---|---|---|---|---|---|---|---|---|---|---|---|---|---|---|---|---|
| 10 | Mathematical Sciences | 46 | | 36 | 6731 | 17 | | 1 | 6 | | | | | | | | | | 1 | 21 | 135 | 6994 |
| 11 | Computer Science and Informatics | 32 | 3 | 112 | 5551 | 1898 | 12 | 8 | 3 | 2 | 1 | | 3 | 12 | 9 | | 1 | | | 1 | 3 | 7651 |
| 12 | Aeronautical, Mechanical, Chemical and Manufacturing Engineering | 2 | | 9 | 4101 | 24 | 2 | | | | | | | | 4 | 1 | | | | | | 4143 |
| 13 | Electrical and Electronic Engineering, Metallurgy and Materials | | | 3 | 3982 | 28 | 10 | 2 | | | | | | | | | | | | | | 4025 |
| 14 | Civil and Construction Engineering | 3 | | 9 | 1348 | 16 | | 1 | | | | | | | 7 | | | | | | | 1384 |
| 15 | General Engineering | 7 | | 17 | 8539 | 90 | 18 | | | | | | 1 | | 5 | 1 | | | | | 1 | 8679 |
| 16 | Architecture, Built Environment and Planning | 229 | 38 | 266 | 2934 | 77 | 2 | 1 | 8 | 1 | | 114 | 17 | 16 | 58 | | 2 | 1 | | 13 | 4 | 3781 |

| UOA | Name | Authored book | Edited book | Chapter in book | Journal article | Conference contribution | Patent/published patent application | Software | Website content | Performance | Composition | Design | Artefact | Exhibition | Research report for external body | Devices and products | Digital or visual media | Scholarly edition | Research datasets and databases | Other form of assessable output | Working paper | Total |
|---|---|---|---|---|---|---|---|---|---|---|---|---|---|---|---|---|---|---|---|---|---|---|
| 17 | Geography, Environmental Studies and Archaeology | 380 | 121 | 459 | 4969 | 23 | | 3 | 11 | | | | | 1 | 29 | | | 3 | 2 | 9 | 7 | 6017 |
| 18 | Economics and Econometrics | 12 | | 28 | 2388 | 2 | | | | | | | | | 1 | | | | 1 | | 168 | 2600 |
| 19 | Business and Management Studies | 160 | 6 | 179 | 11668 | 52 | | 1 | | | | | | | 31 | | | | | 2 | 103 | 12202 |
| 20 | Law | 745 | 25 | 1219 | 3454 | 1 | | | 4 | | | | | | 47 | | | | | 3 | 24 | 5522 |
| 21 | Politics and International Studies | 775 | 63 | 415 | 3082 | 1 | | | | | | | | | 16 | | | 1 | | 2 | 10 | 4365 |
| 22 | Social Work and Social Policy | 440 | 34 | 435 | 3703 | 5 | | | | | | | | 2 | 153 | | | 1 | | 5 | 6 | 4784 |
| 23 | Sociology | 350 | 36 | 230 | 2002 | 1 | | | | | | | | | 8 | | | | 3 | | | 2630 |
| 24 | Anthropology and Development Studies | 215 | 83 | 316 | 1355 | 1 | | | | | | | | 4 | 8 | | 2 | 3 | 2 | 10 | 14 | 2013 |
| 25 | Education | 405 | 22 | 548 | 4322 | 64 | | 3 | 1 | | | | | | 143 | | | | 6 | 1 | 4 | 5519 |

| UOA | Name | Authored book | Edited book | Chapter in book | Journal article | Conference contribution | Patent/published patent application | Software | Website content | Performance | Composition | Design | Artefact | Exhibition | Research report for external body | Devices and products | Digital or visual media | Scholarly edition | Research datasets and databases | Other form of assessable output | Working paper | Total |
|---|---|---|---|---|---|---|---|---|---|---|---|---|---|---|---|---|---|---|---|---|---|---|
| 26 | Sport and Exercise Sciences, Leisure and Tourism | 39 | 1 | 33 | 2668 | 6 | | | 1 | | | | | | 9 | | | | | | | 2757 |
| 27 | Area Studies | 262 | 53 | 414 | 975 | 4 | | | 1 | | | | | 1 | 2 | | | 4 | | 1 | 7 | 1724 |
| 28 | Modern Languages and Linguistics | 760 | 238 | 1397 | 2380 | 44 | | | 9 | 2 | | | | 1 | 4 | | 5 | 57 | 9 | 8 | 18 | 4932 |
| 29 | English Language and Literature | 1678 | 397 | 2026 | 2472 | 11 | | 1 | 25 | 38 | 3 | | | 4 | 2 | | 10 | 139 | 6 | 98 | 13 | 6923 |
| 30 | History | 1320 | 290 | 1815 | 2832 | 20 | | | 14 | | | | | 1 | 3 | | 2 | 47 | 13 | 16 | 58 | 6431 |
| 31 | Classics | 284 | 125 | 517 | 401 | 5 | | | 8 | | | | | 1 | | | | 21 | 2 | 7 | 15 | 1386 |
| 32 | Philosophy | 243 | 25 | 525 | 1344 | 2 | | | 6 | | | | | | | | | 5 | 1 | 1 | 21 | 2173 |
| 33 | Theology and Religious Studies | 391 | 63 | 492 | 579 | 6 | | | 2 | | | | | | | | 2 | 6 | 3 | 9 | 5 | 1558 |
| 34 | Art and Design: History, Practice and Theory | 590 | 230 | 1133 | 1657 | 198 | 22 | 5 | 31 | 119 | 18 | 68 | 675 | 1131 | 38 | 19 | 204 | 6 | 3 | 170 | 4 | 6321 |
| 35 | Music, Drama, Dance and Performing Arts | 461 | 170 | 873 | 1264 | 41 | 2 | 4 | 19 | 324 | 638 | 3 | 21 | 48 | 11 | 1 | 165 | 58 | 6 | 132 | 5 | 4246 |
| 36 | Communication, Cultural and Media Studies, Library & Info. Management | 488 | 97 | 811 | 1845 | 49 | | 3 | 6 | 3 | 6 | | 9 | 23 | 33 | 2 | 88 | 5 | 10 | 33 | 6 | 3517 |

Table 5 Summary of studies of correlating indicators and outcomes of peer review (using data from the 2001 and 2008 RAEs). Note: all references are provided in the references section of Supplementary Report I.

| Authors | Butler and Mcallister (2011) | Mahdi; D'Este and Neely (2008) | Norris and Oppenheim (2010) | McKay (2012) |
|---|---|---|---|---|
| Overall aims | Applied a metrics-based model developed in earlier studies of political science to the field of chemistry, using data from the 2001 RAE. The model identified the best predictors of the RAE results in political science (Butler and McAllister, 2009). | Analysed all 204K individual submissions to the 2001RAE. Citations were counted at the level of the individual submissions for all journal articles covered by the WoS (55% of the submissions). | Examined whether the collective h-index and its variant the g-index correlate with the outcome of the UK 2008 RAE rankings. | Applied a metrics-based model to identify potential predictors of the 2008 RAE (for environment and outputs). |
| Academic field(s) | Political Science Chemistry | All 2001 RAE disciplines | Library and information science; Anthropology; Pharmacy | Social work and social policy and administration |
| Assessment exercise | 2001 RAE | 2001 RAE | 2008 RAE | 2008 RAE |
| Study findings presented by the authors | The most important and statistically significant predictive variables were: citations (inc to journal articles, books and book chapters) and departmental size (represented by student numbers). Research income was not a strong predictor, nor was departmental size if measured by staff numbers. Whether or not a department had a member on the assessment panel was as | The citation counts were a reasonable proxy for the RAE results in the biological sciences, clinical sciences, chemistry and psychology. The correlations were much weaker for RAE results for a large number of disciplines, | In the field of pharmacy, a strong correlation existed between the RAE ranking and the median bibliometric scores. Library and information science showed a moderate correlation, whereas in anthropology the correlation was negative or non-existent. | A metrics-based assessment can predict reasonably well the overall outcome of the 2008 RAE in terms of research environment, but not research outputs. Authors did not always choose to submit their most highly cited work to |

| | | | |
|---|---|---|---|
| strong predictor of the RAE outcome. This model was able to explain 60% of the variance in RAE outcome in political science, and 86% of this variance in chemistry. However, in political science, citation count was the best predictor, while in chemistry research income correlated strongest with the RAE results. The latter indicator had almost no predictive power in political science. The study also analysed in what sense the RAE results would have been different if the model had been applied. For 34% of the 113 departments, the results would have been different if the RAE had been purely metrics based. However, the results point to strong differences between SSH and STEM disciplines. | including fields in the biomedical and engineering sciences, and including fields that are well covered in WoS. The citation counts are even less valuable for fields not well covered in the citation index. | | the RAE. It is possible to explain a great deal of the variation in scores awarded for research environment, "but rather more difficult to find a quantitative counterpart to the peer assessment of research outputs". This supports the panel's insistence on reading the particular works, rather than using shortcuts based on the identity of the journal. The output measures applied in the study related to the type of output and their journals and publishers. "At least in this subject, metrics are more suited as handmaiden to peer review than its replacement". |
| **Authors** | Taylor (2011) | Kelly & Burrows (2012) | Mryglod, Kenna, Holovatch, & Berche (2013) | Allen & Heath (2013) |
| **Overall aims** | Studied the extent to which the outcomes of the RAE 2008 can be explained by a set of quantitative indicators | Developed an exploratory model to predict the RAE 2008 | Analysed the correlation between peer review scores in a range of academic disciplines for RAE 2008, at the level of the research group. | Study of the relation between RAE 2008 results and reputations rankings |

| Academic field(s) | Business and management; Economics and econometrics; Accounting and finance | Sociology | A range of academic disciplines from natural sciences to social sciences and humanities | Politics and International Studies |
|---|---|---|---|---|
| Assessment exercise | 2008 RAE | 2008 RAE | 2008 RAE | 2008 RAE |
| Study findings presented by the authors | Each of the three components of research activity (namely, research output, esteem and research environment) was highly correlated with quantitative indicators. The judgement of the panels was biased in favour of Russell Group universities. The study also showed some evidence of bias by the economics and econometrics panel. The authors support the use of quantitative indicators in the research assessment process, they propose in particular a journal quality index. "Requiring the panels to take bibliometric indicators into account should help not only to reduce the workload of panels but also to mitigate the problem of implicit bias." | They found that 83% of the variance in outcomes can be predicted by a combination of simple metrics: the quality of journals in the submission, research income per capita and the scale of research activity. The most powerful single predictor of how well a submission did in the 2008 RAE was how well it did in the 2001 RAE. The model used a sophisticated indicator to measure both the normalised citation rate and the centrality of a journal for the field. Measured in this way, the percentage of journal articles included | The citation measure in Thomson Reuters Research Analytics was poorly related to RAE scores. The study concludes that these indicators should not be used in place of peer review. However, a measure of total impact in which the size of the department was taken into account, strongly correlated to overall strength according to the RAE in a number of fields. This is especially the case for large research groups. For smaller groups the correlation becomes weaker or disappears. This correlation is moreover stronger for the hard sciences than for other fields. In the more specific comparison of academic impact and quality, the study finds weak correlations for the majority | The number of articles in top journals (defined by rankings) as percentage of all submissions was associated with the institutes top grading in the RAE (4*). The types of output also mattered. Top press monographs were most strongly associated with 4* grades. The proportion of articles in top-ten journals also had a positive and significant association with 4* work. The study concludes that publisher reputations are good predictors of research quality as graded by the RAE. The explanation is that the panels are based in the same communities that review manuscripts. If the |

in a submission that were published in the 'top' quartile of journals proved to be the best citation based predictor of the outcomes of the 2008 RAE. It should be noted that the study restricted itself to those submissions that involved publications in journals covered in Thomson Reuter's Journal Citation Reports (34% of all submissions).

of disciplines: chemistry, physics, engineering, geography and environmental studies, sociology and history. The authors conclude that citation indicators should not be used in isolation to compare or rank research groups or higher education institutes.

correlation would not exist, it would mean that the panels were not representative of the discipline as a whole, the authors argue. The study also found that large departments that submitted many outputs did better in the RAE on average. Having a member on the RAE sub-panel also contributed to the score. Overall, the study concludes that both RAE judgements and reputational rankings are based on peer review. The advantage of using the latter is that they are based on the opinion of more people.

# CHAPTER 9

Table 6    Background information on the use of citation data by REF2014 sub-panels

The units of assessment (UOAs), grouped by main panel, are listed below; those that were provided with citation data within the REF process are highlighted.

| Main Panel | Unit of Assessment | |
|---|---|---|
| A | 1 | **Clinical Medicine** |
| | 2 | **Public Health, Health Services and Primary Care** |
| | 3 | **Allied Health Professions, Dentistry, Nursing and Pharmacy** |
| | 4 | **Psychology, Psychiatry and Neuroscience** |
| | 5 | **Biological Sciences** |
| | 6 | **Agriculture, Veterinary and Food Science** |
| B | 7 | **Earth Systems and Environmental Sciences** |
| | 8 | **Chemistry** |
| | 9 | **Physics** |
| | 10 | Mathematical Sciences |
| | 11 | **Computer Science and Informatics** |
| | 12 | Aeronautical, Mechanical, Chemical and Manufacturing Engineering |
| | 13 | Electrical and Electronic Engineering, Metallurgy and Materials |
| | 14 | Civil and Construction Engineering |
| | 15 | General Engineering |

| Main Panel | Unit of Assessment | |
|---|---|---|
| | 16 | Architecture, Built Environment and Planning |
| | 17 | Geography, Environmental Studies and Archaeology |
| | **18** | **Economics and Econometrics** |
| | 19 | Business and Management Studies |
| | 20 | Law |
| C | 21 | Politics and International Studies |
| | 22 | Social Work and Social Policy |
| | 23 | Sociology |
| | 24 | Anthropology and Development Studies |
| | 25 | Education |
| | 26 | Sport and Exercise Sciences, Leisure and Tourism |
| | 27 | Area Studies |
| | 28 | Modern Languages and Linguistics |
| | 29 | English Language and Literature |
| | 30 | History |
| | 31 | Classics |
| D | 32 | Philosophy |
| | 33 | Theology and Religious Studies |
| | 34 | Art and Design: History, Practice and Theory |
| | 35 | Music, Drama, Dance and Performing Arts |
| | 36 | Communication, Cultural and Media Studies, Library and Information Management |

# LIST OF ABBREVIATIONS AND GLOSSARY

| | |
|---|---|
| AHRC | Arts & Humanities Research Council |
| AMRC | Association of Medical Research Charities |
| ANVUR | National Agency for the Evaluation of the University and Research Systems (Italy) |
| ARMA | Association of Research Managers and Administrators |
| BA | British Academy |
| BIS | Department for Business, Innovation and Skills |
| CASRAI | Consortia Advancing Standards in Research Administration Information |
| CERIF | Common European Research Information Format |
| COPE | Committee On Publication Ethics |
| CRIS | Current Research Information System |
| CWTS | Centrum voor Wetenschap en Technologische Studies (Centre for Science and Technology Studies) |
| DOI | Digital Object Identifier |
| DORA | (San Francisco) Declaration on Research Assessment |
| EARMA | European Association of Research Managers and Administrators |
| ERA | Excellence in Research for Australia (also European Research Area in annex) |
| ERC | European Research Council |
| ERIH | European Reference Index for the Humanities |
| ESRC | Economic & Social Research Council |
| GERD | Gross expenditure on research and development |
| h-index | Hirsch-Index |
| HEFCE | Higher Education Funding Council for England |
| HEI | Higher education institution |
| HEP | Higher education provider |
| HEPI | Higher Education Policy Institute |
| HESA | Higher Education Statistics Agency |
| H2020 | Horizon2020 |

| | |
|---|---|
| ISBN | International Standard Book Number |
| ISNI | International Standard Name Identifier |
| ISSN | International Standard Serial Number |
| JIF | Journal Impact Factor |
| Jisc | Formerly the Joint Information Systems Committee |
| LSE | London School of Economics and Political Science |
| MENA | Middle East and North Africa |
| MRC | Medical Research Council |
| NCURA | National Council of University Research Administrators |
| NERC | Natural Environment Research Council |
| NIH | National Institute for Health |
| NISO | National Information Standards Organization |
| ORCID | Open Researcher and Contributor ID |
| OSIP | Overview of System Interoperability Project |
| PLOS | Public Library of Science |
| PLOS ONE | A multidisciplinary open-access journal published by PLOS |
| PRF | Performance-based research funding |
| PubMed | A free search engine accessing primarily the MEDLINE database of references and abstracts on life sciences and biomedical topics |
| PVC | Pro Vice Chancellor |
| RAE | Research Assessment Exercise |
| RCUK | Research Councils UK |
| REF | Research Excellence Framework |
| RO | Research Organisation |
| RRI | Responsible Research and Innovation |
| RS | Royal Society |
| SCI | Science Citation Index |
| SCOPUS | Bibliographic database containing abstracts and citations for academic journal articles owned by Elsevier |
| SJR | SCImago Journal Rank |
| SPRU | Science Policy Research Unit |
| SRA | Society of Research Administrators International |
| SSH | Social Sciences and Humanities |
| STEM | Science, Technology, Engineering and Mathematics |
| UKPRN | UK Provider Reference Number |
| UOA | Unit of Assessment |
| WoS | Web of Science |